Royal Transport

For my grandfather, Fred Selwyn, who was a Justice of the Peace in Imperial India

PETER PIGOTT

An Inside Look at the History of Royal Travel

ROYAL TRANSPORT

THE DUNDURN GROUP

TORONTO

Copy-Editors: Kate Pedersen and Patricia Kennedy
Design: Andrew Roberts
Printer: Friesens

Library and Archives Canada Cataloguing in Publication

Pigott, Peter
    Royal transport : an inside look at the history of royal travel / Peter Pigott.

Includes bibliographical references.

ISBN-10: 1-55002-572-4
ISBN-13: 978-1-55002-572-9

1. Great Britain--Kings and rulers--Transportation--History--20th century. I. Title.

DA566.9.A1P545 2005   388'.086'21   C2005-903476-9

1   2   3   4   5   09   08   07   06   05

Conseil des Arts du Canada
Canada Council for the Arts
Canada
ONTARIO ARTS COUNCIL
CONSEIL DES ARTS DE L'ONTARIO

We acknowledge the support of the Canada Council for the Arts and the Ontario Arts Council for our publishing program. We also acknowledge the financial support of the Government of Canada through the Book Publishing Industry Development Program and The Association for the Export of Canadian Books, and the Government of Ontario through the Ontario Book Publishers Tax Credit program, and the Ontario Media Development Corporation.

Care has been taken to trace the ownership of copyright material used in this book. The author and the publisher welcome any information enabling them to rectify any references or credit in subsequent editions.

J. Kirk Howard, President

Printed and bound in Canada.
Printed on recycled paper.

www.dundurn.com

Dundurn Press
3 Church Street, Suite 500
Toronto, Ontario, Canada
M5E 1M2

Gazelle Book Services Limited
White Cross Mills
Hightown, Lancaster, England
LA1 4X5

Dundurn Press
2250 Military Road
Tonawanda, NY
U.S.A. 14150

Royal Transport

ACKNOWLEDGMENTS

Detail of photo from page 73.

I am indebted to many people without whom this book would have been difficult to write. Some, for reasons of sensitivity to the subject matter, have asked that their contribution remain anonymous. But I am pleased to be able to publicly acknowledge my obligation to the following:

In Canada:

I owe a special debt of gratitude to all whom I interviewed in the Canadian Forces. Not only did they give their time willingly and with unfailing courtesy, but some did so in what must have been periods of great stress — replying to my queries even as they loaded and flew the first CC-150 flights in the tsunami relief operations.

They are:

Captain Randy Henning
2 Lt Eric Martinat
2 Lt. V.G. Winter
Captain Steve Thompson
Major John Komocki
Captain Mike Chaytor
Major Mat Joost
Captain Al Mclean
Major Al Mornan
Master Seaman John Bourne

For speedily locating archival material and photographs, once more I relied on the skills of Janet Lacroix at the National Defence Imagery Library, Réjean Tremblay and Michel Meilleur in the Lester B. Pearson Library, and Anthony Pacey at the Science and Technology Museum. Vern Bethel, the owner of the 1939 McLaughlin-Buick, was unfailingly helpful, providing me with copious material on the use of his car by royalty.

In Britain:

When I began this book, I saw myself combing through the archives at Windsor Castle, accessing previously untapped sources at Buckingham Palace, and attending informative luncheons at Clarence House and Highgrove. Unable to do any of this (my day job just would not allow it), like Miss Blanche DuBois, I have depended on the kindness of strangers. Taking full advantage of the good nature and sympathies of several Brits, I have drawn heavily from their resources on the Windsors and their transport. They are:

Mrs. Nicky Colman, The Estate Office, Sandringham
Julia Stephenson, Head of Marketing and Visitor Experience, The Royal Yacht *Britannia* Edinburgh, Scotland
Miss Frances Dimond, Curator, Royal Photograph Collection, Windsor Castle
Mrs. Nicola Hunt, Crown Copyright Administrator, Intellectual Property Group, Defence Procurement Agency, Bristol

Sqn. Ldr. Ross Mattinson, 32 Squadron, RAF Northolt
David Pennington, Librarian and Archivist, LNWR Society
Morag Reavley, Web Editor, Buckingham Palace, London
Chris Hallewell, Helicopter Museum, Weston-super-Mare
Lisa Heighway, Royal Collections, Windsor Castle
Peter Sharp, authority on the Canadian Pacific liner *Empress of Scotland*

Labouring as I do in the Legal section of Foreign Affairs Canada, I have assiduously sought permission to use many of the photographs in the book, a difficult task when much that is available on the internet has no provenance. Where I have been unable to ascertain copyright, I can only hope that the author will forgive me.

In the course of writing this book, I have read thousands of words on the Windsors and scanned hundreds of photographs. Rather than bore the reader by listing all of the books, newspaper cuttings, websites, and magazines consulted, I have selected only those from which I derived exceptional pleasure.

Beginning with the basics: *George VI* by Patrick Howarth, *Edward VIII* by Frances Donaldson, *The Queen Mother* by Donald Zec, *Prince Philip: First Gentleman of the Realm* by Douglas Liversidge, *Mountbatten* by Philip Ziegler, *Philip* by Basil Boothroyd, *Queen Elizabeth II: A Celebration of Her Majesty's Fifty-Year Reign* by Tim Graham, and *The House of Windsor (A Royal History of England)* by Andrew Roberts and Antonia Fraser.

For the royal motor cars:

Rolls-Royce and Bentley: The Crewe Years by Martin Bennett, *Rolls-Royce and Bentley Motor Cars: From the Dawn of the 20th Century into the New Millennium* by Klaus-Josef Roßfeldt, *Rolls-Royce State Motor Cars* by Andrew Pastouna, and *Royal Daimlers* by Brian Ernest Smith

For the royal aircraft:

A History of the King's Flight and the Queen's Flight: A Celebration of Royal Flying, 1936-1995 by The Queen's Flight Association, edited by Sqn. Ldr. Brian Sowerby LVO MBE RAF (Retd)

For the royal trains:

C. Hamilton Ellis's *The Royal Trains* and *Royal Journey: A Retrospect of Royal Trains in the British Isles*

As for the Royal Tours, Tom MacDonnell's *Daylight Upon Magic: The Royal Tour of Canada, 1939*, Gustave Lanctot's *The Royal Tour of King George VI and Queen Elizabeth in Canada and the United States*, and The William Lyon Mackenzie King Diaries on the National Archives website capture it all.

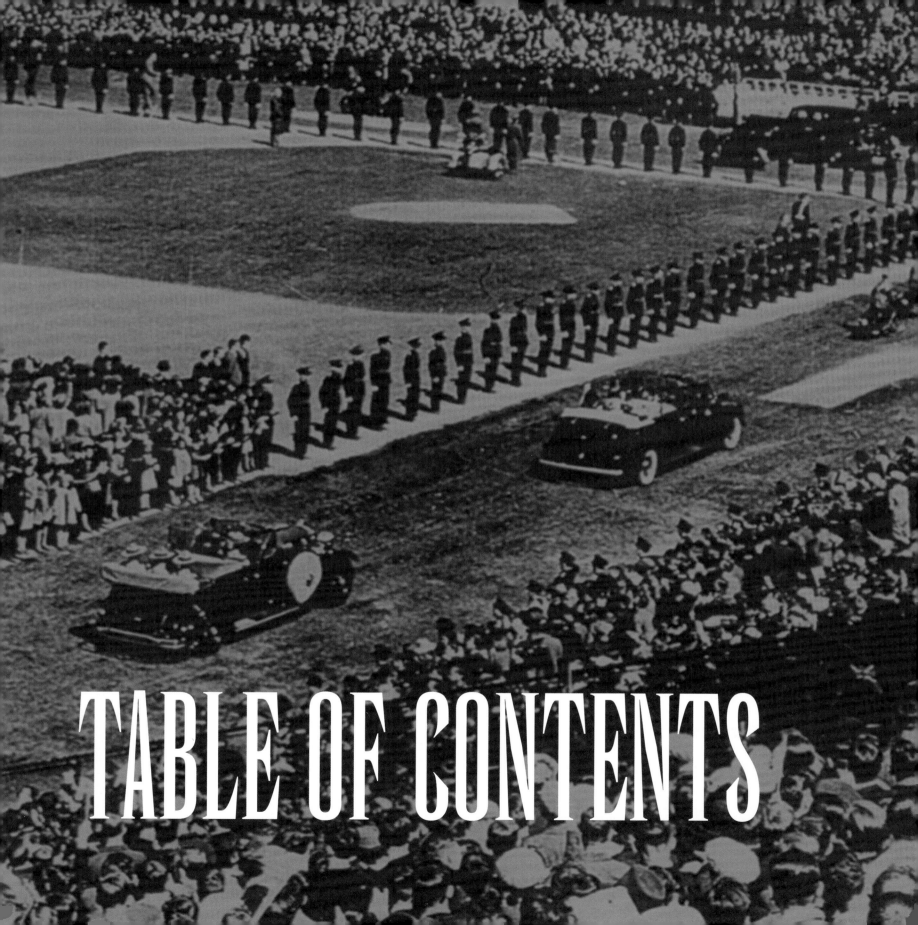

TABLE OF CONTENTS

Detail of photo from page 103.

INTRODUCTION

Detail of photo from page 101.

When I told my aunt that a title I was considering for this book was *One's Royal Transport* (said with an upper-class British accent), she warned me not to be facetious about the royal family. At the age of eighty-five, she had grown up in Imperial India, and the trappings of majesty, whether car, ship, or train, were traditional, reassuring, and immutable.

In the years I was posted to the Canadian Embassy in The Hague, members of the Dutch royal family famously got around by bicycle. There is a (probably apocryphal) story of the Queen of Sweden, who, because she travels without pomp and circumstance, carries in her handbag, in case of accident, a card that reads: "I am the Queen of Sweden." But this pared-down approach that European (i.e. continental) monarchies take in the twenty-first century is not for the House of Windsor — at least not yet. No longer able to send those who disagree with them to the Tower or claim distant countries as Crown colonies, when it comes to what they ride in and how, this royal family can still give us a lesson in majesty. Each year they carry out about 2,900 official engagements in the United Kingdom and overseas. These involve a significant amount of travel that has to be undertaken in a way that meets presentational, efficiency, and security requirements. The family has successfully accomplished this since the steam engine was invented, and that is what this book is about.

In pre-railway, pre-steamship days, royalty rarely went far from the palace. Contrary to what we see in movies, Queen Elizabeth I did not attend the Globe theatre to enjoy Shakespeare's plays — spectacle was brought to the palace. To leave it meant moving the entire royal household, which was a major undertaking and rarely done. Although when taken the royal progress lived off the local nobility for food, shelter, and entertainment — in effect bankrupting them and thus ensuring their loyalty — it still entailed a large number of horses and carriages for courtiers and their baggage. Even in the early years of Victoria's reign, the monarchy was never popular and had to be escorted by troops, on foot and mounted, to provide security as well as pageantry. As for travel away from Britain, whether by land or sea, it was wholly unsafe and uncomfortable, and no dynasty was about to risk its sovereign or the presumptive heir to the throne on a foreign tour.

The first member of the royal family to come to Canada was Prince William Henry, Duke of Clarence, the third son of King George III. Serving in the Royal Navy, he arrived in Halifax in 1786 and behaved much as any seafaring officer of the period did — brawling publicly, drinking to excess, and visiting brothels on Halifax's Water Street. His younger brother Prince Edward Augustus, the Duke of Kent, was hardly an improvement. Banished to Canada in 1791 because he flogged his soldiers incessantly (even for those times), he brought with him his mistress, Alphonsine Thérèse Bernadine Julie de Montgenet. But while in command of the Halifax garrison, His Royal Highness had its fortifications rebuilt and, in thanks, the locals changed the name of Île St. Jean to Prince Edward Island. The Prince returned to Britain in 1800 and nineteen years later fathered the future Queen Victoria.

Her Majesty did not cross the ocean to Canada, disliking travel and barely tolerating the new technology of trains and steamships. But her son Albert Edward, the Prince of Wales, changed it all: he toured Canada in 1860, not on a posting but because he saw his role as "Britain's first salesman." On tour, he opened bridges, shook the hands of selected Canadians, reviewed regiments, and postulated his government's views of the current scene. In doing so, His Royal Highness had discovered a role for royalty and set the pattern for all future tours, each monarch utilizing the new technology of the railway, motor cars, and aircraft to do so.

There have been many royal biographies. Other books have painted pictures of the personalities themselves, but on researching the transport of each successive generation, with the idea that objects can speak louder than the people themselves, I was able to understand better the monarch that favoured them. Queen Victoria kept two hundred horses at the Royal Mews, a hundred more at Windsor and Balmoral, and never really accepted trains. With the enthusiasm with which he took to everything, her son Edward VII embraced all forms of transport, even meeting with the Wright brothers. He also favoured the Daimler, a make of motor car that the royal family would use for half a century. His son George V so loved the racing yacht *Britannia* that he ordered it scuttled when he died. Edward VIII — the only royal matinee idol until Princess Diana — loved jazzy American cars and was the first member of the family to fly. His brother George VI's choice of transport was less bold, but his consort Queen Elizabeth, the future Queen Mother, was more adventurous, keen for anything from jet airliners to helicopters to a golf cart. Denied a naval career, Prince Philip took to aircraft. Denied a role at all, Prince Charles has always loved James Bond's Aston Martins, while his mother the Queen is reportedly never so happy as when driving herself around in a Land Rover.

There is no question that the royal family are privileged, that their only qualification for living in the royal palaces in London and Windsor and for enjoying the executive jet aircraft and Rolls-Royces is that they were born into the House of Saxe-Coburg-Gotha, renamed Windsor.[1] Even years after his abdication, the Duke of Windsor still expected royal privilege, part of an enchanted world he had always known. "Trains were held, yachts materialized, aeroplanes stood waiting," explained Wallis Simpson. When that no longer happened, "It was pathetic to see HRH's face. He couldn't believe it," remembers the Duke's best friend, Major Edward "Fruity" Metcalfe, who accompanied him on many Royal Tours. "He'd been so used to having everything done as he wished."

But it should be remembered that, like the Crown jewels and the Gold Coach, the planes, trains, and limousines are only held by Her Majesty the Queen as sovereign. She cannot sell them, and they must be handed on to her successor. She does have a driving licence and operates her own Daimler Jaguar saloon and a Vauxhall estate (station wagon). The Duke of Edinburgh has a Range Rover and a Metrocab to get through London's traffic. All of these vehicles are expensive but hardly in the super-rich category. And when it was in service, the idea of using the Royal Yacht *Britannia* for a pleasure cruise was always out of the question. Her Majesty has always been a poor sailor; as a princess on her 1947 South African tour, when HMS *Vanguard* hit rough weather, she wrote, "I for one would have willingly died." And as for hopping about in helicopters, Her Majesty's childhood dream was "being married to a farmer and having lots of horses and dogs." Her father too was quite content to be a country squire. For, despite the luxury and deferential treatment, the Queen, in common with her father, has found travel a duty like everything else.

The costs of official royal travel by air and rail used to be shared by the Ministry of Defence, the Department of Transport, and the Foreign and Commonwealth Office. At the royal household's suggestion, responsibility for the expenditure was transferred to the household from April 1, 1997. The royal household now receives annual funding to meet the costs of official royal travel, in the form of a Royal Travel Grant-in-Aid from Parliament, through the Department of Transport. Today the majority of royal travel expenditure goes toward the Queen's helicopter and the chartering of scheduled fixed-wing aircraft

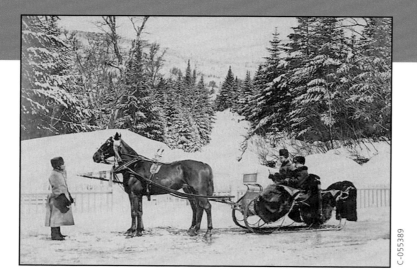

HRH Prince Arthur on a sleigh,1869, Montreal, Quebec.

Probably the most unusual royal transport: the royal party running the Chaudière timber slide on a timber crib, September 1901, Ottawa, Ontario.

Her Majesty Queen Elizabeth II and Prime Minister Lester B. Pearson on the mini-rail at Expo '67.

provided by airlines for overseas state visits. The aircraft provided to her by the RAF's 32 Squadron serve the requirements of the Royal Air Force 80 percent of the time. The Queen's official travel by car is paid for from the Civil List and for the Duke of Edinburgh from his Parliamentary Annuity. Payment for official travel for other members of the royal family comes from their private sources.[2] In 2004, Britons paid the equivalent of about $1.10 each in taxes to support Queen Elizabeth II and the royal family — the price then of a loaf of bread; they were getting a bargain.

Royal visitors to Canada have travelled by horse-drawn sleigh, by rafts on the Chaudière timber slide, and by specially built trains. A remnant from that era (and most familiar to Canadian television viewers) is the state landau, the usual mode for royal travel in Ottawa. In 1911, at the end of his term as Governor General, Earl Grey sold his landau, which he had purchased from the Governor General of Australia, to the Canadian government. The carriage received widespread use during the Royal Tour of 1939 but was put away during the Second World War, only to be brought out again in 1953 by Governor General Vincent Massey. The state landau is still used for the opening of Parliament and during official state visits.

As of 2004, in her twenty-one Canadian visits as queen (and once as princess), Her Majesty has ridden in the state landau, in convertibles, on stagecoaches, and on a mini-rail. This last took place when the Queen was invited to help celebrate Canada's centenary in 1967. Her Majesty unexpectedly asked Prime Minister Lester B. Pearson if she could tour the Expo '67 site on the specially built mini-rail. Security

C-055389

HRH Princess Elizabeth leaving the stagecoach at the Stadium, assisted by Mr. Jim Cross, President, Calgary Stampede Association, October 18, 1951, Calgary, Alberta.

Their Majesties King George VI and Queen Elizabeth ride through Ottawa in the state landau, May 1939.

C-055389

DND photo

Her Majesty Queen Elizabeth and HRH the Duke of Edinburgh ride to the Parliament Buildings, Ottawa, in the same state landau that King George VI and Queen Elizabeth used.

1951 tour: Princess Elizabeth and the Duke of Edinburgh leave Dorval Airport in a convertible.

officials scrambled to accede to her wish and were initially going to completely restrict access to the entire site during the royal visit. In the end, however, only a part of Île Notre-Dame, where the pavilions of Great Britain and Canada were located, was made off-limits to visitors. Fairgoers cheered the Queen along the route, a journey that lasted forty minutes. The ride was a symbolic journey to celebrate Canada's coming of age.

But no Royal Tour will ever equal (in the memories of a certain generation of Canadians) the 1939 visit of George VI and Queen Elizabeth, when for the first time in history, a reigning monarch and his consort, in the King's words,

PL-52760

"shook the hands of everyone in the country." The Queen Mother remembered the tour years later: "I lost my heart to Canada and to Canadians, and my feelings have not changed with the passage of time." It was this tour that gave birth to that royal staple, the walkabout. In Ottawa, beside the War Memorial, Her Majesty plunged into the crowds to meet with the veterans. One young soldier memorably said, "I wish Hitler could see this." The cynical would say that the whole tour had been designed to achieve that very purpose, that is, to bring Canada into a European war. Whatever the opinion, the outpouring of goodwill and affection that was evident as Their Majesties made their way across the continent has never been equalled, and has been immortalized in history texts, newsreels, and radio broadcasts. A single anecdote sums it up: As the royal train wound through the Rockies, it stopped one night for water at a small station. A crowd of locals gathered around the balcony of the last car, hoping to see Their Majesties. The King and Queen took the opportunity to stretch their legs, and stepped down into the crowd. At that moment, the moon came out, illuminating the scene, and a young man within the crowd began singing "When the Moon Comes Over the Mountain." He sang like Nelson Eddy, the Queen's favourite singer, and first she and then His Majesty joined in. Soon everyone took up the song. The royal train was soon on its way, and the locals dispersed into the deep Canadian forests, with the memorable scene destined to pass not into history but surely into the hearts of those who witnessed it. The public interest in Royal Tours has abated little since 1939.

If the travellers were not the royal family, who would care what cars, aircraft, or yachts they use? Air Force One, the Boeing 747 of the President of the United States, is far larger than the aircraft of the Queen's Flight, the Saudi royal family has many more Rolls-Royces, and the fittings on Saddam Hussein's former presidential yacht *al-Mansur* definitely outnumbered those on the now-decommissioned *Britannia*. Her Majesty now shares her aircraft with ministers and military personnel. The furnishings of the royal train have been described as rather dowdy, and the Rolls Royce Phantoms manage to convey a hearse-like, antiquated splendour. With the exception of the state coaches, the transport of the royal family is hardly noteworthy.

Perhaps because of this, there has been as far as I could ascertain, no complete study on all the family's modes of transport. That is a pity, because, whether the Queen travels in the Gold Coach or a Canadian Forces aircraft, by the mere fact that she has done so, the vehicle becomes a link with our heritage. The grandeur of the monarchy, however faded one might hold it to be, provides continuity in a rapidly changing, increasingly globalized world. How it will adapt when Prince Charles comes to the throne (and if he will still be the King of Canada then) cannot be known. But my aunt is right. One tampers with such institutions at one's peril.

ROYAL TRAINS

Buckingham palace on wheels — the Canadian National Railways carriages used by Their Majesties in the Royal Train in 1939.

On June 13, 1842, Her Majesty Queen Victoria took her first train ride. Precisely at noon, the Great Western Railway (GWR) steam locomotive *Phlegethon* departed Slough (at that time the station for Windsor Castle), pulling the royal saloon and six other carriages for Paddington. The stimulus for this trip had been her consort, Prince Albert, who had been riding in trains since 1839 and had finally been able to convince Her Majesty to try the newfangled, steam-hissing machines. Along with the rest of her household, Victoria dreaded the prospect, and it was only the trust in her beloved Albert that gave her the courage to attempt it.

The *Phlegethon* was a 2-2-2 locomotive and not yet a month old. Sharing the cab with the driver was the great engineer (and principal shareholder in the GWR) Isambard Kingdom Brunel and his Superintendent of Locomotives, Daniel Gooch. Built at the Swindon railway works, the royal saloon consisted of three compartments, with Her Majesty and her consort in the centre one. Brown in colour, the compartments were typical of the day: stagecoach-like boxes that were unheated and brakeless, with weak couplings, the passengers' comfort and safety depending on an entanglement of chains to keep the train together. Her Majesty's personal coachman rode on the footplate of the locomotive, as though behind horses. Repeatedly told that the engine had no need for his vigilance, he still insisted on pretending to handle the controls during the journey. Sadly, the smoke and soot so blackened the poor man's magnificent scarlet coat that he never repeated the experience. When the train pulled into Paddington (then a small station, as the present building had not been built), the journey taking twenty-five minutes, Her Majesty pronounced herself charmed by the whole experience. A fortnight later, she returned to Windsor by train, bringing her infant Albert Edward (later the Prince of Wales) with her. Queen Victoria was not the first European monarch to ride in a British train — the King of Prussia had already enjoyed the comforts of the GWR, as had the Queen's aunt, the dowager Queen Adelaide, consort of William IV.[3]

Her Majesty's ride set the template for all royal train journeys to come, and many of the measures adopted during her reign have remained in use until recently. Even then, special precautions were taken to provide Her Majesty with privacy, comfort, safety, and security. Fearing that the event would attract crowds that might spill onto the tracks, the railway positioned employees on platforms, bridges, and in all towns en route until the royal train had passed. Other trains along adjoining tracks were halted and their contents examined. In later years, a pilot train would be sent ahead, and when there was more than one railway line, trains running parallel to the royal train were forbidden to match its speed, so that passengers could not look into Her Majesty's saloon. As for speed, Queen Victoria forbade the royal train to travel faster than forty miles per hour during the day and thirty miles per hour at night. Later, her carriage would have its own semaphore signal: a small disc erected on the roof by which Her Majesty's attendant could let a lookout man on the locomotive tender know that the Queen wished the train to slow down. Also, afraid that they might fall asleep on duty, Her Majesty periodically commanded that both the driver and fireman take sufficient rest periods, whether they wanted to or not. Finally, when the royal train went by, so as not to offend the royal eye by their attire, all railway employees, from station master, foreman, plate-layers, signalmen, gatemen, and shunters to guards and porters, were ordered to be dressed in their finest — even the firemen had to wear whites gloves while handling the coal. The *Phlegethon* set the trend for all royal locomotives in being lavishly decorated with flags and bunting. Taking it to the extreme, on later royal trips, the top layer of coal on the tender was painted white.

For travelling on the continent, Her Majesty personally owned a twin pair of six-wheeler saloons that were maintained at Calais. These were an exception to the rule, for unlike the other royal means of transportation, royal trains were never owned or maintained by the government (like the Royal Flight and the royal yacht) or by the royal household (like the carriages and cars). Except for those two saloons, neither the state nor the royal family ever purchased their own carriages or locomotives and, to this day, royal trains have been provided by railway companies, with the present royal train owned and managed by Railtrack.[4] A total of twenty-two carriages were constructed during Victoria's reign by the railway companies for her and her family, and while the cars were maintained for their exclusive use, they were never provided free, as the railways charged for their use.

It was with the acquisition of the rural residences — Osborne in 1845, Balmoral in 1852, and Sandringham in 1862 — that the royal family began to travel great distances out of London. For the honour of transporting them, the railway companies went to prodigious lengths, not only with the building of ornate and luxurious saloons but also elaborate stations at the royal residences of Sandringham (Wolferton), Osborne House (Whippingham), and Balmoral (Ballater). No railway station conveyed its royal origins better than Wolferton. Two miles from Sandringham House, the station's origins date to the opening of the King's Lynn-to-Hunstanton branch railway line in 1862, the year in which the Sandringham Estate was purchased by Queen Victoria for the young Prince of Wales. In 1863, the Prince of Wales and his bride, Princess Alexandra of Denmark (later Queen Alexandra), arrived by the royal train at Sandringham after their marriage and honeymoon. As the railway link between Sandringham and London, the station grew in importance, and its buildings were rebuilt in 1898 in Tudor style by W. N. Ashbee, the architect of the Great Eastern Railway buildings. Between 1884 and 1911, a total of 645 Royal Trains arrived at Wolferton, conveying Queen Victoria and many of the other crowned heads of Europe to Sandringham, including the German Emperor Wilhelm II and the future Russian Emperor

British Railways Board

The GWR carriage built for Queen Victoria did not have a dining car or toilet, as Her Majesty would not use either while the train was in motion. It did have a signal on the roof to tell the engine driver to slow down.

One of the royal saloons built for the use of Queen Victoria in 1869 by the London and North Western Railway.

Nicholas II. Politicians and statesmen also arrived on its platform to seek royal favour, and local railway employees never forgot the mad Russian monk Rasputin showing up to harangue the royal family — only to be sent packing back to London. As with the railway that built it, Wolferton Station was the scene of many great royal occasions. In 1925, the funeral procession of Queen Alexandra, who had come to Sandringham as a young bride, departed from the station on its way to London. From here too departed the royal train conveying the body of King George V to London for his state funeral in 1936, and in 1952 the funeral train of King George VI also began its journey at Wolferton. In later years the station was used regularly by the royal family, becoming associated in particular with the traditional Christmas and New Year holidays at Sandringham.[5] The last time a royal train was used at Wolferton was in 1966, and the railway branch line closed in 1969.

Having a member of the royal family use your company's carriages bestowed honour far out of all proportion, and from the earliest days of train travel, royal trains always encompassed the very latest in rail technology, with each of the railway companies, whether in Britain, Australia, or Canada, vying to outdo their rivals. It was also a means for the railways to try out, on the most fastidious, most discriminating passengers, innovations like heating, toilets, and dining cars before introducing them to the general public. If the GWR built the first eight-wheeler coach for Queen Victoria in 1842, the following year the London and Birmingham Railway was the first to put heating into the saloon they hired out to the royal household. Ingeniously hidden between the plush ottomans, the Louis XIV chairs, and the Axminster carpet was a closed-circuit hot-water pipe heated by four oil burners. In 1851, the South Eastern Railway built the most conspicuous royal carriage to date. A six-wheeler, with the principal saloon twelve feet in length between two coupes, it was highly ornate, the walls padded in amber, white, and damask. At one end was a huge state chair, as the saloon was to be a travelling Throne Room. There was also for the first time a closet at one end that contained a lavatory, which, so as not to offend Victorian sensibilities, was cleverly disguised to look like anything but a toilet. Before that, if the Queen wanted to use such facilities, her train stopped at the nearest station — which meant that every station en route had to be prepared for a royal visit.

In 1861, the London and North Western Railway (LNWR) put the first full-length bed on a royal train, and eight years later the same company also built the first British railway coaches to be connected by a flexible concertina "bellows," or gangway. It would be another two decades before these appeared on the trains that Victoria's subjects used. But Her Majesty mistrusted these gangways and still insisted that the train be stopped whenever she wanted to walk from one carriage into the other. Similarly, Her Majesty refused to take her meals while the train was in motion. She felt the same about the use of gas and electricity for illumination, which in 1893 the LNWR fitted to her carriages, preferring instead oil

C-081691

Specially built observation car used by the Prince of Wales in 1860 for the opening of the Victoria Bridge, Montreal.

Royal saloon built for the use of King Edward VII in 1902 by London and North Western Railway.

lamps and candles. Her apprehension of electricity did not prevent her ringing the immense electric bells that were mounted in the compartments of her ladies-in-waiting to summon her staff. Finally, the Queen was also sensitive about what she viewed from the train. When passing through the slums of industrial Britain, not wanting to be affected by the suffering of her people, she had the blinds in her carriage lowered.

Queen Victoria's best-known saloons were the twin six-wheelers built by the LNWR in 1869 to take her to Balmoral twice a year, and today one is preserved at the National Railway Museum, York. In 1897, now an old lady, Her Majesty was even more cautious: when the GWR wanted to honour her by building a replacement for her old saloon, she warned them: "Build a new train and as fine as you wish, but leave the private apartment in my carriage as it is." Through the skill of the Swindon craftsmen, her old salon was successfully incorporated into the very latest design. It had three different types of lighting — gas in the brake carriages, electricity in the remainder of the train — but only oil lighting in Her Majesty's saloon.

It was her son Edward VII who was truly the Railway King. Born in 1841, he had never known (as his mother had) a world before steam, and had no qualms of sleeping, dining, or doing anything else on a train. During his nine-year reign, he would travel by royal train constantly (and quickly, insisting that the speed be raised) in England, Scotland, Wales, and Ireland and on the continent. As he smoked cigars, his mother did not like him using her personal saloon. In any case, he would not have been seen in his mother's old LNWR carriages — as a true gentleman, His Royal Highness preferred to be surrounded by furnishings of teak and leather, rather like a moving gentleman's club. In 1897, Edward had his own royal train built for him by the London, Brighton & South Coast Railway (LBSC). His Royal Highness bestowed his patronage on this line because it connected a number of racecourses together, places that his mother frowned upon but which her son frequented. The Brighton Royal Train, as it was called, consisted of five eight-wheel bogie carriages: two saloons for the household, two for the luggage, and one for His Royal Highness — and sometimes Princess Alexandra.

The Prince of Wales was the first member of the royal family to use a train in Canada during his 1860 tour. The Canadian Pacific Railway, then barely begun on its transcontinental route, built a special carriage and an observation car for him. His Royal Highness travelled from Montreal to Toronto, opening public gardens, dancing at balls, planting trees, and chatting with specially selected "ordinary people." He took to the tour with gusto.

Prince Edward's brother, the almost unknown Prince Alfred, was less fortunate. The first member of the royal family to visit Australia, he arrived by battleship in 1867 and toured Adelaide, Melbourne, and Sydney, receiving everywhere a tumultuous welcome — except in Clontarf, Sydney, where on March 12, 1868, Irish patriot Henry James O'Farrell shot him. O'Farrell was arrested (before he could be lynched), convicted, and then hanged. The prince made a quick recovery and was able to leave Australia by early April, but the national disgrace persisted until the turn of the century, when the country was once more thought safe for Royal Tours.

When Edward became king in 1901, the LNWR retaliated against the LBSC's Brighton train by designing its own grand creation. Costing an estimated $300,000, this train was constructed at its works in Wolverton, following the King's suggestion that "it look as much like a yacht as possible," and presented along with its own locomotive to His Majesty in December 1902, causing one American newspaper to comment that His Majesty had been given the ultimate boy's Christmas gift of a complete train. This was untrue, as the train (like all royal trains) remained the property of the company, and the royal household was always charged first-class fare plus the rate per mile for a special train. Of the two suites on the LNWR train, the King's had a smoking room, a day compartment, a bedroom with dressing room attached, and a saloon. Mahogany, inlaid with rosewood and satinwood, featured heavily in the smoking room; the leather chairs were comfortably upholstered, and the curtains, carpet, and general fittings harmonized in this dark colour scheme. In contrast, the adjoining compartment used by Her Majesty was in white enamel, decorated in the Colonial style, and the furniture was in satinwood, with inlays of ivory and green predominating. Electric heaters were built in, so that Their Majesties could adjust the temperature, while for the summer, electric "waving" fans were provided. Modern comforts supplied in the royal saloon even included the provision of electric cigar-lighters. Queen Alexandra's bedroom was draped in delicate pink with silver-plated fittings. Adjoining was Her Majesty's dressing room, similar in design, but with inlaid satinwood furniture, while next to it was another dressing room, no less ornate, for the use of Princess Victoria.

His Majesty's annual schedule meant commuting between the royal residences of Buckingham Palace, Sandringham (a palace he disliked, but from it, he could go to Newmarket for the races), Balmoral, and Windsor. In between, he attended shooting parties in Scotland, supper parties and the theatre in London, all interspersed with romantic rendezvous. For example, he made several rail trips to Gopsall Hall, Leicestershire, not because its garden was where George Frederick Handel had composed the music for the *Messiah* but to meet with Lillie Langtry, a popular actress of the period and his mistress.

Then there was also holidaying on the Continent by train in the summer. As Prince of Wales, he travelled across Europe to advise his nephew the Kaiser or to discuss the Entente Cordiale with the French or to visit the spa at Marienbad to cure his obesity. Once he went as far as Bad Ischl near Salzburg, to speak to the aged Emperor Franz Josef.

For travelling over the European railroads, Edward VII also owned and maintained a royal saloon, a twelve-wheeler that was the longest in use then, which was kept in the same shed at Calais with his mother's. At a time when every royal family, from the grand dukes of the Russian court to Indian maharajahs, maintained their own trains in Europe, this was not unusual. Edward's saloons would be hitched to the famed Orient Express, and his portly figure (travelling as the Duke of Lancaster) was commonly seen in the company of one of the beauties of the day. The Prince of Wales journeyed on occasion with Princess Alexandra, in three private coaches, all built for comfort with enormous arm-chairs, thick pile carpets, toilets, and spacious cupboards for the luggage. His Royal Highness's personal compartment was furnished in the style of a gentleman's smoking room — leather armchairs, card tables, books, newspapers, drinks, and cigars. The King took with him thirty servants and his fox terrier, Caesar, who, the staff knew, could do no wrong. In his rail travels, His Majesty made the Baie des Anges at Nice, with its palm trees and ornate hotels, so fashionable that the French renamed it the Promenade des Anglais. On April 4, 1900, the royal saloon would be the scene of an attempted assassination of the Prince of Wales when the train was leaving Nord Station, Brussels.[6]

In contrast with Edward's own Canadian railway tour of 1860, when his son and daughter-in-law, the Duke and Duchess of Cornwall and York (later King George V and Queen Mary) arrived in September 1901, the Canadian Pacific Railway had grown into a multi-modal transportation giant, operating trains, ocean liners, banks, telegraph companies, hotels, and ferries across the world. A royal train was assembled to take the Duke and Duchess across Canada from Quebec City to Vancouver and back to Saint John, New Brunswick, and Halifax. It was conducted by Andrew Rainie of Saint John, the oldest conductor on the Intercolonial Railway, and the carriages were provided by the rival Canadian Pacific Railway.

Each of the nine cars was 730 feet long, lit by electricity and equipped with electric bells, telephones, and facilities for hot and cold water. "Cornwall," the day coach, had an expansive observation platform at the rear, and its glass door opened into a reception area and an apartment decorated in Louis XV style. The entire room, except the framing and half the sidewalls, was constructed of plate glass to give the royal party an unobstructed view. From the reception area, a winding corridor led to the Duchess's

British Railways Board

The Britannia Class 4-4-0 locomotive that hauled King Edward's VII's royal train in 1902.

boudoir, which was upholstered in silk, its walls hung with original oils. The dining room walls were panelled and adorned with a number of armorial bearings, including those of His Majesty the King and of Their Royal Highnesses the Duke and Duchess, as well as the coat of arms of the Dominion of Canada. Entered through a vestibule with soft green plush curtains, the night coach, "York," contained the bedrooms and bathrooms of the Duke (in grey and crimson), the Duchess (in blue), the ladies and gentlemen-in-waiting, and the servants. "Canada," the third coach, was a compartment car with five staterooms, a dressing room, lavatory and shower bath, and parlour. The remainder of the train consisted of "Sandringham," the staff dining car, and the sleepers "Australia," "India," and "South Africa," which held the secretaries' office and medical dispensary. The royal train was always preceded by the viceregal train carrying the Governor General and his staff, the Prime Minister, Sir Wilfrid Laurier, and members of Parliament, and the premier of whichever province it was then in.

Between 1914 and 1941, no new royal saloons were built and, with some modifications, the existing royal trains served both Edward VIII and George V. Queen Victoria's old saloon would be used as the hearse coach for both her funeral and that of her son, Edward VII. The period of opulence had ended with the Great War, and with hard financial times, railway companies were reluctant to spend on decor in the hope of attracting royalty. Also, the motor car was usurping the train for short Royal Tours.

At Ottawa.

The Prince of Wales (centre) standing next to a Canadian National Railways passenger car, Ottawa, Ontario, 1924.

PA- 38861

King George V and Queen Mary made extensive use of various carriages owned by the LNWR, GWR, and the LBSC. Of the many industrial areas they visited by train — the pair loved to press switches and unveil plaques — particularly historic was their trip to the huge railway yards at Crewe on April 21, 1913: no member of the royal family had until then ever been to a rail yard. During the First World War, Their Majesties continued their inspection trips by train, but now to munitions factories and hospitals. Because they did not wish to stay overnight at homes of friends (for one thing, all the domestic staff in the big houses were now in uniform), they slept more and more on board the royal train and even bathed on it — so much so that, in 1915, two bathtubs, silver plated and encased in mahogany, were installed in the dressing rooms of the saloons used by Their Majesties. On April 28, 1924, the King personally drove a Castle class locomotive, number 4082, appropriately named "Windsor Castle," from the Swindon Works to Swindon Station.[7] Plaques were mounted on the side of the cab to commemorate the occasion.

Through his short eleven-month reign, Edward VIII never warmed to the royal trains — they represented the formality of his father's era. His Majesty preferred instead fast cars (preferably Canadian) and aircraft. But his dislike did not extend to those trains he used overseas. On his first visit to Canada in 1919, accompanied by Captain Alan Lascelles (later to be Governor General Lord Bessborough's secretary), the handsome, unattached, twenty-six-year-old Prince Edward set out on a two-month rail tour across Canada. "I progressed westwards in a magnificent special train provided by the Canadian Pacific Railway. My quarters were in the rear car, which had an observation platform. This last ... while providing me with a continuous view of the varied Canadian landscape had however the drawback of making me vulnerable to demands for ad lib speeches from the crowds gathered at every stop," he remembered. "Getting off the train to stretch my legs, I would start up conversations with farmers, section hands, miners, small town editors or newly arrived immigrants from Europe. It was the first time that a Prince had ever stumped a Dominion." In 1923, he came back for a seven-week tour, and even tried his hand as driver at the controls of a Canadian Pacific 4-6-2 locomotive. The Prince returned to visit his Alberta ranch several times, including in 1927 to celebrate the country's Diamond Jubilee of Confederation.

His Royal Highness was not as fortunate with rail travel in Western Australia when on tour there in 1920: as his train entered Bridgetown, it derailed. Only by luck did the heir to the throne escape unhurt. But when he returned home on HMS *Renown* and stepped ashore at Portsmouth on October 11, the royal train was waiting to take him to Victoria Station, the front of the 4-4-0 locomotive decorated with the Prince of Wales's feathers. It was a mark of respect well meant by the railway but wholly unappreciated by the Prince.

On the Continent the Prince of Wales made frequent trips to Vienna, preferring the anonymity of the Orient Express to the royal train. The Wagons-Lit Compagnie converted Sleeping Car No. 3538 for his private use, with a salon and shower.[8] On one trip, the Prince claimed he was in Vienna consulting a physician for a chronic ear problem, when His Highness and friend Major Edward "Fruity" Metcalfe

Visit of Their Majesties King George VI and Queen Elizabeth. Her Majesty is accepting flowers from a little girl. The royal party has just alighted at Beavermouth, B.C., July 1939.

PA-210047

were seen at the Viennese night spots Chat Noir and Cocotte, and rumours spread that they were meeting with prominent Nazis. Edward VIII had no liking for either Sandringham or Balmoral, and did not use trains as much as his father or grandfather, choosing to isolate himself in his residence at Fort Belvedere, which could be reached only by car. Even a Mediterranean cruise had unfortunate results: the hostility of the Italian Fascist government prevented him from embarking on the yacht *Nahlin* in Venice, and his party had to travel by train to Yugoslavia, "an indescribable journey that I subjected myself to," he wrote (blaming the Foreign Office for this inconvenience), to meet the yacht at the little fishing village of Sibenik.

One of the rare occasions when Edward VIII did use a British train was on November 18, 1936, when he toured depressed areas in Wales. Scorning the royal train — and even the red-carpet treatment — His Majesty travelled in a special GWR carriage, arriving bareheaded in the freight yards, and completing much of the tour by car. His flair for public relations asserted itself this one final time and, moved at the plight of the destitute miners, he declared, "something must be done." However, Edward knew he would not be the man to do it, and had already told his brothers, his mother, and the prime minister of his intention to abdicate. After his abdication, there were no more royal trains and the new Duke took the Orient Express from Austria to France to be married at the Château de Candé, near Tours. This time, a retired Orient Express employee recalled, to escape the media circus, or "hounds" as Wallis Simpson termed the press, his meals were taken by tray into an ordinary compartment, where the former king ate off two suitcases balanced between the seats.

During her son's brief reign, it was Queen Mary who kept the old LNWR Royal Train in use, and after Edward's abdication, it became a perfect means for King George VI, Queen Elizabeth, and the two little princesses to vacation at Balmoral. The children were thrilled at sleeping on a train that had been built for their beloved grandfather, who had doted on little Elizabeth. As soon as he acceded to the throne, as if exorcising his brother's irresponsibility, George VI immediately paid visits by train to Scotland, Wales, and Northern Ireland.

Unlike his brother, the new king had always enjoyed trains. As Duke of York, he had travelled on the Orient Express to Belgrade in 1922 to attend the marriage of King Alexander of Yugoslavia to Princess Marie of Romania. Shortly after his own marriage, the Orient Express had taken him and his bride, the Duchess of York, to Belgrade for the christening of Crown Prince Peter. In 1925, they attended the centenary celebration of the opening of the Stockton and Darlington Railway, the first passenger railway in Britain. On August 6, the following year, His Royal Highness drove the first train on the fifteen-inch-gauge Romney, Hythe and Dymchurch Railway in Kent. On October 20 he visited the Southern railway works at Ashford and even rode on the footplate of the locomotive *Lord Nelson*. Little did he know of the marathon railway adventure to come.

Through the winter of 1938-39, London and Ottawa were busy working out the details of a royal visit to North America. As Prime Minister Neville Chamberlain had just returned from Germany with Hitler's assurance that there would be no war for at least a year, it was considered safe to allow Their Majesties to leave the country and drum up support from Britain's closest Dominion and its mighty neighbour. The royal train trip would be from one coast of Canada to the other and back, with a side trip to Washington and New York. The plan was that Their Majesties would visit every province and provincial capital, with day trips in large cities and whistle stops in smaller ones. The train would pull off into quiet (and secret) sidings at night so that all on board could sleep. If the city to be honoured was in the riding of a powerful Liberal politician, so much the better, for then, as now, the photo opportunity for a politician of greeting Their Majesties at the station was worth thousands of votes. This precipitated local politicians, mayors, Rotary clubs, and society hostesses to badger the Prime Minister's Office for a few precious royal minutes and to warn of dire consequences in the next election if that did not happen. Where the train could not stop, the plan was that it would slow down and Their Majesties would drop everything and rush out to the platform and wave, affording the throngs of locals who had been waiting for hours a quick view of the King and Queen on the rear platform.

It was a heavy schedule, exhausting for everyone involved with the royal party—the Mounties, the press, the ladies-in-waiting, the hairdressers, the postal workers, and everyone on board. But no one was to work harder than Prime Minister Mackenzie King, who at every stop got off the train first and then

Joyce Evans, daughter of the Port Arthur City Clerk, presents a bouquet to the Queen, as W.L. Mackenzie King and C.D. Howe look on, May 23, 1939.

rushed over to the royal car to greet Their Majesties, welcoming them to whichever city they were in and introducing them to the local politicians, their wives, and the aldermen.

The grand railway tour was to begin on May 18, when Their Majesties would be driven from the Citadel at Quebec City to the railway station. Engineer Eugène Leclerc of Quebec, who had worked on the Royal Train in 1901 and had been in CPR service between Quebec City and Montreal for forty-eight years, had the honour of being the first engineer. The Royal Train would leave for Montreal, making sure it stopped on the way at Trois Rivières, Quebec, Premier Maurice Duplessis's hometown. After Montreal it was on to Ottawa, then Toronto, with a brief stop at Kingston and Cobourg on the way. Through the Ontario highlands it would go, and then along the north shore of Lake Superior to Port Arthur, C.D. Howe's riding. The train was to stop at Raith, Ontario, for servicing but only slow down at Kenora before arriving in Winnipeg. The Prairies would follow, with stops at Brandon, Regina (named for the King's great-grandmother Victoria Regina), Moose Jaw, Swift Current, Medicine Hat, Calgary, and Banff, where the royal party was to rest. Through the Rockies they were to stop at Craigellachie, Salmon Arm, and finally Vancouver. On the return east, it was Vancouver to New Westminster, through the Fraser Valley to Jasper for a rest, and then on to Edmonton. They would stop at Wainwright, Biggar, Saskatoon, Waitrose, Melville, Portage la Prairie, and Sioux Lookout, then travel through to Toronto and then west to Guelph, Kitchener, Stratford, Chatham, and finally Windsor, where the royal party would stay overnight — quite a coup for up-and-coming local MP Paul Martin. In the evening the royal train was to arrive at Niagara Falls. Then it would traverse the undefended border into New York State, go down to Washington, and then make for Manhattan. At the New Jersey shoreline, the train would halt to allow Their Majesties to take a United States naval vessel to The Battery, Manhattan. The train would be waiting for them at Hyde Park Station, where the President's home was, to take them back to Canada. Across the border, they would go through Levis, Rivière-du-Loup, and on to New Brunswick. They would reach Prince Edward Island by a destroyer, and then the royal train would be picked up again at New Glasgow. The last stops would be Truro and finally Halifax, where a liner would wait to take them home.

There were only two organizations in Canada capable of planning and executing the logistics of such a complex visit: the Canadian Pacific Railway and the Canadian National Railway. Both railways were already proficient at VIP tours across Canada. CPR President Sir Edward Beatty set out on one annually, in his luxurious carriage "Wentworth" — named, like his golf club, with his middle name — to inspect his domain. More frequently, the CNR would take the Governor General about in his private carriage. With the first company private — and most of its shareholders British — and the second wholly owned by the Canadian government, it might be assumed that Mackenzie King (who loathed the CPR and its president) would give S.J. Hungerford, president of the Canadian National, a free hand in the whole royal trip. But in a typically Canadian gesture, both railways divided the trip — on land and sea, in hotels and lodges — between them, so that, if Their Majesties arrived at a Canadian National station, as in Montreal at Jean Talon, they would leave from Windsor Station, where the CPR had its headquarters. From Vancouver to Victoria they crossed on a CPR ferry the *Princess Marguerite*, but, on the return voyage, they used the government-owned ship *Prince Robert*. The trip west would be made on CPR tracks, the return journey on CNR tracks. Neither railway was to be given preference, and the King and Queen were told not to mention either in speeches or interviews. So important were the two railway presidents that, when Their Majesties stepped on shore at Wolfe's Cove on May 17, after the Prime Minister and Minister of Justice Ernest Lapointe, the next to be introduced were Beatty and Hungerford.

Of the royal train's twelve cars, six were prepared in the Point St. Charles shops of the Canadian National Railways and six at the Angus Shops of the Canadian Pacific Railway. The former included the Governor General's two private cars, in which the King and Queen travelled; No. 7, which the Lord-in-Waiting and the Lord Chamberlain used; the Canadian National compartment cars "Atlantic" (No. 6) and "Pacific" (No. 4), in which other members of the royal party were accommodated; and one of the new Canadian National diners, the most modern type recently put in service by the Canadian National and capable of seating forty people. The Canadian Pacific Railway also supplied the private car "Wentworth" (No. 5), which was used by the Prime Minister and his official staff;

C-014455

When the royal train couldn't stop: Their Majesties leaning out of the carriage, May 1939.

The King's sitting room in Car No. 1 of the royal train used in the 1939 tour.

The map in the sitting room on which Their Majesties plotted their progress across Canada in the royal train.

CN003705

the Chambrette car "Grand Pré" (No. 8), which accommodated the Train Office and provided sleeping quarters for a number of officials; a Chambrette car (No. 3) for the personal servants of Their Majesties and the Mounties; a compartment sleeping car (No. 9), which was used chiefly by the protective forces, but also included a barber shop; a combination baggage and sleeper for part of the train staff (No. 11); and a baggage car (No. 12). In one end of the baggage car, an electric power plant was installed to furnish power for the passengers' needs and to provide a refrigerated storage compartment for food supplies.

Canadian National Railways locomotive No. 6400, which hauled the royal train in 1939.

The King and Queen travelled at the rear of the train, as far from the noise and soot of the locomotive as possible. Car No.1 contained two main bedrooms with dressing rooms and private bath, a sitting room or lounge for the King and Queen, and two bedrooms for members of the Royal Staff. The living room was furnished with green chairs and apricot-coloured upholstery. It had a radio and small library that was appropriately stocked with books by Canadian authors such as Bliss Carmen, Mazo de la Roche, and Stephen Leacock. Popular authors of the day like Pearl S. Buck, Anne Morrow Lindbergh, and of course John Buchan (the Governor General) were also represented — as was a translation of Hitler's *Mein Kampf.* Family photos and mementos were scattered about, including two little canoes that had been given by a First Nations community for the princesses. There was also a set of specially designed maps of North America that rolled up and down like blinds. In the tiny but fully equipped dining room, the china was a white Limoges pattern with bands of maroon and gold surmounted by an embossed crown.

Perhaps reflecting his naval upbringing, His Majesty's rooms were in blue and white chintz. Close at hand were his field glasses and cine camera — he was constantly running in to grab it and record sightings of moose and deer that he thought his daughters would like to see. His bathroom was done in pale blue. The Queen's sitting room was blue-grey with damask coverings and curtains of dusty pink. Her bedroom was in soft peach with brocaded satin drapes. On her bedside table were her *The Book of Common Prayer* and a pile of the ghost-story books that she loved. Her bathroom was in lavender.

Car No. 2 had a large lounge, as well as an office, a dining room and kitchen, and two bedrooms with a bathroom for members of the Royal Staff. Car No.7 had two main bedrooms with bath, lounge, dining room, kitchen, and also a bedroom for servants. The cars "Pacific" and "Atlantic" accommodated the ladies-in-waiting and other persons of Their Majesties' staff. "Atlantic" had six rooms with lounge and a shower. "Pacific" had five rooms, a lounge, and a shower. The lounges on "Atlantic," "Pacific," and car No. 7 were used as sitting rooms for all members of the royal party.

The exterior colour scheme of this "Buckingham Palace on wheels" (so dubbed by the press) was royal blue, with silver panels between the windows and a horizontal gold stripe above and below the windows, the blue extending above the windows to the roof line, which had a gun-metal colour. The last two cars of the train, cars Nos. 1 and 2, were dubbed "The Married Quarters" by the press. Their two carriages, in which the King and Queen travelled, bore the royal coat of arms in the centre of each car below the windows. The other cars in the train bore the royal cypher and crown in the centre below the windows, and a royal crown at each of the blue stripe between the top of the windows and the roof line. All of the cars were air-conditioned, which was more and more appreciated as the Canadian summer began.

It had been on the King's express command that a buzzer was installed between the engine and the royal cars, and the locomotive engineer had instructions that, whenever he saw a crowd at any station ahead where they were not going to stop, he was to press the buzzer and slow down. This was a signal for Their Majesties to run out to the observation platform and wave. Through the trip, Her Majesty spent much time arranging the bouquets of flowers that were handed to her at every station. The King and Queen also spent time talking, reading, or playing games of solitaire. They also listened to the radio[9] and talked on the phone to London and their daughters — facilities were provided at all stops for an outside telephone service. On one such phone call, Princess Elizabeth assured them that she was looking after Margaret, and her sister burst out with the news that she had passed her Girl Guide tracking test. Outside Port Arthur, the royal couple heard that Her Majesty Queen Mary had had an accident in her old Daimler. In between calls, His Majesty worked away on his "boxes," the dispatch cases from London.

The royal train heads through the Rockies on its way to the Pacific coast during the 1939 Royal Tour.

The royal train was preceded, throughout the tour, by a pilot train, its purpose to protect and serve those on the train behind them. It carried the press, photographers, members of the Royal Canadian Mounted Police, and excess baggage that could not be accommodated on the royal train. The pilot train consisted of twelve cars, of which the Canadian National furnished seven. These included: one drawing-room sleeper, and three baggage cars. Two of the baggage cars were specially equipped to carry the baggage of the royal party, and the third baggage car was converted into a unit that included an electric power plant for generating all electric current, a darkroom for photographic purposes, and a postal-service section. The Canadian Pacific furnished five cars, including two drawing-room sleepers, a diner, a combination baggage car and sleeper, and a lounge car ("River Clyde"), which occupied the rear of the pilot train.

The Canadian National prepared locomotives for hauling the royal train, a 6400 type,[10] a 6000 type, and one "Pacific" type, all finished in royal blue. Weighing 660,080 pounds, 95 feet long, and 15 feet high, the Canadian National 6400 steam locomotive had been built by the Montreal Locomotive Works in 1936 and, with the help of the National Research Council, was planned with an aerodynamic design that could prevent smoke from obscuring the engineer's vision and could also reduce costs. The final bullet-shaped configuration, the result of wind-tunnel tests conducted in Ottawa, was so streamlined that it was often mistaken for a diesel locomotive. In addition to these, a CN oil-burner was used for hauling it through the mountains. The Canadian Pacific prepared two of its new Class H-1-d 4-6-4 locomotives for the royal train, which were the Hudson type, 2800 class. The Royal Hudson 2850,[11] reconditioned at the CPR's Angus Shops in Montreal, hauled Their Majesties across Canada, the first time that one engine had made a continuous journey of this length. Specially refitted and decorated for the occasion, the Canadian Pacific locomotive was a mass of shining stainless steel, royal blue, silver, and gold. The semi-streamlined engine bore the Royal Arms over the headlight, and Imperial Crowns decorated each running board. The crest of the Canadian Pacific appeared beneath the window of the cab and on the tender. The general decorative scheme comprised a background of deep blue on the underframe, the smoke-box, the front of the engine, and all the marginal work on the engine and tender. The sides of the tender, cab, and running boards were painted royal blue. The jacket of the locomotive, its handrails, and other trim were of stainless steel with gold leaf employed on the engine numbers. With His Majesty's approval, the Royal Arms and replica crown were applied to all forty-five of the CPR's H-1-c, H-1-d and the H-1-e 4-6-4s built between 1937 and 1945, and they became known as the "Royal Hudsons."

The only time Their Majesties did not travel on the royal train was in New Brunswick between Fredericton and Saint John, where the track wasn't strong enough to take it. A smaller, lighter train, consisting of a drawing-room car and four day-coaches, was used instead.

At a time when most of Canada seemed to live beside or near the two main railway lines, everyone had a good chance of seeing the royal train. Their Majesties met the famous, like air ace Billy Bishop, actor Raymond Massey, and the Dionne quintuplets, and the First People of Canada, like representatives of the Ojibway, Blacks, Stoneys, and Sarcees — some of whom had met the King's father in 1901. They heard "God Save the King" sung many times in English, fewer times in French, and twice in Cree. Obviously missing their own daughters very much, they had lifted up to their carriage balcony dozens

Crowds wait for the royal train at Kitchener, Ontario. Boys placing coins on track over which it will pass.

of bewildered children, and once at a remote station, Her Majesty, seeing two mothers with their babies, rushed into the kitchen and ran out with a bag of cookies for them. They met the future of the country through thousands of Boy Scouts and Girl Guides, many chosen because they were thirteen-year-olds like Princess Elizabeth (a Girl Guide herself), and they met its past, shaking hands with seven holders of the Victoria Cross. The press did not need to look far for copy and anecdotes abounded. At tiny La Station du Côteau, Quebec, the Queen made His Majesty remain still and pose for a little girl who was struggling with a box camera. Later, at the White House, Her Majesty delicately tried to eat the first hot dog she had ever seen with a knife and fork until President Roosevelt leaned over and advised, "Just push it straight into your mouth, Ma'am."

When she learned the house prices at British Pacific Properties in Vancouver, Her Majesty wondered aloud if even she could afford to live there.[12] The pair got off to visit dozens of veterans' hospitals, placed wreathes on a dozen memorials, and must have planted a forest of trees. The blue train stopped at all major Canadian cities as well as specks on the map for water. Such a one was Fire River, Ontario (population twelve), where Her Majesty asked a trapper, "How cold does it get here in the winter?"

"Sixty-five below, Ma'am, and the snow, she's six feet deep," was the stoic reply.

When the royal train crept into Halifax on June 16, having covered 8,377 miles, in its freight compartment was a variety of gifts. Among them were the two tiny birchbark canoes for the princesses, dozens of stamp albums (everyone knew that the King, like his father, was a keen philatelist), twelve-pound cheeses, braided gauntlets from Duck Chief of the Blackfoot, a silver desk telephone, a solid gold trylon and crystal glass perisphere (with a thermometer in the trylon) from the New York World's Fair, and a portrait of the late King George V by Sir Wyly Grier.

When the *Empress of Britain* docked at Southampton, the party boarded the old LNWR Royal Train for Waterloo Station. There they were met by Princess Alice of Connaught, and the Countess and the Earl of Athlone, all of whom had viceregal connections with Canada. Also on the platform was the Canadian High Commissioner Vincent Massey, another future Governor General. At Waterloo, the King and Queen boarded a landau for the ride to the palace, and as it emerged from the station, they were visibly moved by the cheering crowds outside. Through Trafalgar Square and the Mall, massed ranks of spectators applauded, the King noticing some carrying signs that said simply, "Well Done." The Queen later told Prime Minister Mackenzie King, "The tour made us! It came at the right time, particularly for us."[13] A *New York Times* headline summed it all up: "The British Take Washington Again." The North American rail tour had given His Majesty the confidence he would need to face the rigours of the war that was just around the corner.

At the start of the Second World War, the old LNWR train built in 1902 was repainted the same colour as other trains, so that it would not stand out. As George V and Queen Mary had done, Their Majesties began tours of munitions factories and

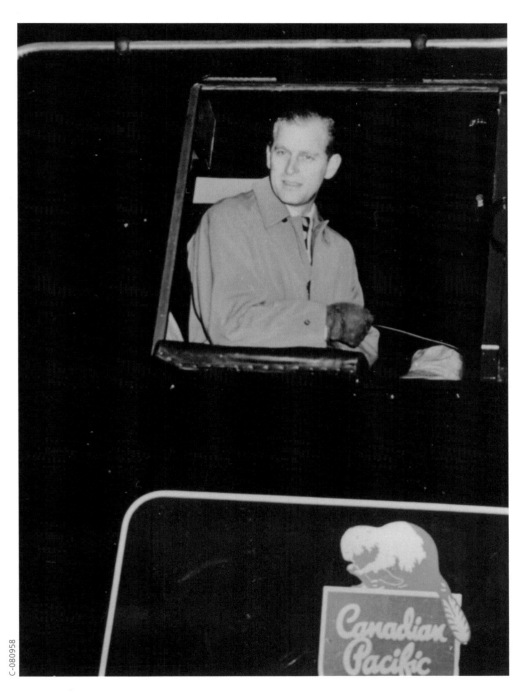

C-080958

Prince Philip in the cab of the royal train locomotive, Kamloops, B.C., October 1951.

army camps and — with the Blitz — of bombed cities. Having slept on the train en route, they could appear at bomb sites in Coventry and Nottingham the morning after an air raid to comfort survivors and chat with Civil Defence workers. Everyone understood that the old train would not withstand a direct hit by a bomb or even shrapnel, and in the event of a German invasion, the saloons would splinter before a machine-gun attack. It was, of course, more likely that the train would be caught in an air raid, and the safest place was thought be in a tunnel. At the first sound of a siren, the train was to make for the closest one, remaining there until the "all clear" was sounded. Because of the threat of invasion, three new twelve-wheel cars were built for the royal family by the LMS at Wolverton: the King's saloon (No. 798), the Queen's saloon (No. 799), and one for the brake, power generators, and accommodation staff (No. 31209). The old LNWR royal saloons were withdrawn and later given to the National Railway Museum in York. Gone too was the ornate Victorian decoration; in its place were massive steel armour plates, including armour-plate shutters for the windows. Inside, the basic design was similar to the 1902 LNWR saloons, but they were now meant for extended day and night use. The walls, curtains, and carpets in the royal compartments were finished in pastel colours to provide a "country house" touch, contrasting with the armour plate outside. A rudimentary form of air-conditioning was attempted, with ice stored in boxes under the floor. It had to be frequently changed. Both saloons remained in use with the royal family until 1977, when they were sent into retirement. Today they stand next to their LNWR predecessors at the National Railway Museum.

Also made in 1940 were two special saloons by the GWR. Without sleeping accommodations, they were used for daytime trips by the royal family, as well as by Prime Minister Winston Churchill and General Dwight Eisenhower. After the war, both continued to be used by Her Majesty the Queen Mother to go to the races at Cheltenham and, now restored, one is at the Birmingham Railway Museum and the other at the Didcot Railway Centre.

At 4:15 p.m. on November 20, 1947, a very special royal train was preparing to pull out of Waterloo and the station masters at Clapham Junction, Surbiton, Woking, and Basingstoke were told to phone as soon as it passed their stations. There were also to be standby locomotives and crews waiting at Woking and Basingstoke. The main part of the train would be two Pullman cars called "Rosemary" and "Rosamund." At the termination of the train at Winchester, a chalk mark was to be made at the exact spot at which the footplate of the engine (a Lord Nelson class) stopped at the down platform. A signalman with a red flag was to stand on the platform side of the engine at the chalk mark to ensure that the train halted exactly at the appointed place so that the red carpet could be put down. The whole railway — indeed, in the frugality of post-war Britain, the whole country — was participating in this ride. For this was the honeymoon train for Her Royal Highness Princess Elizabeth and Lieutenant Philip Mountbatten, RN, ready to take them to Lord Mountbatten's home, Broadlands, in Hampshire. The young couple arrived at the station directly from their wedding reception at the palace in an open carriage. Concealed beneath the rugs were hot water bottles and the bride's favourite corgi, Susan, with whom she couldn't bear to part.

As His Majesty King George VI became ill, he tired more easily, and going to or from an event, he slept more often on board the royal train, his equerry asking that speed be reduced so as not to disturb

His Majesty's sleep. After he died on February 6, 1952, at Sandringham, his remains were conveyed on February 11 from Norfolk for the lying-in-state in London and on February 15 from Paddington Station for the burial at Windsor. The same saloon had been used as a hearse vehicle for the funerals of Queen Alexandra in 1925 and King George V in 1936. The sides were painted black, with the King's coat of arms mounted centrally on each side, while the roof was finished in white.

On January 1, 1948, all the railways in Britain were nationalized but the royal family's LMS Royal Trains were unaffected. Two saloons were built for Princess Elizabeth and the Duke of Edinburgh. Thus, when she became queen in 1952, Her Majesty inherited three royal trains: the 1941 LNWR armoured train, the 1940 GWR daytime train, and the two saloons. The Queen used her mother's saloon, 799, while Prince Philip used the former king's saloon, 798. All three trains were hauled by the Lord Nelson-class locomotives, each of which was decorated with the royal plaques above their smoke boxes.

In 1955, Wolverton Carriage Works built a new saloon for the royal children, Prince Charles and Princess Anne. No. 2900 was fitted out in nursery furniture and nicknamed "the nursery coach" by the railway staff. By the end of the 1970s, the last of the old LNWR coaches that had been built in 1941 had been retired and the royal train was very much a product of British Railways. The present royal train came into operation in 1977 with the introduction of four new saloons to mark the Queen's Silver Jubilee. The carriages were built in 1972 as prototypes for the standard Inter-City Mark III passenger motor carriage and subsequently fitted out for their royal role at the Wolverton Works, where much of the work on the royal train has been done. The Queen and Prince Philip were both consulted as to design, as seen in the inward-opening, double-door entrance vestibule at the end of her saloon. The windows in the doors opened inward so that Her Majesty could take leave of her hosts after the doors had closed. Other smaller royal trains were still in use for daytime journeys or by Her Majesty's guests. Visiting royalty or heads of state were met by the royal train whether they entered the country at one of the Channel ports or at Gatwick Airport. Unlike her father and grandfather, Her Majesty has travelled by ordinary trains (first class), and on March 7, 1969, she rode the Underground from Green Park to Oxford Circus, a trip that surely brought back memories of when her governess Crawfie had taken her and her sister on the Underground while the King and Queen were in Canada. Characteristic of his appreciation of history, on September 27, 1975, Prince Philip opened the National Railway Museum at York, where so many of the saloons made for royalty by such companies as the GWR, LMS, and LNWR have been preserved.

But what the world's television viewers remember most are the great events in the royal family's (and the nation's) history in which the royal train is featured. One such event was the funeral of Earl Mountbatten of Burma on September 5, 1979, when a combined royal and funeral train took Her Majesty and the Earl's body from Waterloo to Romsey. A happier occasion was the honeymoon special on July 29, 1981, when the Prince and Princess of Wales used the train to travel on the same journey from Waterloo to Romsey to spend part of their honeymoon at the Mountbatten estate, Broadlands, as the Queen and Prince Philip had also done. This time, able to follow their every move on television, thousands of well-wishers crowded the route, cheering as the train was led by the locomotive "Broadlands," which bore at its head the code "C.D." — the initials of the royal couple.

The royal train enables members of the royal family to travel overnight at times when the weather is too bad to fly, and to work and hold meetings during lengthy journeys. The designation "royal" train is actually incorrect, because the modern train consists of carriages drawn from eight purpose-built saloons, pulled by one of the two Royal Class 47 diesel locomotives, named "Prince William" or "Prince Henry." The exact number and combination of carriages forming a royal train is determined by factors such as which member of the royal family is travelling and the time and duration of the journey. While it is owned by Railtrack, an American company, it is operated by the English, Welsh and Scottish Railway Company. Journeys on the train are always organized so as not to interfere with scheduled service, and royal train drivers are drawn from an elite pool working in the railway industry. One of the most demanding skills they have to master is the ability to stop at a station within six inches of a given mark, a feat that fascinated Prince Charles when he was a boy.

Fitted out at the former British Rail's Wolverton Works in Buckinghamshire, the carriages are a distinctive maroon, with red and black coach lining and a grey roof; they include the royal compartments for sleeping and dining, and support cars. On board are modern office and communications facilities. The Queen's saloon is seventy-five feet long, air-conditioned and electrically heated, and has a bedroom, a bathroom, and a sitting room with an entrance that opens onto the platform, as well as accommodation for her dresser. The Duke of Edinburgh's saloon has a similar layout, with a kitchen. Scottish landscapes by Roy Penny and Victorian prints of earlier rail journeys hang in both saloons. A link with the earliest days of railways is displayed in the Duke of Edinburgh's saloon: a piece of Brunel's original broad-gauge rail, presented on the 150th anniversary of the Great Western Railway.

For the Queen's Golden Jubilee celebrations in 2002, the royal train came into its own, covering 3,500 miles across England, Scotland, and Wales, taking Her Majesty from as far south as Falmouth in Cornwall and as far north as Wick in Caithness, Scotland. The train was to be sold off after the Queen and her family had made use of it during the Golden Jubilee celebrations, but Buckingham Palace told Members of Parliament that there were benefits for the Queen in allowing a new train to replace the old one. Helicopters were often grounded by bad weather or found it difficult to land at night, at dawn, or at dusk. But a train allowed the Queen to go to the very centre of cities, stay on board overnight, and have meetings or entertain people on board. Prince Charles, who used the royal train more frequently than the others, argued (through his staff) that he enjoyed the isolation and convenience it brought to a heavy schedule. It gave him invaluable time to read his briefings and prepare speeches, all the while travelling towards his destination.

The future of the royal train is once more in doubt as the government has launched an inquiry into its cost to the taxpayer, which in 2003 was £596,000 for seventeen journeys, or £35,059 per trip. When Prince Charles took the royal train overnight to Cumbria to launch a rural revival project, the trip cost £16,729. A royal train journey taken by the Prince of Wales from London to Kirkcaldy, Scotland, to visit a farm ecology centre cost £37,158. The Queen and the Duke of Edinburgh's trip from Slough to Lincoln for the annual Maundy Service in April 2002 cost £34,263. Their journey from London to Bodmin to visit the Royal Cornwall Show cost £36,474. The cost of maintaining and using the train is met by the royal household from the Grant-in-Aid that it receives from Parliament each year for air and rail travel. It cost taxpayers £872,000 in 2003, compared with £675,000 in 2002 and was used for a mere nineteen journeys, four more than in the previous year, averaging 827 miles per journey. To mitigate the expense, the royal family has indicated that it had cut the cost of its rail travel by 64 percent in the last five years, reducing the number of coaches from fourteen to nine. Of the five carriages of the royal train that were given up, three were sold for £235,000, while the other two were kept for spare parts. The remaining nine carriages were also offered for rent. But in three years, only the Foreign Office has rented — and only once, in 1998. Lack of conference facilities and dining facilities is cited as the reason, but the train is probably seen as rather too pretentious for modern conferences. In any case, unused for three-quarters of the year and then used only around twenty times, it would require airing out and dusting. Expensive to maintain and underused, it could be replaced by a commercial service, and its critics point out that using a helicopter or renting a single carriage and connecting it to the end of a regular train would be cheaper.

Its future in doubt even before 9/11, a journey by the royal train is now a security official's nightmare. The miles of tracks are impossible to secure, and the train is old and slow. Industrial action by railway employees (while not directed against Her Majesty) has disrupted royal journeys many times. Vulnerable especially when the royal passengers are asleep, the royal train itself is heavily protected by uniformed members of the royalty and diplomatic protection squad armed with 9-mm Austrian Glock machine pistols. But having just lost her beloved HMY *Britannia*, Her Majesty is devastated at the thought of surrendering the very last exclusive and familial means of royal transport left.

Ultimately, what might save the royal train is its nemesis: the motor car. As Britain becomes increasingly urbanized and its road system even more congested, traffic jams will multiply. Only a train will allow Her Majesty to get from the middle of one big city to another comfortably, easily, and on time.

ROYAL YACHTS

Detail of photo from page 92.

"People criticize the expense of the Royal Yacht *Britannia*," Lord Mountbatten once remarked. "But when the Queen arrives, no matter where it is, she brings not just a ship but part of the Court of St. James, part of Buckingham Palace with her. She comes in, this beautiful ship with its escort … and it is a tremendous and majestic way of arriving."[14] When he heard the media attacking the expenditure on *Britannia*, Prince Charles said, "It's not a sort of private yacht. It goes with the position. It is part of the process of representing Britain abroad." But who had the use of a yacht almost the size of a small ocean liner for a honeymoon?

Royal Yacht *Victoria and Albert II*. After Prince Albert's death, it was rarely used by Queen Victoria.

The history of royal yachts can be traced to 1660, when the Dutch East India Company presented Charles II with a fifty-foot miniature man-of-war called *Mary*. After the death of her consort, Queen Victoria had no use for the Royal Yacht *Victoria and Albert II*, an old paddlewheel steamer, and it was only in 1899 that the third of the royal yachts of that name was launched. The government of the day had convinced Her Majesty that, as both the Kaiser and Czar had royal yachts, Britain could not be left behind, and a royal yacht, the larger the better, was an absolute necessity. At its completion in 1901 (delayed after design problems arising from confusion over Imperial and metric measurements), *Victoria and Albert III* was the largest royal yacht in the world (4,700 tonnes, 380 feet long, and with a crew of 367 officers and ratings). Besides its crew, it also took a staff of thirty personal servants for the royal family. Queen Victoria was never destined to sail in her, as she had died seven months before the launch, but the yacht would serve three future sovereigns.

Her son Edward did sail in the new yacht annually, cruising the Mediterranean every April and returning to London in May to preside over the social season, which culminated at Ascot in June. His

The brand new Royal Yacht *Victoria and Albert III*, then the largest royal yacht in the world.

most historic voyage was to France in 1904, when His Majesty's diplomacy sealed the Entente Cordiale between the two nations, effectively checking Germany's ambitions in Europe until after the King's death. But as Prince of Wales and King, Edward was much happier and more relaxed on HMY *Britannia*, a racing yacht that had been built for him as Prince of Wales. The fastest in its class in the world, in 1895 alone *Britannia* won thirty-eight of fifty regattas she took part in, and in 1897, to the glee of the Prince, she even outraced *Meteor*, the yacht owned by his nephew, German Kaiser Wilhelm II, and winning the Challenger Cup. The next year, when the Kaiser's yacht *Meteor II* avenged this defeat at Cowes,[15] the Prince of Wales sold *Britannia* and concentrated on golf. But as king, he was able to have *Britannia* bought back and, although it had lost its racing edge, the King's sons crewed the yacht several times, as did his grandchildren.

During the Great War, the yacht was laid up, and, although it was overhauled in the 1920s, with its one-mast gaff rig it was no longer able to win races. Re-rigged in 1926 and again in 1930, it managed win a final few, but it never attained its pre-war status as the fastest yacht in the world.

Rather than have it broken up, His Majesty George V willed that, on his death, *Britannia* be taken out to sea and scuttled, and this occurred on July 9, 1936.

For Canada, royal visits by sea began on March 16, 1901, when Prince George and Princess Mary, the Duke and Duchess of Cornwall and York — later King George V and Queen Mary — embarked from Portsmouth on a Royal Tour. The general intention was to thank as many of the colonies as possible for their aid in the Boer War, and specifically to open the first Parliament of the new Commonwealth of Australia. Two weeks before they left, Edward VII returned to England from a European tour on the brand new Royal Yacht *Victoria and Albert III*. The Duchess of York knew the yacht well, having launched her at Pembroke Yard on May 9, 1899. But it was unsuitable for a long voyage, and an Orient Line steamship, RMS *Ophir*, was hired for the world tour, with the Royal Navy providing the destroyer HMS *St. George* as an escort. Built by Napier & Son, Glasgow, in 1891, the *Ophir* was 6,814 gross tonnes, with twin funnels, two masts, and a twin screw, and she cruised at eighteen knots. Named appropriately from the John Masefield poem "Cargoes," she was well-suited for the tour, as she regularly sailed between London, Suez, Melbourne, and Sydney.

The stopovers of the tour ranged from tiny naval bases like Gibraltar, Aden, and Singapore, to the major dominions of Australia, New Zealand, and Canada. The King was not in favour of his son undertaking such a long and arduous trip so soon after the death of his grandmother, Queen Victoria. Besides, Prince George had already been away, having served as captain of HMS *Thrush* in 1898. But the Prime Minister, Lord Salisbury, was convinced that, after the Boer War, the tour was the ideal way to strengthen the bonds of Empire. As for the young couple themselves, both Prince George and Princess Mary found the separation — from their parents and from their four children, Edward, Albert, Mary, and Henry — very hard to bear. George and John were not yet born.

Besides the Duke's three closest friends (and future equerries), the party on the *Ophir* included Major Derek Keppel, (the brother-in-law of Mrs. Alice Keppel, at that time the mistress of the King) and Prince Alexander of Teck. The younger brother of Princess Mary, Alexander was soon to marry Princess Alice, the granddaughter of Queen Victoria, and, as the Earl of Athlone, one day would be Governor General of Canada. As the King wanted a visual record of the trip, there were for the first time a number of photographers on the *Ophir*.

In Canada, Prince George and Princess Mary undertook a two-month visit from the east coast to the west, using a specially fitted-out rail carriage provided by the Canadian Pacific Railway. They performed the duties typical of a royal visit to Canada: watching a lacrosse match, reviewing troops, even attempting a lumberjack's hearty meal of pork and beans outside Ottawa. As during future Royal Tours, they ensured that the accompanying press would not have any juicy tidbits to report.[16] When the couple visited British Columbia and travelled from Vancouver to Victoria on October 1, they sailed on the Canadian Pacific's latest ship, the *Empress of India*. The royal party returned to Vancouver on October 3, and the Duke was so impressed by the ship and its captain, O.P. Marshall, that he made him an Elder Brother of Trinity House. Through the years, many members of the British royal family favoured the Canadian Pacific's ships for transport, but *Empress of India* was the first to be so honoured.

PA-028956

The royal party from the *Ophir*. Front row (L to R): Earl of Minto, Duke of Cornwall and York, Duchess of Cornwall and York, Countess of Minto. Back row (L to R): ?, Hon. Mrs. Derek Keppel, Lady Mary Lygon, others unidentifiable. Niagara-on-the-Lake, Ontario, October 16, 1901.

The Canadian tour was a good test for Prince George, who on his return to England was created the Prince of Wales. From October 1905 to April 1906, the Prince and Princess would visit India and Burma on the battleship HMS *Renown*, and in 1908, His Royal Highness returned to Canada on the battleship HMS *Indomitable* to celebrate the tercentenary of Quebec City. The former temporary Royal Yacht *Ophir* was sold by the Orient Line in 1913 and during the Great War was commissioned as an Armed Merchant Cruiser and later a hospital ship.

On wishing his son and daughter-in-law farewell in 1901, Edward VII must have recalled pleasant memories of his own tour to Canada. In 1860, as Prince of Wales, the nineteen-year-old had arrived in North America on the latest British battleship, HMS *Hero*, disembarking at Quebec City on August 18. The object of the tour was to rebuild the Anglo-North American transatlantic ties that had become somewhat strained during the American Civil War. His Royal Highness threw himself into this as a goodwill ambassador and visited Ottawa, the lumber town on the Ontario-Quebec border that had been chosen by his mother to be Canada's capital, where he laid the cornerstone for its parliament buildings.[17]

Prince of Wales's visit to Canada. Shooting the rapids on the Nipigon River, Ontario, September 5-7, 1919.

PA-022368

Travelling by wood-burning locomotive, by ship, and carriage, the Prince charmed crowds from St. John, New Brunswick, to Windsor, Ontario — even breaking the royal prohibition by dining publicly. His mother had never been seen to eat in public, and the last British monarch to do so had been George IV in 1821. Edward met an ancient Laura Secord and the last surviving veterans of the war of 1812, drove in the last spike on the Victoria Bridge that connected Montreal with the South Shore of the St. Lawrence, and hunted and fished. Gifts of stuffed moose and birds were presented to him, and he was danced off his feet by Montreal matrons. The Prince went as far west as Niagara Falls, where he watched the French acrobat Charles Blondin cross the raging waters by a tightrope. His Royal Highness presented Blondin with a bag of gold coins, and when Blondin offered to take him across in a wheelbarrow, the Prince readily agreed to do so — until dissuaded by his entourage. Easily his most memorable experience on the Canadian tour was running the Chaudière timber slides on a raft during the Ottawa portion of the visit. When he returned from the tour on November 15, Queen Victoria noticed that he had become more talkative, and even the politicians who had previously depreciated his strengths agreed that the Prince of Wales had found his metier, and that henceforth, foreign visits by members of the royal family were to be encouraged.

Edward VII's eldest grandson, whose full name was Edward Albert Christian George Andrew Patrick David (he was called David by his family), first went to sea as a seventeen-year-old. In August 1911, Edward served as a midshipman on the old battleship *Hindustan* and learned how to read flag signals, keep watch, and run a picket boat. It wasn't that his father had planned a naval career for Edward (he was, after all, going to accede to the throne) but that, as a former naval officer himself, George V thought it would teach him some concept of duty. Writing about the experience fifty years later, the Duke of Windsor recollected the voyage from Cowes to the Firth of Forth. He got to mix with boys his age, drink a glass of port on "guest nights," and begin smoking cigarettes. It all ended in three months when he was summoned home to the library at Sandringham and told by his father that he was going to Oxford. "If I cannot stay in the Navy," he is supposed to have begged his father, "please let me go around the world and learn about different countries and their peoples at first hand." In the summer of 1913, he was sent on a tour of Europe to improve his languages, and also made an officer in the Royal Navy, his commission jointly signed by his father, Winston Churchill, the young First Lord of the Admiralty, and his relative Prince Louis of Battenberg, First Sea Lord.[18]

Second sons in the royal family (such as both George V and Prince Albert, the Duke of York) were trained for a career in the Senior Service, the Royal Navy. It would thus be as a member of the crew of an old training ship, HMS *Cumberland*, that Prince Albert (Bertie to his family), the future George VI, first visited Canada in 1913. Known as Mr. Johnson by all on board, the seventeen-year-old had never even crossed the English Channel, let alone the Atlantic, and now he was stoking coal with the other middies (midshipmen), seeing exotic Tenerife, and drinking beer. With lifelong gastric problems, the Prince was never a good sailor and was plagued with seasickness throughout his life. Without his father's authoritarian bearing and perpetually in the shadow of his older brother, Albert stammered and was

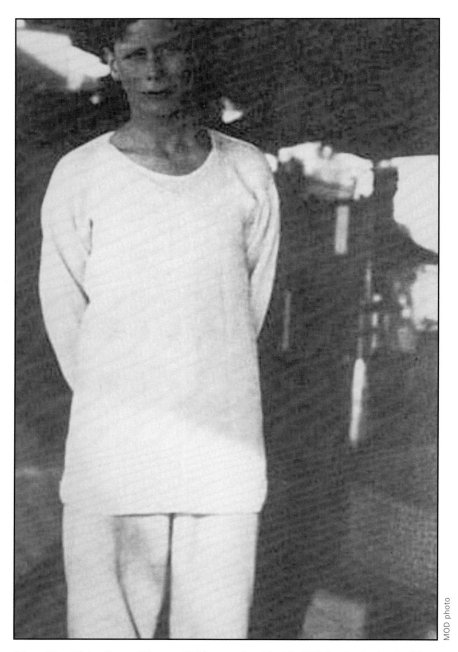

Prince Albert (later George VI) as a midshipman when his ship HMS *Cumberland* arrived in Canada in 1913.

MOD photo

remembered as too shy to meet the young ladies of Montreal. Interviews with the press terrified him even more. Harassed by North American reporters, he hired a shipmate to impersonate him. The Canadian tour was part of his education, and besides Halifax and Montreal, he visited Niagara Falls. On the way home, in Charlottetown, the Prince refereed a cricket match between the crew and the local team. HMS *Cumberland* would soon become a familiar sight to Canadians, since, because of the First World War, the 9,800-tonne armoured cruiser got a second lease on life, doing convoy duty between the U.K. and Canada until 1917. Three years after the Canadian visit, as a sub-lieutenant, the future George VI would take part in the Battle of Jutland on HMS *Collingwood.*

Even before the war had ended, Prime Minister Lloyd George had conceived the plan for a whole series of Empire tours for the heir to the throne, to strengthen relations with the peoples of the Commonwealth. His Majesty approved them, as his father had approved his own worldwide tour in 1901. But now twenty-five, the Prince of Wales had been changed by the war and the gap between his generation and that of his father's was becoming more obvious daily.[19] His first Canadian tour was devised for him. On August 5, 1919, the Prince of Wales left Portsmouth for St. John's, Newfoundland, on the battleship HMS *Renown.*[20] He was accompanied by a retinue of twenty-two, which included friends, clerks, valets, orderlies, and two detectives from Scotland Yard. The *Renown* was too large for the harbour at Charlottetown, and the Prince transferred to HMS *Dragon,* returning to the battleship for his arrival at Quebec City on August 21. Between Vancouver and Victoria, His Royal Highness sailed on the Canadian Pacific ferry *Princess Alice,* and the next year, when he returned, it would be the *Princess Louise.*

When George V went to France in 1923, instead of taking the *Victoria and Albert III,* he travelled rather bizarrely on the Southern Railway Steamship *Biarritz,* which flew a White Ensign, a Royal Standard, and an Admiralty flag. As for the royal yacht, the King used it for short cruises, like his father, going as far as the Mediterranean Sea. An escape from the rigours of the court and press, the yacht belonged intimately to the family, its symbolism never so obvious as in the 1920s, when Queen Mary threatened to ban the Prince of Wales from it as punishment for his unorthodox social life.[21]

When the Prince of Wales returned to Canada in 1923, the Canadian Pacific liner *Empress of France* became the Royal Yacht *Empress of France*. His Highness returned the following year via New York on the SS *Berengaria* (it was on this ship that a female reporter asked the Prince, "Would you marry an American gal if you fell in love?"). In 1927, the Prince of Wales accepted the invitation of the Canadian government to celebrate the country's sixtieth year in Confederation. This time he brought his younger brother George, Duke of Kent. Also accompanying His Royal Highness on this Canadian tour, with His Majesty's blessing, were Prime Minister Stanley Baldwin and his wife, Lucy. Baldwin had left a fractious Cabinet and a failed international conference to come to Canada, but he thought it justified if his presence would help curb what was more and more seen as the Prince's irresponsible, immature excesses. He failed to do so, like many others before and after him; the Prime Minister had overrated his influence on the young man and was setting the stage for future conflict. On Lake Ontario, the Prince boarded the *Cayuga* and later, to make the now familiar crossing from Vancouver to Victoria, used the *Princess Adelaide*.

As it had done in previous royal tours, the Canadian Pacific stepped in to help. Its *Empress of Australia* served for the transatlantic trip over and the *Empress of Scotland* home. The choice of a Canadian Pacific liner over the usual battleship was no doubt influenced by Edward Wentworth Beatty. Succeeding Lord Shaughnessy as president and chairman of the mighty Canadian Pacific (and becoming its first Canadian-born president), Beatty was an unabashed anglophile, idolizing two things: British royalty and his *Empress* ships. Putting both together for this tour allowed Beatty, who would be knighted in 1935, to fawn over the princes on the tour.

MOD photo

The training ship HMS *Cumberland* that brought Prince Albert to Montreal in 1913.

Courtesy of Australian Archives

The popularity of the Prince of Wales was never more evident than with the Australian compliment "Digger." The battleship HMS *Renown*, used by His Royal Highness for both his Canadian and Australian tours, is shown.

Rather like the royal family itself, the *Empress of Australia* had recent German origins. In 1914, as the 21,498-tonne *Tirpitz*, it had been the pride of Kaiser Wilhelm's merchant navy. Fortunately, she had spent the Great War safely in port, and in 1919 was handed over to the British steamship line Cunard in reparations. Although lavishly outfitted, the former *Tirpitz* was a coal-burner at a time when it was becoming impossible to find stokers. Like many German ships of her era, she was also top heavy and needed a lot of ballast to secure her. For these reasons, Cunard was quick to sell her to Canadian Pacific. On July 25, 1921, renamed the *Empress of China*, the former *Tirpitz* was sent to John Brown & Co. on the Clyde to be converted to oil and refitted for the company's Pacific run between Vancouver and the Orient. When this was completed on June 2, 1922, as China was in turmoil, the company thought better of the name, and the ship was renamed *Empress of Australia*. On September 1, 1923, as she was about to cast off from Yokohama, Japan, the port was devastated by an earthquake and, through subsequent days, the *Empress* provided shelter for thousands of Japanese. The ship and its crew were commemorated for their efforts and a plaque on deck testified to this. In May 1926, the *Empress of Australia* was sent once more to the Clyde shipbuilders, where she was refitted with new boilers and single-reduction Parson turbines and made into a temporary royal yacht.

As flagships of the Canadian Pacific, the *Empresses* were hosts to the wealthy and famous many times, but no one personified the image that the company wanted to cultivate (that of a charming loafer in best P.G. Wodehouse style) better than His Royal Highness, the Prince of Wales. The Prince availed himself of the lifestyle on board the *Empresses* on several occasions, attempting halfheartedly to pass incognito as Lord Renfrew. On one memorable trip on the *Empress of France,* he played the drums with the ship's orchestra. Cameras, both movie and still, recorded his unabashed enjoyment of shipboard life away from his father's strictures. Movie stars and millionaires may sail out of New York on Cunard, but for Canadian Pacific (and Canada) the sight of the heir to the throne playing shuffleboard, lounging in a deck chair, and giving interviews gave the CPR's *Empresses* a social cachet in which the company, and the country, took pride. After his 1927 voyage on the *Empress of Australia*, there were so many stories of the Prince's Cabin, No.140, that it became a much-sought-after venue for passengers, and even Prime Minister Mackenzie King asked to use it on his trip in 1937. "I was like a man caught in a revolving door," the Duke later said of his Empire travels.

On July 26, 1933, King George V and Queen Mary officially opened The King George V Graving Dock, the largest in the world at the time, steaming into it aboard the royal yacht. Three years later, with Edward VIII, the royal family returned to the site to inspect the RMS *Queen Mary* and Queen Mary presented her personal standard to the ship.[22]

When he acceded to the throne on January 20, 1936, as Edward VIII, the former Prince of Wales mistakenly thought that he had the power to do as he pleased. With Wallis Simpson not accepted by his side in public, that summer he rented a villa in the south of France for a party of close friends and planned to take the divorced American with him. Not wanting to be drawn into what promised to be a royal fiasco, the canny British Ambassador in Paris cited the Spanish Civil War nearby and persuaded him against it. Stealing off in the *Victoria and Albert III* was also out of the question. For the King, the yacht had too many memories of his father — like Buckingham Palace, which he referred to as "that mausoleum," Edward would always hate the ship. His family would also have been aghast if the American divorcée were allowed on board. Instead, the *Nahlin* was charted for a cruise down the Adriatic and on to Istanbul. That Wallis Simpson was to be on board attracted great media attention (American newspapers were now calling her "The Prince's Moll"), and even the prime ministers of the Dominions were appealing to Downing Street to do something.

With a handsome clipper bow, 250 feet in length and 36 feet beam, and with an approximate speed of 18 knots, the *Nahlin* was an elegant yacht belonging to the heiress Lady Yule. Built in 1929 on the Clyde by John Brown & Co. it had already circumnavigated the world. "The special charm of a yacht lies," His Majesty wrote, "in that it enables presumably responsible people to combine … the milder irresponsibilities of a beachcomber's existence with all the comforts of a luxury hotel and in this respect the *Nahlin* did not disappoint me."

Under the old rules, the fiction that His Majesty was to be called the Duke of Lancaster for the duration of the tour was preserved. Arriving by train in the Yugoslav fishing village of Sibenik on August 10, the party found not only welcoming crowds of Yugoslavs curious about Mrs. Simpson and shouting "Zivila Ljubav" — Yugoslav for "Vive l'amour" (obviously, the American tabloids were popular here) — but also two Royal Navy destroyers, HMS *Grafton* and HMS *Glow Worm*, that were to accompany their floating hideaway everywhere.

Their hope for an unobtrusive vacation now blown, the party made the best of it, proceeding on a leisurely tour of the Mediterranean on the *Nahlin*, even nicknaming the two destroyers "nanny boats." His Majesty practised his golf swing on the deck of the yacht, putting an estimated three thousand balls into the sea. On hearing that Istanbul had a particularly fine golf course, the King asked that a match be arranged for him there. Downing Street was appalled, the Foreign Secretary Anthony Eden pointing out that to play there, without first meeting with the Turkish President Kemal Ataturk, would be an insult. Eden then tried to make the best of it and asked that His Majesty formally call on Turkey, which had just regained the strategic Dardanelles and was to be courted. Edward did play golf and meet with Ataturk (who was thrilled — the last European monarch to visit Turkey had been the Kaiser), and he charmed the Turkish President by speaking fluent German.[23] Considering Turkey's neutrality in the Second World War, the visit paid off for the British in dividends.

But it was the King's devotion to Mrs. Simpson and his contempt for protocol that the press of a dozen nations (except the British) captured. His grandfather had taken his mistresses abroad as well, but unlike him, Edward VIII lacked the maturity to combine the role of lover with that of monarch. Wearing sandals and shorts, he met local officials, who were always in top hats, morning coats, and striped trousers. His Majesty is "so Robinson Crusoe," said Wallis, "that the locals try to guess which of the party is the King." Passing through the Corinth Canal, lined by fascinated Athenians, the King stood on the bridge of the yacht in nothing more than his shorts, wearing his binoculars around his neck. "Do you think you could get the King to put his shirt on," the other guests begged Wallis "until we get out of sight of the Greeks?" The cruise was an embarrassment to both the royal family and the British government and one from which His Majesty's reputation did not recover. As for the yacht, now made infamous by the part it had played, in 1937 the *Nahlin* was bought by King Carol II of Romania. When he lost his throne during the war, the yacht was forgotten in a backwater of the Danube.[24]

In the end, for King Edward VIII, it all came down to December 11, 1936, when, after broadcasting to the world that he found it impossible to discharge his duties as King without the help and support of the woman he loved, the former King (once again His Royal Highness Prince Edward and soon to be the Duke of Windsor), stepped aboard his last royal naval vessel, the destroyer HMS *Fury*, at Portsmouth and went into exile. There would be other ships in his life — he caught the *Queen Mary* out of New York on February 7, 1952, to go to his brother's funeral in London — but his Royal Standard would never fly from one again.

His brother, now George VI, used the royal yacht in 1937, with young Princess Elizabeth on board, for his coronation review. But *Victoria and Albert III* was then nearly forty years old and, in 1938, the Admiralty considered building a ship that would not only replace her, but which could be used as a hospital ship in the event of a war. A statement of essential requirements for such a vessel were drawn up and sent to principal shipbuilders in the country, inviting them to submit proposals. But with the preparations for impending hostilities, the whole matter was dropped.[25]

That year the threat of war with Germany was also preoccupying the government of Prime Minister Neville Chamberlain. A royal tour to Canada and the United States, as we have seen, was considered an important public relations exercise.

The King did not want to go. He (like his brother the Duke of Windsor) still harboured ideas that Hitler could be talked out of his territorial ambitions if spoken to by a monarch. It was his duty he felt to remain at home and be ready to play some part in a Europe moving inexorably to conflict. Hitler had just taken over Czechoslovakia and was now hoping to do the same in Poland. His Majesty did not feel confident enough to win the former colonists over. After his naval service, Prince Albert had been quite content to settle down with his wife, Elizabeth, and two daughters to a life as a country squire. It was not even two years since that he had been plucked from that and the crown had been thrust on him. Lacking his brother's charm and trained only as a naval officer, George VI was nervous before crowds. He also smoked heavily, and his health in 1939 was increasingly delicate. The opinion of those who knew him was summed up by his cousin Louis Mountbatten who had been at Cambridge with him: "Dear old Bertie," he wrote, "honest, loyal and a bit stupid."[26]

In those last months of peace, Prime Minister Neville Chamberlain persuaded His Majesty that he was of more use on a Royal Tour than waiting at Buckingham Palace for something to do. After all, in the face of an earlier German threat, his grandfather Edward VII had made a personal visit to France and bonded the two countries to each other in the Entente Cordiale. Therefore, on October 8, 1938, an announcement from Balmoral Castle revealed that Their Majesties had accepted the invitation of the Prime Minister of Canada for a visit of three weeks duration the next May, with a side trip to the United States.

Because of rumours of German submarines prowling the Atlantic and a German battleship lurking off the Spanish coast, there was fear that Their Majesties would be kidnapped and the entourage was slated to use the battleship HMS *Repulse* with an escort of two destroyers. This His Majesty, as a naval officer, refused to do: at a time like this, Britain needed her capital ships around her, not being wasted as a royal yacht, berthed safely away in the St. Lawrence. The *Victoria and Albert III* was too small for an ocean voyage and not in her prime. The old *Renown,* fortunately for the royal couple, was being refitted for the coming war. As it had done for other Royal Tours, the Canadian Pacific stepped in. The *Empress of Australia* was once more taken off its schedule, brought over to Portsmouth from its home base at Southampton, and refitted into a royal yacht. At the same time, the Duke of Windsor, the former Prince of Wales, now living in France and scheduled to visit the United States in May, was suddenly told that permission had been refused and his visit had been cancelled. At this critical time, Their Majesties were not going to be upstaged by the King's older brother and Wallis Simpson.

When the press made known the German origins of the *Empress of Australia* to the British public, questions were asked in the House of Commons as to Their Majesties' safety. Chamberlain mollified the opposition by replying that at least her engines had been made on the Clyde. As the ship had a normal capacity for 1,200 passengers and 400 crew, the royal couple with their eighteen staff were somewhat lost on board. It had taken a week of frenzied work to convert the liner into a royal yacht (fortunately it had been designed with very large staterooms to accommodate the Kaiser and his court), and the smell of the paint had to be concealed with buckets of water filled with sliced onions. Furniture was brought over from the *Victoria and Albert III*, including His Majesty's bed, and extra ballast was added to lessen its notorious pitch and roll. The royal entourage consisted of two ladies-in-waiting for Her Majesty, a lord-in-waiting for His Majesty, the Lord Chamberlain, the Earl of Airlie, a doctor, a press secretary, two equerries, dressers, a page, the royal hairdresser, maids, valets, and footmen. Although the Royal Canadian Mounted Police were to handle security, a detective from Scotland Yard Special Branch was also in evidence.

The tour began at Waterloo Station on May 6, when Their Majesties boarded the train that would take them to Portsmouth. Once on board, wearing an Admiral's uniform, with the Queen by his side, His Majesty stood on the *Empress*'s promenade deck to wave goodbye to the crowds that had come to see them off. The latest RAF fighters flew overhead, bands played, and two columns of battleships escorted the liner, now flying the Royal Standard, into the Channel. As parents, Their Majesties had just endured a tearful farewell from their daughters on "A" deck below: the thirteen-year-old Princess Elizabeth had hugged her mother and cried, while nine-year-old Margaret Rose, who refused to smile for the photographers —

Canadian Pacific Photo

The two princesses bidding Their Majesties farewell aboard the *Empress of Australia*.

she never liked flashes — entirely out of character, kissed her father goodbye three times. The Queen said to Princess Elizabeth: "Be good and look after Margaret." At 3:00 p.m. the *Empress of Australia* moved out of the harbour for Canada. The Canadian Pacific House Flag was flown at the bow and the White Ensign at the stern.

In fact, the eight-day voyage was just what His Majesty needed. Although the news from Europe was broadcast on board, in the Atlantic, it seemed from another world. All there was for the King to do on the cavernous, empty ship was relax: bundle up and pace the deck, watch the two escort cruisers HMS *Glasgow* and HMS *Southampton* like sheep dogs by its side, and take photographs, both still and cine. The *Empress*'s catering supervisor, Abe Toole, ensured that there were plenty of Their Majesties' favourite treats on board: haggis, Black Sea caviar, thirty-three cases of wine from His Majesty's own cellar, and the hand-rolled Havana cigars that the King loved. The sea was stormy; the *Empress*, at fourteen knots, bounced about (as Cunard had known it would), and the royal entourage were seasick. Then there were the icebergs. With thirty years of experience under sail and steam, Canadian Pacific Captain Archibald Meikle knew the best route in the spring was as far south as possible, away from the ice packs. But he was overruled by the Sea Lords in London and especially by Vice-Admiral Sir Dudley Pound, whom His Majesty had invited along. To discourage German submarines, they wanted the *Empress* to be as far north as possible, open to the fog and iceberg fields. And the expected occurred: when the storm had subsided on the fifth day out, the trio of ships ran into both thick fog and mountainous icebergs. Everyone on board the royal ship now took to watching the cathedral-sized icebergs off the bow, the destroyers having vanished into the mist. The *Empress*'s foghorn blew constantly, and they listened for the answers from the *Southampton* and *Glasgow*. By now the Captain was tired of being reminded that the RMS *Titanic* had sunk in these very waters — and at this time of the year, too. But none of this bothered Their Majesties. They rested, talked to any of the crew they met, watched Walt Disney cartoons, and, with the use of books and movies, studied up on Canada.

When, on Saturday, May 13, just before a fog bank covered them, an iceberg the ladies-in-waiting said was the size of Windsor Castle came into view, Captain Meikle reversed engines around it and cut his speed to five knots. He also radioed the waiting Canadian government that the ship was going to be two days late, arriving not on May 15 but May 17 in the morning. This caused a flurry of meetings and phone calls in Ottawa. Where should the tour be cut? Which unfortunate cities would lose out on the royal visit?[27]

Through the whole voyage, the Queen came into her own. She talked with everyone, asking questions, and was interested in everything. What, she asked the crew, were those large canisters on deck? Depth charges, they told her and, to explain what they did (after alerting the destroyers), fired one off. The explosion directly below the *Empress*'s hull sent a torrent of freezing seawater up into its drains. The poor royal steward Frank Knight, who had been sitting happily on the toilet at that moment, felt a sudden flood and was uncomfortably soaked. He thought they had hit an iceberg, and ran out of the bathroom. The fog and ice pack kept pace with the ships until Sunday, May 14, when they were met by two ships of the Royal Canadian Navy, HMCS *Skeena* and HMCS *Saguenay*.

Now the shores of the Gaspé could be seen, and on May 16, rather than risk making for Quebec City at night, the captain dropped anchor near St. Jean on the Île d'Orléans, twelve miles before Wolfe's Cove. It was the last night on board the *Empress*, and, as if to relieve the tension of the voyage — and allow the packing to be done — the dining room was decorated with balloons and streamers and a dance was held, the passengers enjoying the lights of bonfires and automobile headlights along the shore. The crew were given gifts, customary at the end of any voyage, and Captain Meikle was made a Commander of the Royal Victorian Order. The captain had not slept for three days and the next morning, when the sun emerged, could not believe his luck. Wanting to get the voyage over with as quickly as possible, he had the anchor hoisted at 8:15 a.m. and surprised the four naval vessels by steaming alone straight ahead towards Quebec City.

Prime Minister Mackenzie King sat waiting for notification of the ship in his suite on the eleventh floor of the Château Frontenac. A few months earlier, the late King George V had appeared to him in a seance to reassure him how much his son and daughter-in-law loved him. He had planned, schemed, and dreamed about the visit for months, and had successfully manoeuvred Governor General Lord Tweedsmuir (the author John Buchan) out of the welcoming party, saying this was a completely Canadian affair. As a result, at 10:30 a.m. only he and his Quebec minister, Ernest Lapointe, both awkward in their black wool and gold braid, with cocked hats under their arms, walked up the ship's gangplank to meet the King and Queen.[28] The King, in an admiral's uniform, and the Queen, wearing lavender crepe de Chine, with a silver fox stole around her shoulders, were waiting for them in one of the ship's saloons. Mackenzie King took His Majesty's hand and bowed low. "Welcome, Sire, to Your Majesty's realm of Canada," he said. Then they all walked down the gangplank, the King now wearing his cocked hat.

The first moment when the King touched Canadian soil was a historic one. Never before had a reigning monarch done so and while the newsreel cameras took it all in, artillery sounded, the Royal 22nd Regiment snapped to attention, church bells pealed and thousands of Quebecers — who had been waiting for hours — cheered. The Royal Tour of 1939 had begun.

With all eyes on the *Empress of Australia*, the *Glasgow* and *Southampton* could unload their cargo without attracting attention. This was fortunate, since in their holds were steel boxes containing 3,550 gold bars from the Bank of England. The Royal Tour had been the perfect cover for the first shipment of British gold sent for safekeeping in Canada.

On the overland tour, Their Majesties would embark on ships five times. They left from Sandy Hook, New Jersey, for Manhattan in the USS *Warrington*, the first time that the Royal Standard was hoisted from an American naval vessel. In Washington they were received by President Roosevelt on board the presidential yacht USS *Potomac* for a short voyage of fifteen miles to Mount Vernon. Between Vancouver and Victoria, they sailed on the CPR's *Princess Marguerite*, and returned on the government's auxiliary cruiser *Prince Robert*. When the King and Queen boarded the *Princess Marguerite* for the trip to Victoria, Captain Clifford Fenton, according to naval custom, proffered command of the ship to His Majesty, who accepted, becoming the official captain of the ship for the

Rt. Hon. W.L. Mackenzie King and Ernest Lapointe with King George VI and Queen Elizabeth at the gangplank of CPS *Empress of Australia*, Wolfe's Cove, Quebec, May 1939.

C-035115

voyage. As the CPR ferry, now flying the Royal Standard, turned its bow outward bound, a twenty-one-gun salute was fired from Stanley Park and four Canadian destroyers, the *Fraser*, the *Ottawa*, the *Saint-Laurent*, and the *Restigouche*, went ahead of it. Above, Canada's total air force on the Pacific coast — two flights of antique Blackburn Sharks — circled and dived in salute while three Hawker Hurricanes patrolled the route until the ship had passed Point Grey. But what impressed the royal party the most were the eight First Nation war canoes that kept pace on either side of the Princess, "manned by braves stripped to the waist, driving deep into the water their red, white, and blue paddles."[29] On the voyage back to Vancouver, it was Captain H.E. Nedden, Commander of the *Prince Robert*, who was presented to Their Majesties. Once more there was a twenty-one-gun salute, this time from Work Point, Victoria, and again the same four Canadian destroyers appeared before them. The royal couple went straight to the bridge and, charmed by the islands they passed, Her Majesty remarked to Captain Nedden. "I wish we could buy one of these islands."

"Why buy them?" was his reply. "They are all yours now."

Finally, to visit Prince Edward Island, the King and Queen crossed the Northumberland Strait on HMCS *Skeena*, accompanied by her sister ship HMCS *Saguenay*, the two-and-a-half-hour voyage made in a violent storm. It was the first time that the Royal Standard was flown from a Canadian naval ship. It rained through the whole visit and, this far into the exhausting schedule, His Majesty was in poor form (translation: bad mood), so much so that Mackenzie King felt sorry for the fumbling of the local politicians. Worse, because alcohol was prohibited on the Island, the King could not even get a therapeutic Scotch.

For the return home from Halifax, the Canadian Pacific had been able to get their flagship, the *Empress of Britain*. The fastest, largest, most luxurious ship ever built for the CPR, its keel had been laid at the John Brown shipyard on November 28, 1928. The Duke of Windsor must have read of this with some sadness. As the Prince of Wales, he had launched the 42,000-tonne *Empress* on June 11, 1930, the radio broadcasts of the event sent for the very first time throughout the Empire. On May 27, 1931, His Royal Highness personally flew to the Southampton docks to wish the crew bon voyage. Cunard could flatter the royal family by naming their ship the *Queen Mary* after the consort of George V, but appropriately the Canadian Pacific chose *Empress of Britain*, because she represented the ultimate in British engineering, nautical architecture, and style. On her maiden voyage she captured the Blue Riband by steaming between Cherbourg and Father Point, Quebec, in four days, nineteen hours, and thirty-five minutes. In 1934, she reduced the eastbound crossing to four days, six hours, and fifty-eight minutes, and the westbound in four days, eight hours. Not only was she the first Canadian Pacific ship to have ship-to-shore radio telephones, but her roominess, aesthetic appeal, standard of food, crew courtesy, and riding qualities put the *Empress* on the same level as the French Line's *Normandie* and Cunard's *Queen Mary*. Now she carried as passengers only the members of the royal party who, after the closeness of the train, succeeded in getting lost on board. On the first evening out, the King stepped out of the elevator into the main lobby and, seeing all the doors, remarked with a smile, "And now, where do we go from here?"

The Canadian Pacific flagship *Empress of Britain* carried Their Majesties home from Canada in 1939.

The *Empress of Britain* waited for the now-weary royal party at Pier 20 on June 15, 1939, its crew listening in awe as thousands along the quay chanted, "We want the King! We want the Queen!" The royal couple boarded the *Empress*, and a small party was held for the press who had accompanied them across the country. With the tour over, everyone was relaxed, and Their Majesties dispensed small gifts to the Mounties who had guarded them on the tour. Prime Minister Mackenzie King was given a history of the royal oaks that had been planted throughout the Empire, the volume signed by both the King and Queen. Then he and the Governor General said their farewells and, at 7:00 p.m., the gangplank was hauled up. The crowd kept up the chanting throughout and, as the ship moved away from the pier, Their Majesties appeared on the bridge to wave. The crowd then broke into "Auld Lang Syne" and after that, "God Save The King." At 7:32 p.m. the *Empress* began to swing away from the pier and move into the centre of the harbour. She turned and passed the pier again, her escorts *Southampton* and *Glasgow* with the Canadian destroyers now joining her. Overhead lumbered three RCAF Stranraer flying boats. As the ship moved away, a choir sang "Will Ye No' Come Back Again" and everyone on shore continued to wave at the receding figures of the King and Queen.

C-085083

Aircraft escort CPS *Empress of Britain* from the harbour, Halifax, Nova Scotia, June 15, 1939.

"The *Empress* ran past one end of the harbour where she was towed around, then came back the opposite way to pull out to sea. She was accompanied by British warships and our own destroyers. The *Bluenose* and other vessels also in the harbour as an escort," Mackenzie King recorded in his diary on June 15, 1939. "The sun was shining very brightly and as the *Empress* turned, lit up the whole of one side. The King and Queen were at the very top of the ship and kept waving.… The last I saw of them was the King standing at the side of the Queen and the Queen with her hand upraised, the light shining on it. No farewell could have been finer than that given by the day, the people and the country."

Escorted by HMS *Berwick*, the flagship of the British West Indies squadron, the *Empress* steamed towards Newfoundland, the oldest British colony in the Empire, for a quick visit to St. John's on June 17. The ship was too large to enter the harbour and dropped anchor at Conception Bay. In a rainstorm, the royal couple and the Governor of Newfoundland and his wife set off in a blue naval barge for a nine-mile journey to the port. On return to the *Empress*, Their Majesties boarded the ferry *Maneco* (which proudly hoisted the Royal Standard) and made for the *Glasgow*. On board, His Majesty made Captain C. Coltarb a Commander of the Victorian Order. Then they proceeded to the *Southampton* and later the *Berwick* where His Majesty conferred honours on its captains.

Once the King and Queen were back on board, the *Empress* weighed anchor for home. June 18 was Sunday, a day of rest, and Their Majesties attended a sung service of the Church of England in the ship's lounge; before dinner, Queen Elizabeth phoned Princess Elizabeth and Princess Margaret Rose.

On June 22, the Canadian Pacific liner arrived off the British coast to be met by aircraft from the carrier HMS *Ark Royal*. In the Yarmouth Roads, the first ship to greet them was the destroyer HMS *Kempenfelt*, by coincidence about to be transferred to the Royal Canadian Navy and renamed HMCS *Assiniboine*. It carried the two princesses, who boarded the *Empress*, yelled "Hullo, Mummy!," and ran to their parents' arms. Their governess Crawfie wrote that His Majesty couldn't take his eyes off his "Lilibet," commenting that he could not get over how much Elizabeth had grown. The princesses wanted to know all about Canada and had a million questions about the train trip. They also had a few stories of their own to tell: Crawfie had rather unwisely taken them on a ride in the Underground, and they had been recognized by the public — what did Her Majesty think of that? The tour over, everyone relaxed; the *Empress*'s dining room was decorated with streamers and balloons, its orchestra played "The Lambeth Walk," and the whole party drank champagne.

The *Empress* docked at Southampton at 2:40 p.m. and Queen Mary, who had visited Canada on the *Ophir* thirty-eight years before, had sufficiently recovered from an auto accident to be the first up the gangplank. Tumultuous crowds greeted the royal procession as it drove through the Southampton streets on the way to the flag-draped Central Station. As one of those in the crowd, Harold Nicolson wrote, "We lost all dignity and yelled and yelled. The King wore a schoolboy grin. The Queen was superb."[30]

Sadly, the *Empress of Britain* would be bombed by a Luftwaffe Condor on October 26, 1940, northwest of Ireland, and set on fire. The ship was abandoned and taken in tow by tugs. But the Condor had given away the *Empress*'s position and, on October 28, the German submarine *U-32* fired three torpedoes into its hulk. One detonated prematurely but the other two found their target and the *Empress of Britain* sank, the largest Allied merchant ship to be lost in the war.

The ferry *Princess Marguerite* that had carried the royal party from Vancouver to Victoria was also finished, far away from its home. A troop ship in the Mediterranean in 1942, when the British were attempting to reinforce Cyprus, the *Marguerite,* packed with soldiers, was en route from Port Said to Famagusta on August 17. Somehow Kapitään Leutnant Hans Werner Kraus got the U-83 through the protective ranks of destroyers and torpedoed the British Columbia ferry. The escorts on the Royal Tour suffered as well. On June 25, 1940, HMCS *Fraser* was sent to rescue refugees trapped in France by the German military forces. In rough seas and poor visibility, the *Fraser* collided with the British cruiser HMS *Calcutta* and was cut to pieces with forty-five of her crew killed. The destroyer HMS *Southampton* was sunk in January 1941 while escorting a convoy in the Mediterranean,[31] and HMCS *Skeena* survived a torpedoing by an Italian submarine only to be lost in a storm off Iceland on October 25, 1944. But none of this was known as the tour came to an end.

A month after their return, recuperating from it all, the royal family was holidaying on board the *Victoria and Albert III.* On July 22, they embarked on it to visit the Senior Naval College at Dartmouth, which His Majesty had also attended. Because several of the cadets had mumps, the princesses Elizabeth and Margaret were forbidden to mix with them, and were at a loss as to what to do. Lord Louis Mountbatten, the King's aide-de-camp, saw his chance. He ensured that his nephew Philip,[32] a very junior cadet at the college (he had joined in May), be deputized to show the girls around the grounds and have biscuits and lemonade with them. Afterwards, the King invited the officers and senior officer cadets to lunch on the royal yacht, and despite his lowly status as a freshman, Philip was included — legend has it at Elizabeth's personal request. When the *Victoria and Albert III* moved out into Dart Bay, many of the boys escorted it out in rowboats, until the King told the Captain Sir Dudley North: "This is ridiculous and quite unsafe. You must signal them to go back." Slowly, the boats turned around — all except the one rowed by Philip, who now drew the King's disfavour. "The young fool," fumed the King, "he must go back otherwise we will have to heave-to and send him back." Philip eventually turned around, and it would be six years before he saw Princess Elizabeth once more.

When the question of a replacement for the royal yacht was raised by the Admiralty in June 1938, His Majesty replied that, although he realized it was out of date and falling apart, he did not want the construction of a new yacht to "impede, or interfere with, the naval construction programme." Relieved, the government dropped the plan. During the Second World War, the royal yacht would be permanently withdrawn from service and maintained as a depot ship at Portsmouth.

The threat of a German invasion was very real in the summer of 1940, so much so that, like many British parents, Their Majesties were considering sending the princesses away to Canada. But for George VI there were to be no special privileges for his family, even for his children; with duty always coming before family considerations, they spent much of the war isolated at Windsor Castle.[33]

During the war, His Majesty used various naval vessels to visit the troops. In June 1943, with the Italian forces only sixty miles away, at his own request he sailed on the cruiser HMS *Aurora* to Malta. He

stood on the bridge, waving to onlookers as the cruiser entered the Grand Harbour at Valletta. Awarding the island the George Cross, he wished, he said, to pay personal tribute to the Maltese people, who had suffered continuous bombardment since the war began. On June 16, 1944, the Royal Standard was broken out on the cruiser HMS *Arethusa* when His Majesty visited the Normandy beaches. Both he and Churchill had said that they wanted to witness D-Day at first hand, but the decision was the Cabinet's to make, and both had to be dissuaded from attending. A compromise was settled on, and His Majesty was allowed to go ashore on June 16. But because it was only "D-Day plus 10," and the Germans were still within artillery range, the cruiser was closely escorted by two destroyers, HMS *Scourge* and HMS *Urania* with RAF Spitfires wheeling low around the trio. The ship anchored three miles offshore, and His Majesty, in the uniform of an admiral, "jumped for it" into a U.S. Army amphibious "duck." He was met by General Bernard Montgomery, who escorted him to his headquarters at a château six miles from the front. After lunch His Majesty conferred the CBE (Commander of the British Empire) on Major General R.F.L. Keller of the Canadian Third Division. The forty-three-year-old Canadian had been a captain in the Princess Patricia's Canadian Light Infantry just four years before.

With peace, there came an opportunity for family holidays once more. But the old *Victoria and Albert III* was no longer even seaworthy. This was when Lord Mountbatten stepped in with an ingenious plan. He said that he could arrange to buy — at great savings — from a certain Mr. Arida, the yacht *Grille* that had been built for Adolf Hitler but never used by him. It should have come as no surprise that His Majesty refused, replying that he would prefer to have a British-built yacht than one built by the Germans for Hitler.

His Majesty King George VI enters Valletta Harbour, Malta, on HMS *Aurora*.

Although exhausted by the war and not in the best of health, the King still wanted to tour South Africa in 1947 with an idea of helping his old friend General Jan Smuts against the rising Nationalist party. Since he did not want to fly so far and be without a royal yacht, Their Majesties and the two princesses used the brand new battleship HMS *Vanguard*. When, on September 13, 1759, General Wolfe, stormed the Heights at Quebec and made that historic surprise attack on the French at the Plains of Abraham, one of the naval vessels giving his forces covering fire was HMS *Vanguard*, which had also taken part in the siege of the fortress at Louisbourg. Since then, there had been many more ships of that

His Majesty King George VI coming ashore in an amphibious vehicle at D-Day plus 10.

MOD photo

name, and in 1917, in one of the worst British naval disasters, the eighth *Vanguard* blew up in the Firth of Forth with the loss of eight hundred of its crew. The memories of this tragedy delayed the naming of the ninth *Vanguard*. Laid down in 1941 as an armoured battleship to meet those of the Axis of the same size and class, her armament consisted of eight 15-inch and sixteen 5.25-inch guns with close range anti-aircraft guns backed up by a modern fire control and radar system. Launched by Her Royal Highness the Princess Elizabeth on November 30, 1944, the battleship's completion was rushed so that she could participate in the final assault on Japan. But the dropping of the atom bombs and the enemy's sudden surrender deprived her of a place in history. She was commissioned for sea trials on April 25, 1946, when it was announced that *Vanguard* would be used to take the royal family to South Africa in early 1947. This tour was without precedent, as it was the first (and only) one taken by the entire royal family. To be used as a royal yacht, particularly to accommodate Their Majesties, both the princesses, and their retinue, the battleship required considerable alteration.

In an era when the public is accustomed to pop stars and presidents travelling with a retinue, it is intriguing to note how many people Their Majesties needed to bring with them on a tour and who they were. The royal party to South Africa consisted of:

The Lady Harlech	Lady-in-Waiting to the Queen
The Lady Delia Peel	Lady-in-Waiting to the Queen
The Lady Margaret Egerton	Lady-in-Waiting to the Princesses
The Right Honourable Sir Alan Lascelles	Private Secretary to the King
Major T. Harvey, D.S.O.	Private Secretary to the Queen
Major Michael Adeane, M.V.O.	Assistant Private Secretary to the King
Miss E. Leach, W.R.N.S.	Extra Clerk to the Private Secretary
Miss C. Howland (outward trip only)	Extra Clerk to the Private Secretary
Mr. E.F. Grove	Chief Clerk to the Private Secretary
Surgeon Rear-Admiral H.E.Y. White, C.V.O., O.B.E., M.D., F.R.C.S	Medical Officer
Captain (S.) Lewis Ritchie, C.V.O., C.B.E.	Press Secretary
Wing Commander Peter Townsend, D.S.O., D.F.C.	Equerry to The King
Lieutenant-Commander Peter Ashmore, D.S.C., R.N.	Equerry to The King
Deputy Commander Burt (return trip only)	
Superintendent H. Cameron, M.V.O.	The King's Police Officer
Inspector A.E. Perkins	The Queen's Police Officer
Miss C. Wilcox	The Queen's 1st Dresser
Miss M. King	The Queen's 2nd Dresser
Miss M. MacDonald	Maid to Princess Elizabeth
Miss R. MacDonald	Maid to Princess Margaret
Miss Geach	Maid to Ladies-in-Waiting
Miss F. Bamford	Maid to Ladies-in-Waiting
Mr. T.L. Jerram	The King's 1st Valet
Mr. J. MacDonald	The King's 2nd Valet
Mr. R. Evitts	Sergeant Footman
Mr. F.D.T. Dodd	Footman
Mr. R.C. Smith	Footman
Mr. S.J. Gray	Footman

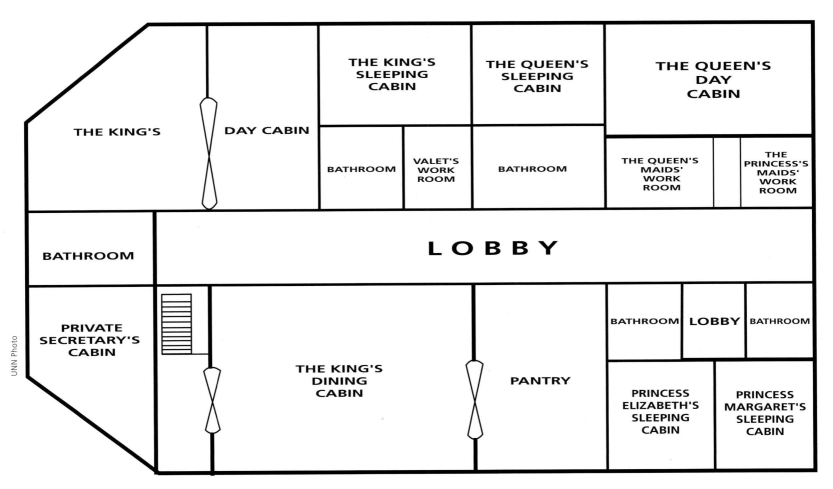

Mr. F.C. West	The King's Hairdresser
Mr. T.H. Joerin	The Queen's Hairdresser
Mr. Wullf	Reuters correspondent
Mr. Nicholls	Exchange Telegraph Company correspondent
Mr. Horton	Press photographer
Mr. Graham Thompson	Newsreel cameraman
Mr. Frank Gillard	BBC commentator
Mr. Unwin	BBC engineer
Mr. Pardy (Warrant Steward)	Keeper of the Royal Apartments
Mr. Bayne	Civilian Cypher Officer

UNN Photo

The royal apartments on HMS *Vanguard* for the 1947 South African tour.

The royal family engaging in target practice on board HMS *Vanguard* on the way to South Africa.

Perhaps the happiest royal tour of them all. The royal party boarding HMS *Vanguard*, bidding farewell to South Africa.

As with the royal party on the *Ophir* forty-five years before, there was a hint of notoriety. Sir Alan Lascelles (known as Tommy) had begun his career as equerry to Edward, the Prince of Wales, only to resign in 1928 because of His Royal Highness's sexual indiscretions while on safari. Perhaps to spite his son, George V made Lascelles his Private Secretary, as would George VI for the Canadian tour. It was Lascelles's skills as a courtier that allowed him to successfully handle the prickliness of Prime Minister Mackenzie King and the nervousness of King George VI on the 1939 tour.[34] Bringing Group Captain Peter Townsend DFC on the voyage was His Majesty's idea — he wanted his equerries to be men of action and had once said, "I would like to have had a son like Townsend." Pining for Philip, to whom she had been engaged since September, 1946, Princess Elizabeth was kept busy writing to him, but letting him know, "The officers are charming and there are one or two real smashers." Margaret Rose was then seventeen, and Townsend, the tall, slim, Battle of Britain hero was thirty-two and very married. It was hero worship at first sight.[35]

One night there was a wardroom sing-song after dinner, and the royal family asked several of the officers to join them. The selection was eclectic: sea shanties, Scottish songs, "Alouette," some of the more respectable wardroom songs, and a family version of "After the Ball Was Over" sung by the King and the two princesses. Princess Margaret played the piano and Princess Elizabeth leaned over the back of it with the King standing behind her. To everyone's amusement, His Majesty also belted out "Don't Fence Me In." The princesses would always remember the voyage as the last time that the whole family was together on a journey.

At the crossing of the equator on February 10, 1947, Their Majesties had to ask permission of King Neptune and his court to do so, and in accordance with custom, forfeits were to be duly paid in the form of duckings or shaves. Fortunately, the delicate problem of Their Majesties having to endure forfeits was avoided as they had crossed the equator some twenty years before on HMS *Renown* — and King Neptune reminded them of it — but the two princesses had not. King Neptune thus addressed the princesses:

> A hearty welcome to you, Princesses,
> Your lot is not one which distresses;
> For we've decided in consultation
> To modify your initiation.
> We seldom make a special case,
> For fear of serious loss of face;
> But on this day Queen Amphitrite

UNN Photo

Princess Elizabeth's bedroom on HMS *Vanguard* for the South African tour, 1947.

Put in a plea to treat you light.
You've been excused the ducking chair,
Which throws its victims through the air;
Razor, brush and lather, too,
Have been debarred for use on you.
Elizabeth and Margaret Rose,
Accept some powder on each nose;
And after this my doctors will
Administer a little pill.
These rites admit you to our realm,
For which we hand you proof on vellum.
Come forward, please.

The princesses were led to the ducking stools and lightly powdered by the "barbers." The "doctors" administered the pills, which tasted suspiciously of glacé cherries. These were swallowed with some trepidation, and the initiation was complete. The press, especially the BBC reporter, were not so fortunate, and Neptune exacted a full payment from them. Although she missed Philip, it was, for the future queen, the happiest tour of her life. As with the Canadian ocean trip in 1939, the voyage to South Africa was also just the holiday that His Majesty needed.[36]

So successful was it that, in the summer of 1948, it was announced that another tour would be made in January 1949, this time to Australia and New Zealand. Now flagship of the Mediterranean Fleet, *Vanguard* was rushed home to Plymouth to prepare for this. Shortly after her arrival, the news that the King was in poor health caused the proposed tour to be cancelled. For *Vanguard* it was a missed opportunity for a last hurrah. Increasingly outmoded, she had no place in the age of jet bombers, and soon of missiles. Her Majesty Queen Elizabeth would be piped aboard her on June 15, 1953, for the coronation review at Spithead, and the last British battleship would linger through the decade, demoted finally to the Reserve Fleet. Her final indignity was taking part in the movie *Sink the Bismarck* in which, ironically, she played the part of the German battleship that she had been built to meet. On October 9, 1959, the government announced that the *Vanguard* would be scrapped, and in August 1960, she was towed from Portsmouth to the breakers yard at Faslane, Scotland. Today, her namesake *Vanguard*, also based at Faslane, lives on as a nuclear submarine, armed with Trident missiles. Whatever her virtues, there will never be a Royal Tour on her.

Philip Mountbatten was born into the Royal Navy — almost literally. His parents, Prince Andrew and Princess Alice, ruled Greece until 1922, when the monarchy was overthrown. Sentenced by the revolutionaries to be shot, Prince Andrew appealed to his British cousin King George V for help. The British royal family, aware of what had happened when their Russian cousins fell into the hands of the Bolsheviks, prevailed on Downing Street to do something. His Majesty phoned the Admiralty personally and directed that a Royal Navy cruiser be detached from the British Mediterranean Fleet and sent to Greece to rescue the Greek royal family.[37] Captain H.A. Buchanan-Wollaston was ordered to pick them up, and, in a scene out of the movies, the Greek royal family was taken on board the cruiser HMS *Calypso*,[38] with sailors making a cradle out of an orange crate for the baby Philip. They got off at Brindisi to go to Rome and seek an audience with the Pope, and then went into exile and poverty in London, living at Brown's Hotel. Captain Buchanan-Wollaston would retire as a vice-admiral, living until 1969, and remembering the dramatic rescue all his life.

Philip was sent to public school at Cheam and, although he later said that he had really wanted to fly Spitfires for the RAF, he was packed off to the Royal Naval Academy at Dartmouth. When war began, he served in the Mediterranean as a midshipman on HMS *Ramillies* and later on HMS *Valiant*. In 1942, Philip was sent back to Britain from the Mediterranean via South Africa, on the Canadian Pacific liner *Empress of Scotland*. En route, the ship's stokers went on strike, leaving him and the other young midshipmen to stoke the furnaces all the way to the United States. For his stoking duties, he was awarded a trimmer's certificate when he returned to Britain. Philip arrived home in Portsmouth, from Gibraltar on January 17, 1946.

After instructing in the Petty Officers' School and attending the Naval Staff College at Greenwich, he was appointed first lieutenant of HMS *Chequers*. He married Princess Elizabeth on November 20, 1947, and shortly before the wedding, he was created Duke of Edinburgh. On August 15, 1950, he was promoted to lieutenant-commander (on the very morning that Princess Anne was born) and appointed in command of the frigate HMS *Magpie*, then in Malta. If there were some who called it "Edinburgh's private yacht," Philip ignored them, and was as determined as his father and his uncle Louis Mountbatten had been before him to make the ship he commanded the best in the fleet. In the annual whaleboat regatta, *Magpie* won with the duke rowing stroke, stripped to the waist. Having just finished nursing the baby, Princess Elizabeth flew out to join him and was given use of the C-in-C's dispatch ship HMS *Surprise*. The two ships with their young royal couple were ideal for British prestige and media relations in the Mediterranean.[39] By the time he was promoted to commander, his personal life and duties as the consort to the future monarch were taking precedence over his career — the government wanted the royal couple to tour North America in 1951. Philip was ordered to London that July, on "indefinite leave." He left the Navy and, on bidding farewell to the crew of *Magpie*, summed up his regret by saying that the eleven months he had served with them had been the happiest of his life. But there was to be one more ship in his future.

For the 1951 North American tour, Princess Elizabeth and the Duke of Edinburgh flew to Montreal, but on the way home they were picked up at Portugal Cove, Newfoundland, on November 12, by the Canadian Pacific liner *Empress of Scotland*. The 26,032-tonne ship had been built in 1929 for the Canadian Pacific by Fairfield's at Govan, Scotland, and, under the name *Empress of Japan*, served on the Pacific route between the Orient and Vancouver until 1939. At an average speed of twenty-three knots, she was fast for her day and beautifully furnished with a dome ceiling, a Palm Court, a ballroom, and a cinema. After the attack on Pearl Harbor, at the express order of Prime Minister Churchill, on October 16, 1942, the *Empress of Japan* was rechristened the *Empress of Scotland*. With its new identity, it began carrying troops, successfully dodging bombs from both the Luftwaffe and the Japanese air force during the war. Her only earlier brush with royalty came in September 1945, when she took the Earl of Athlone and Princess Alice back to Britain after he had served as the Governor General of Canada. The *Empress's* most historic trip to Canada was undoubtedly on November 27, 1945, when she docked at Halifax crammed with 4,269 returning Canadian troops.

After the war she was refurbished once more at Fairfields, and the Palm Court was renamed the Cocktail Room. The ex-trooper was put on the Liverpool—Quebec City (later Montreal) run, and, in this capacity was slated to take Princess Elizabeth and the Duke of Edinburgh to Canada in September 1951. Its fleet depleted by the war, the Canadian Pacific had only three ships on the Atlantic run then: the *Empress of France II* (formerly the *Duchess of Bedford*), the *Empress of Canada II* (formerly the *Duchess of Richmond*), and its flagship, the *Empress of Scotland*.

The Canadian Pacific liner *Empress of Scotland* picked up Princess Elizabeth and the Duke of Edinburgh from Newfoundland, 1951.

The *Empress of France II* was initially chosen to be the royal yacht, and furniture and fittings for the royal suite were made for it. When the *Empress of Scotland* replaced it, these fittings were put in at Quebec City on November 6. On the starboard side of "A" deck — the sunny side when homeward bound — there were three rooms in the suite: the Princess's room, the Duke's room, and a combined sitting and dining room. All three rooms were painted in pastel shades. Princess Elizabeth's rooms had a fitted carpet of turquoise pattern on a grey background. The curtains were beige with blue silk stripes. The easy chairs had a green tapestry with cushions of silk brocade in peach blossom and gold. Her bedspread was turquoise-blue silk brocade decorated with a small gold star pattern and bordered with a pale gold fringe. The chosen furniture for the room was cherry maple.

Canadian Pacific Photo

Flagship of the Canadian Pacific fleet, the *Empress of Scotland* was lavishly refurnished to serve as the royal yacht. This is the Common Room.

The Duke of Edinburgh's room had a fitted carpet in Georgian green and grey; the curtains were green and gold moiré striped damask. The large easy chairs were upholstered in green ribbed tapestry, while the cushions had brown and gold stripes. His bedspread was in old gold stub bordered with a green fringe. The furniture in the Duke's room was blistered chestnut.

The combined sitting and dining room had a fitted carpet with a ruby pattern on a grey background. The curtains were of purple, brown, and cream striped silk. The dining chairs were upholstered in purple brocade shot with gold while the settee was a rich wine-coloured brocade with loose cushions of a mushroom colour and a gold star pattern, piped on the edges with scarlet silk. The furniture in this room was of light Nigerian walnut.

The *Empress of Scotland* crew present HRH Princess Elizabeth and the Duke of Edinburgh with a pair of homemade dolls for their children.

Some of the *Empress of Scotland*'s crew for the royal voyage had historic connections with royalty and the war. Its Master, Captain Ernest Duggan, had joined the Canadian Pacific in 1919 and been second officer on the *Empress of Britain* in 1939 when it met the King and Queen at the end of their Canadian tour. Commander Far East of 11th Minesweeping Flotilla during the war, he rejoined Canadian Pacific after becoming first Master of the *Empress of Australia* and then in 1951 Commodore Captain of the flagship *Empress of Scotland*. His Chief Engineer James Thompson had been badly wounded when the *Empress of Canada* was torpedoed by an Italian submarine in 1943 in the South Atlantic. Chief Stewardess Lilian O'Brien had thirty-three years of uninterrupted service with the Canadian Pacific and had personally attended the Queen when she and the King had come to Canada on the *Empress of Australia* in 1939.

Getting into Conception Bay, Newfoundland, on November 12, then manoeuvring the big ship off Portugal Cove was tricky enough for Captain Duggan without the very rough sea and Force 7 (moderate gale) on the Beaufort scale. But after the hectic schedule of the tour, the young couple enjoyed the voyage home, watching movies in the theatre, dining alone, and arriving at Liverpool on November 17. The staff on board the *Empress* were so taken with the Princess that they made a pair of dolls for her children, Charles and Anne. Two years later, while still Master of the *Empress of Scotland*, Captain Duggan in his position as Royal Naval Reserve aide-de-camp to Her Majesty was invited to attend her coronation. Having survived the Luftwaffe's attentions during the war, the *Empress of Scotland* would be sold in 1958 to the Hamburg-Atlantic Line and renamed the *Hanseatic*.

In October 1951, the Admiralty announced that a medium-sized hospital ship would be built, which could serve a dual purpose in peacetime and replace the Royal Yacht *Victoria and Albert*, which by then was no longer seaworthy. The requirements were that the ship should be, for the first time, truly oceanic and suitable for service in both tropical and arctic waters. It also had to have a continuous seagoing speed of twenty-one knots and an endurance of at least two thousand miles at twenty knots at load displacement. King George VI and subsequently the Queen continually stressed the need for economy, and both made many suggestions to reduce expenditure. Both also made many changes to reduce the size of the ship from the pre-war requirements. But because of the long ocean passages and possible use as a hospital ship in wartime, it was necessary to ensure that the size of the ship was not so reduced as to impair her seaworthiness. The smallest ship to meet these requirements was one of about four thousand tonnes displacement, and every effort was made to produce an acceptable design with a displacement as near to this figure as practicable.

Sharp Family photo

Canadian Pacific Captain Ernest Duggan on the *Empress of Scotland*.

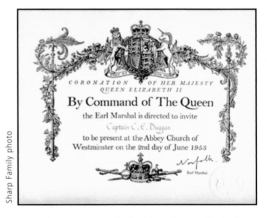
Sharp Family photo

Captain Duggan was invited by Princess Elizabeth to her coronation, a day that he forever cherished.

HMY *Britannia*. Three masts were a requirement for a royal yacht; the Royal Standard is worn at the main, the flag of the Lord High Admiral at the fore, and the Union Jack at the mizzen.

MOD photo

The *Britannia* served Her Majesty for 43 years and 334 days, bringing the grandeur of Buckingham Palace to 135 countries.

As a dual-purpose vessel, the ship would have to suit two requirements. Because she was a royal yacht, she would fly the White Ensign and be manned by a naval crew. But as a hospital ship she would be manned by a merchant-service crew and fly the Red Ensign. The design was developed and statements of requirements were prepared at the Admiralty by the end of 1951. These were approved by His Majesty before his death. Later the plans and a model of the ship were submitted to and approved by the Queen.

HMY *Britannia* was given a clipper bow and modified cruiser stern, rather than the more traditional swan bow and counter stern previously associated with royal yachts. It had been the wish of King George VI that the new yacht would be on modern lines, but still traditional in other aspects. For example, a requirement for a royal yacht was that it had three masts: the Royal Standard was worn at the main, the flag of the Lord High Admiral at the fore, and the Union Flag at the mizzen. But a single funnel was in keeping with a modern design. The royal and state apartments and accommodation for the household and royal staff was to be aft, with the ship's company accommodated forward. This always gave the HMY *Britannia* a slightly larger superstructure, but overall a well-balanced, graceful, and dignified appearance was accomplished.

She cost £2,098,000; one of the most important factors when placing the contract for the construction of the *Britannia* was the requirement, for budgetary reasons, that the vessel be completed by the end of 1953 or by early 1954 at the latest. This was not an easy deadline to meet as there was a shortage of shipbuilding materials and equipment. Of the seven companies invited to bid, John Brown & Co. (Clydebank) Ltd. was given the contract and the order officially placed with them in February 1952. The keel was laid on June 16, 1952, and ship number 691 was named *Britannia* — a personal choice by Her Majesty. *Britannia* was launched by the Queen on April 16, 1953, and was commissioned on January 11, 1954.

But as her grandfather and great-grandfather had, the Queen would also own a racing yacht. In 1952, members of the Island Sailing Club at Cowes presented Princess Elizabeth and her new husband with *Bluebottle*, a Dragon-class racing yacht, for their personal use.[40] The twenty-six-foot wooden sailboat had been built at Gosport by Camper and Nicholsons in 1948. The boat would have a close connection with Canada. To foster yacht racing, in 1953 Prince Philip established The Duke of Edinburgh Trophy in Canada for supremacy in Dragon-class racing. Twice, he sent his own sailboat *Bluebottle* to Canada for the national Dragon competition. On July 6, 1967, His Royal Highness arrived by helicopter from Government House at the HM Yacht Britannia Yacht Club on the Ottawa River to present the trophy to the winning crew from Toronto's Royal Canadian Yacht Club. Until the HMY *Britannia* was ready, the sailboat would be all that the royal couple had, as the former Royal Yacht *Victoria and Albert III* was now a rotting hulk; in 1955 it was taken to Faslane and broken up.

Queen Mary, who had come to Canada on the *Ophir* in 1901, died at Marlborough House on March 24, 1953. Her death must have been on the mind of the Queen as she and Prince Philip planned the worldwide Royal Tour that year. Her Majesty had just become, under the Royal Titles Act of 1953, Head of the Commonwealth, and now, on the advice of her ministers, had to enact that title and office in each of the Commonwealth's countries. As HMY *Britannia* was not yet ready, they used the Shaw Saville ship, SS *Gothic*. When it entered Sydney harbour, millions of Australians lined the shores and, everywhere the royal progress went, people marvelled because, as one historian put it, "they could finally see the face on the money, smiling in their own streets." It was the longest official tour of the Queen's reign: an epic round-the-world Commonwealth tour that lasted six months from November 24, 1953, to May 15, 1954, and covered 43,618 miles. Considering that Her Majesty had been crowned only five months before and was leaving her children, Prince Charles (aged five) and Princess Anne (aged three), behind for five months, it must have required all her strength.

At the end of the tour, the Queen and Prince Philip met the new royal yacht with their two children on board in Tobruk harbour, and, reunited, the family sailed home in it. Now Admiral of the Mediterranean Fleet, Lord Louis Mountbatten staged a naval review of the *Britannia*, with every warship going smartly close by. At The Needles off the British coast, Churchill came aboard and the old warrior shared the bridge with the Queen and Prince Philip as *Britannia* came down the Thames. Its arrival was commemorated in a famous painting now at the naval museum in Greenwich.

While Her Majesty was abroad, HMY *Britannia* was accepted by the Admiralty on January 11, 1954. Its principal dimensions and other leading particulars were:

- Length overall: 412 feet, 3 inches
- Length on waterline: 380 feet
- Length between perpendiculars: 360 feet
- Maximum breadth moulded: 55 feet
- Breadth at upper deck moulded: 54 feet, 6 inches
- Depth moulded to upper deck: 45 feet; abaft amidships: 32 feet, 6 inches
- Depth moulded to upper deck at fore perpendicular: 40 feet, 4 inches
- Depth moulded to upper deck at aft perpendicular: 33 feet, 10 inches
- Load displacement: 4,715 tonnes
- Mean draught at load displacement: 15 feet, 7.5 inches
- Gross tonnage: 5,769 tonnes
- Shaft horsepower: 12,000
- Speed on trials at 12,000 shp 22.75 knots (at 4,320 tonnes displacement), corresponding rpm 286
- Continuous seagoing speed: 21 knots
- The foremast was 133 feet high (from the waterline), the main mast 139 feet, and the mizzen 118 feet; the top 20 feet of two of the masts were hinged and could be lowered to allow the yacht to pass under low bridges.

In the load condition the ship motor carried 330 tonnes of oil fuel, which is more than sufficient to obtain the design endurance of 2,000 miles at 20 knots, and 120 tonnes of fresh water, which was considered sufficient for two days' supply without evaporators working. The yacht's diesel generator was first used as a propulsion engine in HM Submarine *Vampire* and was removed from her in 1943. (At the time of decommissioning, it was probably the oldest seagoing operational diesel in existence.)

HMY *Britannia* was equipped with the royal barge, with a top speed of nineteen knots, and two thirty-four-foot motor boats (built in 1970), which were used as escorts for the royal barge and for ferrying liberty men and guests.

The royal apartments were on the shelter deck between the main and mizzen masts with a veranda at the aft end leading to a sun deck. The deck of these apartments was two feet higher than the general-shelter deck level, so that the external fore and aft gangways were below the windows of the royal apartments. The main staircase from the royal apartments on the shelter deck led to a vestibule on the upper deck, about which were grouped the state apartments. Her Majesty's and His Royal Highness's sitting rooms were at either end of the vestibule. The dining room, drawing room, and anteroom extended the full width of the superstructure, without obstruction from pillars. Sliding screens were fitted at the entrance to the anteroom and between the anteroom and the drawing room and could be folded back when required to provide a large reception space from the aft end of the drawing room to the foot of the main staircase. The main staircase came down from the upper deck to the main deck, where the household and guest cabins,

Over the years, the dining table on the *Britannia* has been host to many world leaders.

Architect Sir Hugh Casson aimed for a simple "country house feel," with much of the furniture brought from the *Victoria and Albert III*.

sitting rooms, and cloak rooms were located. The royal staff were accommodated on the lower deck, and had use of an elevator near the main staircase operated between the main and shelter decks.

The crew of 21 officers and 250 men were accommodated forward in a manner generally in accordance with Royal Naval practice, except the Chief Petty Officers, who slept in four-berth cabins. There would never be women among the crew. All the officers underwent a two-year tour of duty, as did half the crew. For this honour they received no extra pay, allowances, or leave.

The suitability of the decorative design and the furnishing of the royal and state apartments were, of course, very important. Her Majesty and His Royal Highness the Duke of Edinburgh both took a great interest in the work and personally approved the decorative treatment of the walls and ceilings and the design of new furniture and chose the soft furnishings. Prince Philip, an artist himself, chose several of the paintings on board and on one occasion, after viewing works by members of the Royal Society of Painters in Watercolours, bought four etchings by Alan Carr Linford for the private rooms of HMY *Britannia*.

There were separate messes on the royal yacht for the seamen (called "Yotties"), the petty officers, the engineers, and the royal household. The senior officers' accommodation was located on the shelter deck. The admiral's day cabin was the most spacious and comfortable room outside of the royal apartments. His sofa and armchairs were brought from the previous Royal Yacht *Victoria and Albert III*. Nine admirals had the honour of serving on the *Britannia*. They were responsible for a crew of 19 officers and 220 yachtsmen. When the Queen was on board, the admiral dined in the royal quarters.

The shipbuilders, Messrs. John Brown & Co., appointed Messrs. A. McInnes Gardner & Partners as their decorative architects for this work. A specialist in this field, Sir Hugh Casson, was appointed as consultant to the Admiralty. A favourite architect of the royal family — he would design interiors at Balmoral and Windsor Castle — Casson was also president of the Royal Academy, and the artwork on board reflected his influence. He would later write that the Queen was anxious to keep costs down but also to link the new ship with the old and incorporate a sense of tradition. Her Majesty had very strong views about every detail, from the door handles to the lampshades. HMY *Britannia*'s state apartments also contained furniture and fittings from the former royal yacht, including a small gimbal table designed by Queen Victoria's consort, Prince Albert.

The wheel in the wheelhouse came from George V's racing yacht HMY *Britannia*, while the binnacle on the veranda deck was first used in the *Royal George* (built in 1817) and since fitted in each successive royal yacht. To economize, use was made as far as possible of furniture from the *Victoria and Albert III* and of new pieces made for the SS *Gothic* for the Commonwealth tour.

Thus, from its birth, Her Majesty became extremely attached to the *Britannia*, in part because of the connection with her father and also because it could bring the formality of Buckingham Palace anywhere in the world and yet maintain the holiday atmosphere of Balmoral.

In the initial stages of the design, the Medical Director General of the Navy was consulted about the requirements for the vessel in her role as a hospital ship. It was thus possible to proceed with the designs for a hospital ship and a royal yacht concurrently, so that the conversion could be made economically and efficiently. The wards, which could accommodate two hundred patients, would be located to the aft part of the ship. While most of the patients would have been medical and surgical cases requiring normal hospital conditions, provision was also made for infectious cases and those suffering from tuberculosis. Infectious patients would be accommodated in glazed cubicles built within the drawing room. Tuberculosis cases requiring fresh-air beds would be accommodated on part of the veranda, while others suffering from this disease would have been berthed in wards in the space occupied by the royal bedrooms. The remaining wards, including the cabins and wardroom for sick officers and the cabins for a few female patients, would be sited in the other royal apartments and in spaces later allocated to members of the royal household and staff. Particular care was taken in the layout of bathrooms and sanitary facilities to ensure that as little alteration as possible would be necessary upon conversion. The operating theatre, with its annexes and its adjacent sterilizer and anaesthetic rooms, would be on the lower deck, along with the other specialist facilities, including an ophthalmic room, a physiotherapy room, a pathological laboratory, and an X-ray room with adjacent darkroom. Full facilities for dental treatment, including a laboratory, would be located on the main deck. (The hospital ship role was formally deleted in 1992.)

The ship's royal quarters were spartan in taste, which was exactly what the Queen desired. The original plans had been much more ornate, but the Queen rejected these proposals in favour of a more simple, "country house" feel for her floating home. Hundreds of original items from the Royal Collection were always in evidence. These included prints and paintings, the baby grand piano, furniture, silverware, and gifts given to the Queen from nations around the world.

The teak-lined sun lounge on the shelter deck was one of the Queen's favourite spaces on HMY *Britannia*. A true family room, it offered privacy from the rest of the ship. It was Prince Philip who chose and purchased the room's lightweight, colourful furniture in 1959 during a visit to Hong Kong. The Queen was fond of breakfasting in this room, enjoying the spectacular scenery through the large windows. The Queen and the Duke of Edinburgh's sleeping quarters consisted of two suites. Both their bedrooms were unexpectedly simple. Each had a private bathroom, and a connecting door linked the two rooms, which were mirror images in design, though each reflected the individual's tastes. While the Queen's pillows had lace borders, Prince Philip preferred a more masculine feel to his room. If either required a midnight snack they pressed a button at the side of their beds to summon a steward, who was constantly on call to tend to their needs. As had *Victoria and Albert*, *Britannia* would always be a refuge for the royal family, keeping them far from the cameras of the media. As a result, it came as no surprise that Prince Charles and Princess Diana spent part of their honeymoon on the vessel in the Mediterranean,[41] as did Princess Margaret and Antony Armstrong-Jones, Princess Anne and Captain Mark Phillips, and the Duke and Duchess of York.

The elegant drawing room, with its chintz-covered sofas, deep armchairs, and luxurious Persian rugs, was used both for official functions and for private entertaining. The baby grand piano in the corner of the room, firmly bolted to the deck, was regularly played by Princess Diana, Princess Margaret, and Princess Alexandra. The State Dining Room was the largest and grandest room on the royal yacht, and throughout the forty-four years of HMY *Britannia*'s life, it witnessed some spectacular banquets and played host to the rich, the famous, and the powerful. Sir Winston Churchill, Nelson Mandela, Bill Clinton, Boris Yeltsin, Ronald Reagan, and Margaret Thatcher all dined aboard the royal yacht. And a banquet on board HMY *Britannia* was an experience to remember. It took three hours to set the fifty-six places for a state banquet, and the position of every knife, fork, and spoon was meticulously measured with a ruler. The grand, polished mahogany dining-room table was adorned with gleaming silverware, sparkling candelabras, and fine china. Guests to this table were presented with the menus, printed in French, as a souvenir of their time on HMY *Britannia*. Even when the royal family dined alone, they always dressed for dinner. When Princess Margaret honeymooned on the royal yacht, she wore her tiara at every evening meal.

It was the only naval ship not to have its name on the bow — the royal crest was sufficient. It was also the only ship in the Royal Navy on which the sailors were called by their first name. But a commission on HMY *Britannia* was never plain sailing. These were not ordinary passengers. For each state visit, the royal family brought with them five tonnes of luggage, including Malvern water for the Queen's tea and forty-five members of the royal household to tend to their needs. Shouting by staff was forbidden at all times to preserve the air of tranquility that existed on board. All orders were relayed by hand signal, and "red hot" notice boards were used if there were any last-minute orders to be posted. Because of the continuous state functions that required instantaneous changes of clothing and linen, the sailors had to run a twenty-four-hour laundry where temperatures could climb above 120°C.

HMY *Britannia* also had several curiosities that originated in its use as a royal yacht. The royal bridge, scene of many famous pictures of the royal family, had a mahogany bar in the middle of the deck. While it appeared to have no function, it was built to preserve royal modesty in case a breeze lifted the ladies' skirts. Within the royal quarters there was a large deck where the royal family relaxed and played, and one of their favourite games was deck hockey. There were unusual cabins like the Jelly Room, where the royal children's desserts were stored, and the Silver Room. A yachtsman polished the massive silverware collection daily, and understandably, a three-month deployment used 240 tins of polish. Then there was the garage. Her Majesty required transport overseas, and HMY *Britannia* had a built-in garage where a Rolls-Royce Phantom V remained. The Rolls-Royce was brought on board in its transporter, which had to be hoisted onto the special track fitted into the deck. The bumpers then had to be removed before the car was squeezed into the garage with only eight inches to spare.

Finally, a shop supplied daily essentials to the crew, and that was where, as children, Prince Charles and Princess Anne first spent their pocket money.

The officers' wardroom, where the nineteen serving officers on HMY *Britannia* ate, was a gentlemen's club at sea. The large dining-room table, where they took their meals dressed in their distinguished red "sea rig," was adorned by fine crystal. Serving as an officer on HMY *Britannia* was an honour that carried some benefits. When the Royal Marine Band was not on royal duty, it provided musical accompaniment to the meal. At the end of every meal, the officers stood and drank a toast to Her Majesty before the musicians played the national anthem.

Designed to be used as a royal yacht in peacetime and as a hospital ship in time of war, HMY *Britannia* served for forty-four years as an official and private residence for the Queen and other members of the royal family. The royal yacht provided reception rooms for up to 250 guests, and included office space and accommodation for staff accompanying the Queen. In addition, HMY *Britannia* was used extensively to support the country by undertaking many diplomatic, representational, and (particularly in the last ten years) commercial duties. The Duke of Edinburgh made two around-the-world voyages in the royal yacht, visiting some of the most remote parts of the Commonwealth as the Queen's representative, travelling some 72,430 miles. The four-month voyage of 1956-57 included visits to the far-flung South Atlantic locations of the Falkland Islands, South Georgia, Tristan da Cunha, Ascension Island, and St. Helena.

HMY *Britannia* first came to Canada in June 1959, when Her Majesty opened the St. Lawrence Seaway with President Dwight Eisenhower. It was escorted up the St. Lawrence to the St. Lambert lift locks by HMCS *Gatineau*. There, the twenty-one-gun salute was fired while Ike and Mrs. Eisenhower arrived on the presidential yacht *Columbine*. The highlight of the visit was on June 26, when Queen Elizabeth joined President Eisenhower in the formal opening of the St. Lawrence Seaway. After addressing the crowd at the St. Lambert lift lock, the Queen and the President boarded the royal yacht, which pulled away and entered the lift locks, formally opening the Seaway for business.

It was in Canada's centennial year that HMY *Britannia* was especially appreciated by those who sailed on her and by the millions of Canadians who saw her on television. After proceeding down the St. Lawrence, she toured the Thousand Islands. In a reception hosted by the Queen on board her yacht, Her Majesty entertained eight provincial premiers and nine lieutenant governors (feeding them duck in orange sauce). Only Quebec premier Daniel Johnson said he had a previous engagement. The Queen wore a gown of yellow with a diamond tiara, and all the premiers were in dinner jackets. Premier Joseph Smallwood of Newfoundland, the only living Father of Confederation, was "walking about with his hands in the pockets of his tuxedo which was baggy at the ankles and his shoes were black basket-work loafers," as the society columnist for the *Globe and Mail* noted. That evening on the veranda deck of the yacht, forty-three scrubbed and polished young Canadians received their Duke of Edinburgh awards from the Duke himself. Security measures included a detachment of naval frogmen inspecting the hull and more in dinghies circling the yacht. Her widest coverage was when she sailed from Cornwall, Ontario, on July 2, 1967, for a seventy-mile overnight journey to Montreal's Expo '67 with Prince Philip and Queen Elizabeth on board. They arrived at the World's Fair on the royal yacht the next day.

HMY *Britannia* at the opening of the St. Lawrence Seaway.

While Queen Elizabeth and Prince Phillip flew home, *Britannia* sailed to St. John, New Brunswick, where Queen Elizabeth the Queen Mother had arrived on July 10 to begin a thirteen-day centennial tour of the Maritime provinces. The royal yacht was used as a floating base while the Queen Mother toured the four Maritime provinces before flying back home on July 22. She had last visited the region in 1939 with her husband, the late king.

During the Queen's 1971 ten-day Canadian visit, HMY *Britannia* was on the Pacific Coast and carried the royal party, Prime Minister Pierre Trudeau, and Premier W.A.C. Bennett between Victoria and Vancouver. Her Majesty used the yacht to visit Canada again in 1983, on this occasion travelling from Victoria to Vancouver, where she laid the foundations on the future site of the Expo '86 Canada Pavilion and offered the "invitation to the world" for Expo '86.

In her 43 years and 334 days in commission, HMY *Britannia* steamed 1,087,623 nautical miles and carried out a total of 968 visits overseas and in home waters, including 696 visits abroad (such as an official visit to seven countries in the Caribbean in 1994 and to South Africa and Russia in 1995) with the Queen or other members of the royal family. HMY *Britannia* also carried out 272 visits at home, including taking part in the V-J fortieth anniversary commemorations in London in 1995. During the last twelve months of her life, the royal yacht hosted 67 major commercial and diplomatic events on board and entertained 10,500 guests. During her last overseas deployment in the first eight months of 1997, HMY *Britannia* carried out twenty-eight visits to seventeen countries; the best-known visit was taken to hand over Hong Kong in June. Although *Britannia* was never required to carry out her secondary role as a hospital ship, in January 1986, while on passage to Australia, the royal yacht coordinated the evacuation of 1,379 civilians of 55 different nations from Aden when that country was being invaded from the north. *Britannia* herself evacuated 1,068 men, women, and children.

Despite all the care that had been lavished on it by the Navy, the royal yacht required frequent refits paid for by the Ministry of Defence. It underwent a £9-million refit in 1960, and when it was due for another in 1968, Harold Wilson's Labour government first considered scrapping it. With Britain still reeling from the effects of devaluation a year earlier, the Wilson government had embarked on a public expenditure review to trim spending to the bone. Buckingham Palace officials wrote to the Ministry of Defence proposing a symbolic tightening of the royal belt by offering HMY *Britannia* for use in other Royal Navy duties. At the same time, *Britannia*'s running costs jumped from £29,188 in 1953-54 to £757,300 in 1970-71. If few grudged Her Majesty taking it annually on a holiday to Scotland, the royals did themselves no favours by using *Britannia* on honeymoons.

By the 1990s, *Britannia* was in dire need of retirement, and rather than undergo the £17-million refit required to keep her in operation for a further five years, after consultation with the Queen, the government decided that there would be no royal yacht to replace her. The prestige she provided to the British government and to companies overseas could be accomplished more economically with the rental of a hotel or conference centre.

The government decided that the final destination for the royal yacht would be Leith, in Edinburgh. The royal yacht was first to be decommissioned, with a paying-off ceremony in which the flags were lowered for the last time. On November 11, 1997, Her Majesty and the Duke of Edinburgh joined with other members of the royal family in bidding the HMY *Britannia* farewell at its paying-off ceremony at Portsmouth. She had launched the ship in 1953, and it had travelled more than a million miles on royal and official duties. As Her Majesty left the royal yacht for the last time, there were tears in her eyes, never seen before. The Queen had allowed her emotions for the old ship to betray her.

Permanently moored in Leith, in August 1998, the former royal yacht opened for visitors and as a conference centre. Immaculately kept, it is now run by a non-profit charitable trust and known simply as *Britannia*.[42]

DND photo

HMY *Britannia* at Expo '67.

MOTOR CARS

Detail of photo from page 114.

In 1898, the Prince of Wales (later Edward VII) was inspecting a company of Highlanders in front of Balmoral Castle when, from the distance, came the noise of a motor vehicle. As it spluttered into view, "a fearsome sight with smoke and steam on all sides," His Royal Highness turned from the parade, exclaiming, "What the devil is this?" Gradually, through the smoke and dust, emerged the outline of the face of one of his ministers. "Good Heavens, it's the devil himself," murmured the Prince. It was not the devil that had been introduced to the royal family but the motor car.

Typical of His Majesty King George V's Daimler limousines in the 1920s: claret coloured and dignified (or dowdy, depending on one's point of view).

The last Daimler limousine — note the police light that all royal motor cars have.

The Bentley's stylists have incorporated a "glass house" design so that there is maximum visibility both into and out of the car — at Her Majesty's insistence.

The Royal Mews on Buckingham Palace Road was designed in 1825 by architect John Nash to be a self-contained transportation centre. Under the Crown Equerry (who still lives there), the quadrangle was to house stables for two hundred horses, shelter multiple barouches, broughams, and state coaches, as well as provide accommodation for the grooms, coachmen, and stable boys. Today, thirty horses and some of the coaches remain, sharing the historic space with Rolls-Royces, Bentleys, and assorted "people carriers," the descendants of that first car that startled His Royal Highness more than a century ago.

To the discerning, the royal motor cars are no less resplendent and unique than the coaches they have displaced. A pop star's Porsche or a computer millionaire's Lamborghini might be flashier, and the Mercedeses used by the rulers of many countries more expensive, but with their burnished claret or black bodywork, rear glass-house design, and silver mascot on the grilles, the royal motor cars are exceptional vehicles. Used for public engagements and some ceremonial occasions, they must transport their passengers in a style that is safe, slow, and dignified, allowing as many people as possible to see the Queen or other members of the royal family. For most, a glimpse of a royal motor car driving slowly by will be their only opportunity to see Her Majesty. Built to unique specifications by firms who once handcrafted the coaches of previous dynasties, they are vehicles of great historical and technical interest in themselves. Through the last century, the royal family have driven and been driven in many cars around the world, but at home certain makes have dominated through generations: Daimler, Rolls-Royce, Bentley, and to a lesser extent Austin, Aston Martin, Rover, and Jaguar.

Queen Victoria was never known to have ridden in any type of motor car, although her consort, Prince Albert, with his scientific bent (to say nothing of his German nationality), would have enjoyed this new form of locomotion. For it all began with a baker's son in Schondörf, Germany. Born in 1834, three years before Victoria came to the throne, Gottlieb Daimler was apprenticed to a local gunsmith. His genius with machines showed itself early, and after graduating from the Stuttgart Polytechnic, Daimler tackled the mysteries of the internal combustion engine. At the age of thirty-eight, he was appointed technical director at Doktor N.A. Otto's workshop, where he hired another talented engineer, Wilhelm Maybach, and in 1892, the pair set out on their own. Between them, Daimler and Maybach invented much of the modern combustion engine. Rejecting conventional designs, they stood their engine upright, enclosed the flywheel, invented a carburetor, and discovered a combustible mixture for liquid fuel that was 91 percent air and 9 percent petrol. In September 1886, Daimler put his two-cylinder engine into a coach body and drove it around Bad Cannstatt. The following month, he set up a small factory to produce and sell copies.

But the German engineer's fame might not have made it to Britain had not Frederick Simms, an Englishman born in Hamburg, seen its potential. Simms, who was later to found the Royal Motor Car Club, bought the British patent rights for Daimler's engine, but to use on motorboats on the Thames. It was only in 1893 that his Daimler Motor Syndicate Ltd. moved into an abandoned linen factory in Coventry and began building cars. Somewhat confusingly, although the Daimler name continued to be used both in Britain and Germany, there would never be any connection between Daimler Benz of Stuttgart and Daimler of Coventry.

To publicize its reliability, in 1897, a Daimler was driven from John O'Groats in Scotland to Land's End, completing the 929-mile run in 93.5 hours. Impressed by this, John Walter Scott-Montagu (soon to be the second Lord Montagu of Beaulieu), bought a 12-horsepower Daimler, beginning the car collection at his home that continues today. He encountered great hostility towards the car; for instance, when he attended the House of Lords, he was not allowed to drive it into the front yard of the Houses of Parliament. All this changed with a single event. In August 1899, when His Royal Highness the Prince of Wales was staying at Highcliffe Castle in Hampshire, Montagu drove over from Beaulieu for lunch. After the meal, he took the Prince out in his Daimler. His Royal Highness sat in the front seat with (naturally) two young ladies in back. At an average speed of forty miles per hour, they drove through the New Forest on the Lyndhurst-Southampton Road for eight miles before returning to Highcliffe. The Prince, teasing the young ladies about the unsuitability of their fashionable hats, presciently remarked that motoring would force female fashions to change. It was the first time that a member of the British

UNN photo

The royal Daimlers in the Sandringham Museum. Note fluted grilles.

King Edward VII and Daimler — the first royal motor car.

Royal Photograph Collection Windsor Castle

royal family had been in a car.[43] On their return, John Montagu asked the Prince to pose for a photo in the Daimler, which was taken by the local schoolmaster. The photo has become famous since it shows the introduction of royalty to motor cars. The next year, Montagu drove his Daimler on the continent to win third place in the 165-mile Paris-Ostend race. The car that introduced motoring to the royal family remains in the Montagu collection today, and in 1970, with the latest Lord Montagu driving, it even ran the Paris-Ostend race again.

While public opinion held that the automobile would never take the place of the horse, His Royal Highness did not. Although he loved horses himself, with foresight (and tolerance) Edward declared, "I shall make the motor car a necessity for every English gentleman." So taken with Montagu's Daimler was he that the Prince of Wales immediately ordered his first motor car: a 1900 Daimler Tonneau with a twin-cylinder poppet valve engine and a registration plate marked A7.

The order, placed with Ernest Instone, the secretary of the Daimler company, began a royal connection that has continued with the manufacturer until very recently.[44] The vehicle was one of the Daimler company's standard type, the frame known as Model A. Its two-cylinder engine not only had an output of six horsepower but a double ignition, both electrical and by means of an incandescent tube. The former was normally relied upon, with the burners being kept as a reserve. Another new feature was that the accelerator was controlled by a foot pedal rather than by a conventional hand lever. In the construction of the motor, aluminum was used as far as possible, with the crankcase and other parts made of that metal. The transmission gear gave four speeds ahead and reverse motion, and the change of speed was controlled by a hand lever at the side.

The first royal Daimler was capable of up to a maximum of about twenty-four miles per hour, an astonishing speed then. As engines increased in size and horsepower, hand cranking became increasingly arduous, and Simms teamed up with Robert Bosch to develop a low-tension ignition magneto. The public was not convinced of its value, as it decreased the horsepower, until E.W. Lewis, the company's chief draftsman, designed and fitted his own contact breaker to the Prince of Wales' first car. When it received royal approval, electric ignition — Daimler and otherwise — became universally accepted.

As for the body, it had been entrusted to Messrs. Hooper and Co. Ltd. (Coachbuilders) of 54 St. James Street, Piccadilly, a company that Daimler would soon take over. The history of royal cars is closely linked with the great British coachbuilder firms of Park Ward & Co. Ltd., H.J. Mulliner & Co. Ltd., Hooper & Co. Ltd., and James Young Ltd. These family firms had handcrafted coaches as far back as 1760, and already had royal warrants, with Hooper receiving theirs from King William IV in 1830. Coaches had been individually made to suit the buyer's needs, pocketbook, and taste, and the wealthy motorist saw no reason to change this.

For His Royal Highness's first car, Hooper chose the form of a mail phaeton, with seating accommodation for four persons. The woodwork was painted in the royal colours, chocolate and black, picked out in red. After he became king, Edward had black mouldings added to outline the bodywork, and finally the crest of the Royal Arms encircled by the collar of the Order of the Garter was affixed to one of the panels behind the lamp on the left side.

The front seat had a collapsible hood, new to English motor cars of the day and closer to the American buggy hoods, the back being made to roll up, thus enabling the hood to be used as a canopy in bright, sunny weather. The wheels were of wood shod with Clipper pneumatic tires, the mudguards of leather and of a much greater width than usual. Steering was controlled by an inclined hand wheel, the standard of which pivoted at the bottom so that it could instantly be placed in a vertical position to facilitate mounting and dismounting.

In 1902, for Ascot week, the new King Edward VII ordered a second Daimler and honoured the company with a royal warrant. From that moment onward, Daimler was the royal car of choice. Eventually, His Majesty would own no less than four Daimlers, and when he travelled to Europe, three motor cars and their chauffeurs would be sent in advance to either Biarritz or Marienbad, supervised by the first royal motor-car engineer, C.W. Stamper. His Majesty did not drive himself — the last British monarch not to do so — but he is remembered as having an addiction to speed and admonishing his engineer with, "Faster, Stamper. Faster!"

The 1902 model had several improvements to the Tonneau that changed the shape of the car. Because of overheating problems (a common fault on this model), the rear-mounted radiator was replaced with one at the front requiring a new hood. This gave the car a very square look at the front. The thin rear seat was removed and a rear-entrance Tonneau body was substituted. The pneumatic tires on the rear were changed for solid tires, and instead of the leather hood, a Surrey top with slight fringe was substituted.

As the royal household bought other cars, the first Daimler was relegated to local work around the Sandringham Estate. The car was stored in the Coach House at Sandringham and was later returned to the Daimler Company in 1930. It was known to be in running order in 1938, when King George VI drove it on the Daimler Test Track during his visit to the Daimler factory. It took part in the Daimler Jubilee Cavalcades in 1946 and appeared on television in 1957. By 1968, it had been passed back to the Royal Mews. After repair work was carried out, the car took part in its first-ever London-to-Brighton run in 1971.

King Edward VII was not the only auto enthusiast. In 1901, Queen Alexandra relished the sensation of travelling at high speed. She wrote excitedly in a letter to the Prince of Wales: "I did enjoy being driven about in the cool of the evening at 50 miles!! an hour! — when nothing in the way of course only! & I must say I have the greatest confidence in our driver — I poke him violently in the back at every corner to go gently & whenever a dog, child or anything else comes in our way!" Although it is unlikely that she herself could drive, a list of royal motor cars in 1908 showed that Queen Alexandra had two, both Siddeleys. In January 1913, she even bought a miniature Cadillac motor car for her grandson, Prince (later King) Olav of Norway; the motor car is now on display in the Norsk Teknisk Museum in Oslo. The Prince of Wales (later King George V) owned a City and Suburban electric car and, since he had often driven in his father's Daimlers, in February 1903 ordered a 22-horsepower Daimler seven-seater himself. The tradition was (and remained until very recently) to buy British cars, but that did not prevent other makes from creeping in to the Royal Mews. Possibly because of the family's German connections, a Mercedes was acquired in 1905, and proved to be better built (Stamper wrote), than the Daimlers.

The year 1904 was a historic one in the British motoring world. Although those of the King's ownership were exempted,[45] there were so many cars now that the general public had to register theirs with the government and affix a metal plate on the vehicle to demonstrate that they had complied. It was also in this year that the King decided to use his Daimlers rather than a carriage for official duties, as well as for private occasions. Within a year of George V's accession to the throne, every member of the royal family had been in a car or was about to own one. From now on, only on great state occasions would they be driven through the streets of London in horse-drawn coaches, as their ancestors once had. Proof of this revolution in transport was the drawing up of terms of employment for "Chauffeurs to Their Majesties." They were paid £3 a week with 6 shillings per day when travelling, and bachelor accommodations for the drivers were provided at Sandringham, Windsor, and Balmoral, where they had their own servant to cook their meals. Two liveries (uniforms) were provided, and the hours were from 9:00 a.m. until Their Majesties retired for the night.[46] By special order, the chauffeur's room had one of the first telephones in a royal residence, installed so that, the Crown Equerry said, "this would give them a sense of responsibility and keep them alert and at their post." Two washers were also employed to keep the cars spotless.

Another significant event of 1904 was the historic meeting on May 4 in Manchester between engineer Frederick Henry Royce and the Honourable Charles Stewart Rolls, a well-connected pioneer aviator and motor-car enthusiast. The foundation for what was to become the most famous car in the world — and a rival in the royal garages to Daimler — was set. Royce's brilliance in engineering and Rolls's moneyed connections ensured that, by 1907, their Silver Ghost had gained a reputation for silence and smoothness in all the best circles.

PA -123472

Riding in a Comet, the Prince of Wales visits Saint-Joachim, Quebec, July 27, 1908. He is accompanied by Earl Grey, Governor General of Canada, and Mgr. O.E. Mathieu, rector of Laval University.

His Majesty King George VI and Queen
Elizabeth drive through the city of Quebec.

Royal Tour, Montreal, May 18, 1939. Fifty thousand schoolchildren gathered in the Montreal Stadium to greet Their Majesties as the royal party motored around the grounds. Note the human Union Jack made by a group of schoolchildren in red, white, and blue.

Canadian Government Motion Picture Bureau Neg. No XGC-12

PA-155397

Queen Elizabeth II and Prince Philip travel in a Lincoln Premier convertible during their visit to Canada. Ottawa, Ontario, October 12–16, 1957.

PA-052480

Queen Elizabeth visiting Toronto, 1959, in a Lincoln Continental Mark IV convertible.

The Queen Mother participating in the ceremonies of the centenary of the Black Watch of Canada. Her Majesty was Colonel-in-Chief.

The Queen Mother in Jeep, Halifax, Nova Scotia. Presentation of the Queen's Colour to Maritime Command.

In Canada, the first use of a car in a Royal Tour took place in 1908, when His Royal Highness the Prince of Wales (later George V) came to the Dominion to celebrate the tercentenary of Quebec City. Accompanied by Earl Grey, the Governor General, and Monseigneur O.E. Mathieu, the Rector of Laval University at St. Joachim, Quebec, he was driven from Quebec City to St. Joachim in a Montreal-made car called the Comet.

The advent of horseless carriages changed Royal Tours completely. Royalty was now more accessible to rural communities away from urban centres, and later itineraries reflected that. When Prince Arthur, Duke of Connaught and Canada's Governor General, toured British Columbia in September 1912, the Prince was driven from Victoria to Shawinigan Lake by car. On September 21, while in New Westminster, he motored to the Colony Farm, had lunch, visited Fraser Mills, and returned to New Westminster, all by early evening, an impossible feat by horse and carriage.

The Daimler company's fluted radiator trademark had become a fixture in the royal garages, and the King's son Prince Edward Albert would spend a good deal of time at Sandringham learning the mysteries of the motor car under the guidance of a Mr. Stratton, the Daimler employee accorded the rank of an upper-class servant in the royal household. In 1913, the Daimler Motor Company was taken over by the Birmingham Small Arms Company and, in the Great War, the motor-car firm, like Rolls-Royce, built military vehicles, as did its German namesake. The government bought motor cars for the royal family, mainly Daimlers and Rolls-Royces, but as they were paid for from the public purse, upon replacement they vanished into history. It is the privately purchased royal motor cars that remain today, lovingly preserved at the Royal Motor Museum at Sandringham. Each tells more of the royal family through the decades than the public vehicles ever could.

July 1, 1999: Her Majesty's Rolls-Royce at opening of the Scottish Parliament.

The Prince of Wales in motor car, High Park, Toronto, August 1919.

In December 1914, George V bought a 45-horsepower Daimler Brougham that had large windows fitted into frames equipped with Hooper's special device, which enabled them to be opened to and maintained at any height without fear of rattle. The interior of the body was roomy, and for the first time, the chauffeur was given some protection from the weather by a leather curtain on a spring roller that extended from the front of the body (which was behind the driver) over his head to the top of the windscreen. The Brougham was painted in the royal colours, with blue morocco being used for the interior, and the driving seat was covered in blue buffalo hide. The leather mudguards were old-fashioned for a car as late as 1914, but "old-fashioned" was to be a Daimler characteristic, and later the mudguards were changed. There was a CAV dynamo lighting set, Autovox friction-driven horn, and two Smith's speedometers.

During the Great War, Daimler made so many staff cars and ambulances that served on the Western Front and in Egypt and Mesopotamia that the Prince of Wales famously remarked, "It seems to me that the Daimler people are running this war." Several wealthy motorists (including the King and Queen) also presented Daimler ambulances to the troops in the field. The King visited the troops both in Belgium and France many times, attending an estimated 1,500 ceremonies, including inspections of hospitals, during the conflict. After an accident in 1915 when a horse on which the King was riding reared at the disturbance caused by cheering soldiers and fell back on him, His Majesty was driven by motor car.

PA-022311

The Prince of Wales leaving City Hall, Nanaimo, B.C., September 1919.

But it was during the General Strike of 1919, when railway staff were on strike between September 26 and October 5, that the royal family really began using motor cars for long journeys. The strike caused King George V and Queen Mary to be stranded at Balmoral after their first summer holiday there after the war (the residence had been closed during the conflict), and to get back to Buckingham Palace they were forced to rely on their Daimlers. It took a relay of cars and an overnight rest at a friend's home to allow the royal couple to drive to London from Scotland.

When he served at the front, Edward, the Prince of Wales, went everywhere on his green Army bicycle; despite all the cars he ever owned, he mentions only the bicycle in his memoirs. But after the war His Royal Highness took delivery in 1919 of his first Rolls-Royce, a Barker Limousine. Disdaining his father's and grandfather's love for Daimlers, in his lifetime, the Prince owned no less than ten Rolls-Royces, including the 20-horsepower Phantom I and Phantom II models. Influenced by the McLaughlin-Buicks on his Canadian tours, His Royal Highness later developed an infatuation with North American cars. This seems to have become common among his set. His great chum of the day, his cousin Louis Mountbatten, did the same in 1932, buying a new Chrysler Six after his MG sports car "fell to bits in six months."

The Prince of Wales captivated North American audiences like no other royal until Princess Diana in the 1980s.[47] Canada was to have celebrated its Golden Jubilee in 1917, but the celebration was postponed until after the war. Considering the sacrifices that the Dominion had made during that conflict, the Prince, who had served on the staff of the Canadian Corps, was ideal for the first post-war royal visit in 1919. Banned from flying by his father, he took to every other mode of transport in the country: driving, canoeing, riding, descending into a silver mine, and hiking out to camp with First Nations guides. The Prince's itinerary was organized by Sir Joseph Pope, (the creator of the Canadian Department of Foreign Affairs,) who had been responsible for his father's tour in 1901, and Pope saw no reason to vary from that plan. There were to be regal state drives in Landaus with mounted escort, mounted military parades, and tours by carriage of local landmarks, about which the Prince of Wales wrote, "It all had a decidedly Victorian flavour" and "the saddle and carriage horses in Canada were unaccustomed to crowds, unlike the trained mounts from the Royal Mews [at Buckingham Palace]." Against his better judgement, the Prince rode a horse at the CNE in Toronto on Warriors' Day before a parade of 27,000 veterans. He had been assured that the horse was specially trained to handle crowds, but, when the veterans broke ranks and mobbed him, it reared up and made to bolt. Fortunately, the Prince was "lifted off the horse's back by strong hands and passed like a football over the heads of the crowd." Having witnessed his father's accident when inspecting the troops in France, from that moment on, the Prince always toured by car.

His Royal Highness's love of Canada led him to buy the E.P. Ranch at Pekisko, Alberta, a property that he owned until 1952 and that inspired him to visit five more times, in 1923, 1924, 1927, 1941, and 1950. It was when he returned in 1927, accompanied by his brother, Prince George, Duke of Kent, to celebrate the Diamond Jubilee of Confederation that the first McLaughlin-Buick was made for him. The McLaughlin family had been closely entwined with that of the American Buick company since the earliest days of motor-car production. R. Samuel McLaughlin first met William C. Durant in 1905 and, in 1908, the company, later the McLaughlin Motor Car Company of Oshawa, Ontario, built 154 McLaughlin motor cars using Durant's engines. Thus, the beginning of the McLaughlin-Buick association would become General Motors of Canada, the largest motor-car manufacturer outside the United States. For the 1927 Royal Tour, two four-door McLaughlin-Buick convertibles were custom built, so that each could be shipped ahead of the other. Their bodies were painted in desert sand with a turquoise stripe, the upholstery was covered in a light brown lizard skin, the bumpers were nickel plated; they were wholly Canadian (only the engines were made out of the country, in Flint, Michigan). Three such McLaughlin-Buick open touring cars were crafted, all for royalty — the third for Prince Mahendra, an Indian Maharajah. After the Royal Tour ended, General Motors sold one of theirs to John Bulloch of Gananoque, Ontario, who gave it to his niece Bernice Marshall in 1956. It was driven locally until December 18, 1985, when the National Museum of Science and Technology in Ottawa was approached to purchase it. On May 20, 1986, the museum bought the remaining McLaughlin-Buick that had been built for the Prince of Wales's 1927 tour for $55,000, putting it on display.

Satisfied with the two specially constructed McLaughlin-Buicks used in his visit, in 1936, the former Prince of Wales, now Edward VIII, ordered a custom-built Buick Roadmaster station wagon to drive at home. Wallis Simpson who was very much in evidence then, described what happened in her memoirs:

> That spring, David bought a new American station wagon, a type of car then almost unknown in Britain. He was extremely proud of it and lost no chance to show it off to his friends. One afternoon David said, "Let's drive over to the Royal Lodge — I want to show Bertie [his younger brother] the car." Turning into the entrance of the Royal Lodge, he made a complete swing around the circular driveway and drew up to the front door with a flourish. The Duke and Duchess of York met David at the door. David insisted that they inspect the station wagon. It was amusing to observe the contrast between the two brothers: David all enthusiasm and volubility, the Duke of York shy, quiet, obviously dubious of this newfangled American contrivance. It was not until David pointed out its advantages as a shooting brake that his younger brother showed any interest. "Come on, Bertie," David urged. "Let's drive around a little. I'll show you how easy it is to handle."

When they returned in the Buick, the brothers and Wallis met the Duchess of York and the two little princesses for cold lemonade. Mrs. Simpson concluded, "I left with a distinct impression that while the Duke of York was sold on the American station wagon, the Duchess was not sold on David's other American interest."[48]

A second Roadmaster would be delivered to His Majesty from the Oshawa plant in 1937, and it was in this car that Edward VIII would be driven to Portsmouth after his abdication speech. When he went into exile, the Duke of Windsor took delivery of yet another Canadian-built Buick in Paris. This was a 1939 series, custom-built formal sedan, the body finished in a rich dark blue with blanked rear quarters. By now, McLaughlin-Buick had delivered six of their cars to various members of the royal family. The last Buick survived the war and, in 1946 the Windsors were driven in it to Cap d'Antibes when they reopened the Villa de la Cröe. Their city mansion at 4 Route du Champ d'Entrainement in the Bois de Boulogne (taken by General de Gaulle in 1953) always housed four cars, one of which was a Cadillac limousine driven by Ronald Marchant, the Duke's long-suffering driver of three decades. Whether to the South of France or their country home at Gif-sur-Yvette in the Chevreuse Valley, the couple never travelled with fewer than three cars — one of which would later be a long, blue Cadillac station wagon for the maids and luggage, the convoy led ironically by a Daimler, which always had "The Duke of Windsor" stamped in metal letters on both of its front doors.

Edward's brother Bertie continued their family's loyalty toward Daimlers for state and personal use, and the coachbuilders Hooper would deliver four new vehicles to the royal family through the pre-war years. The first was a 6-cylinder valve "shooting brake" (a station wagon used for hunting in upper-class

British circles) received on August 24, 1924. The exterior was finished in varnished wood with the scuttle and hood grained and varnished to match. The sleeves were of cast iron and the pistons of aluminum and the Daimler lubrication system. The car could carry eight passengers in the rear and two on the driving seat, and had roll-up curtains all round the body. Two independent ignition systems were provided: one by magneto and the other by coil and accumulator. Fuel was fed to the carburettor from a 22-gallon tank carried at the rear of the chassis. The most striking new feature of the car was the brake system, which employed brakes on all four wheels. This gave additional stopping power and protected against skidding. The chassis and springs were painted in colours of royal claret, picked out with vermilion, but the wings and valances were in black to contrast. The upholstery was in brown leather, and the seats were hinged and divided. A varnished rack to carry twelve guns was included, and the royal crest was hand-painted on the sides and back panel. The original Palmer Cord tires were changed to Dunlop Straight Side Cord tires. Daimler sent a new set of six wheels fitted with 36-by-6 Dunlop tires, which were standard equipment.

When the baby Elizabeth was born to the Duke and Duchess of York in 1926, Their Majesties came to see her at 17 Bruton Street in a royal Daimler. While the baby could not have seen it, in a few weeks she was taken for her first car ride in one of her father's old Lanchester Fortys. The Duke was a fan of Daimlers, and owned four Straight-Eight Lanchesters. Three years later, an Armstrong Siddeley 30-horsepower shooting brake was commissioned for him, and delivered in January 1929, to his residence, now at 145 Piccadilly, London W1. The shooting brake was taken up to the Duke and Duchess's Scottish home, Birkhall, on the Balmoral estate, where it was used for three years. Today, it remains in working order and has been in almost constant use on grouse moors in Scotland and Yorkshire.

Throughout her widowhood, Queen Mary continued her husband's loyalty to Daimlers.[49] Her last, bought in 1924, was the Brougham. It had been built by Mulliner, who had received her warrant, and painted in the royal colours, with the appropriate heraldic decoration. The rear compartment was trimmed with blue Vaumol leather, the inside woodwork was of dark, polished mahogany, and the fittings were of silver and white ivory. The royal identification lamp was fitted on the canopy. Improvements were the windscreen wipers that worked from the top and a force-feed lubrication system, including the automatic oil primer that ensured an adequate supply of oil to vital parts of the engine when it started from cold. Oil consumption had been reduced, and smoking (a characteristic of Daimlers) was eliminated by the special design of piston and piston rings. Another interesting feature of the servo-assisted brake was a handwheel placed in an accessible position under the bonnet, for simultaneously taking up wear on the shoes of all four wheels.

In May 1939, when George VI was on his Canadian tour, his mother was returning in this Daimler from a visit to the Royal Horticultural Society when the royal car was hit by a truck. It slid sideways across the street, hit the curb, and fell over. The Queen Mother couldn't get out until a passing house painter provided a ladder. Once she had managed to climb out, Her Majesty was invited into a nearby home for a good cup of tea. A worried nation learned that Queen Mary had suffered a few bruises, and she received many bouquets of flowers, including one from the embarrassed truck driver. After royal service, the Brougham was returned to the Daimler factory and was presented to Her Majesty the Queen in 1968 after a considerable amount of restoration work had been carried out.

As children, the Queen and Princess Margaret played with a Citroën/Daimler. An electric car, it was one of the reproductions of the Citroën C4 made by André Citroën for his son Miki in 1928, and a limited number were put on the market. Power was supplied by two 12-volt batteries, and it could reach a maximum speed of eight miles per hour. The car was renovated in 1953, and the Citroën radiator was changed for that of a Daimler; it was then given to Prince Charles to play with, the registration number appropriately "PC 1953." This was the first of two Citroëns that the princesses received.[50]

At the end of May 1937, a new Daimler shooting brake was ordered for delivery before the King's visit to Balmoral later that summer. It had a 4.5-litre engine of 32 horsepower, similar to that of the new Daimler state car, which was delivered to Buckingham Palace just before George VI's coronation. The shooting brake was furnished in natural woods and could accommodate ten people. There was a folding luncheon table down the centre, and specially fitted gun racks. Glass windows of the drop-type afforded good visibility all around and gave ample ventilation in hot weather. There was a Luvax Shock Absorber Control System for added comfort, an extra spare wheel and six wheel discs (painted to match), a master switch for the ignition circuit, a battery-charging socket, black finished Lucas wing lamps, and a Pyrene fire extinguisher. This was the last royal Daimler shooting brake and at the end of 1975, its mileage was shown on the clock as 26,404.

With the announcement of the Royal Tour to Canada in May 1939, the three major car companies in Canada — Ford, General Motors, and Chrysler — each embarked on custom-building cars for the event. Although it was still making cars in Windsor, Packard didn't enter the competition, as the company was getting ready to close its Canadian operation that year. The logistics of the tour meant that, as there was no continuous highway across Canada then, the cars would be transported in two teams by train and positioned at the next city that Their Majesties were to visit.

Two McLaughlin-Buicks were chosen, along with one car each from Ford and Chrysler. A patriotic zeal gripped the manufacturers as all outdid themselves to proclaim that their products were "Made in Canada." The Lincoln had actually been built in Detroit, but the Chrysler was built entirely in Canada. Chrysler selected a Canadian-built chassis, the Royal, to which was added the custom-built convertible limousine body. There was a fifth Royal Tour convertible limousine built by Chrysler on the Imperial chassis with custom coachwork by Derham. It was used exclusively on the American part of the tour.

The word *phaeton* has mixed origins: classically, it derives from Greek mythology. Phaeton was the son of Helios and his mistress Clymene, and like all teenagers he liked to drive his chariots fast. The Victorians knew phaetons as light, four-wheeled carriages, and the very early motorcar phaetons were sporty touring cars with little bodywork and a rear underbody engine. By the time the two McLaughlin-Buicks were built as Phaetons, the style had come to mean that they were coach-built, dual-cowl, expensive touring cars, distinguished by a secondary cowl and windshield for the rear seat passengers. The pair were built side by side at General Motors Canada from the Buick 90 Limited limousines in a shop on the second floor of the Oshawa factory. All the work was done by the Passenger Body Tool and Production Engineering Department of the plant. The styling and body design were under the direction of F.E. Hudson of this department, while the chassis changes and mechanical features were directed by A.A. Maynard, General Motors of Canada's chief engineer. First, the sedan tops were cut down to take the special convertible tops. Then, the whole car body was cut under the rear doors. The metal tops were removed and fifteen inches added to the centre section, extending the wheelbase from 140 inches to 155 inches. New collapsible tops were installed made of super fine beige duck, fully seven inches higher than the usual Buick. The additional height was to accommodate the plumed headgear of the royal party. The division glass separating the front and rear compartments was electrically operated. For the early part of the tour it was a two-piece rear quarter glass. When His Majesty complained that it obstructed his view while the royal couple were in Washington, it was removed and new glass panels were installed. The interiors were finished in the finest woods, leathers, and fabrics. Sterling-silver vanity pieces selected by Norman Hartnell, designer of Her Majesty's wardrobe, were

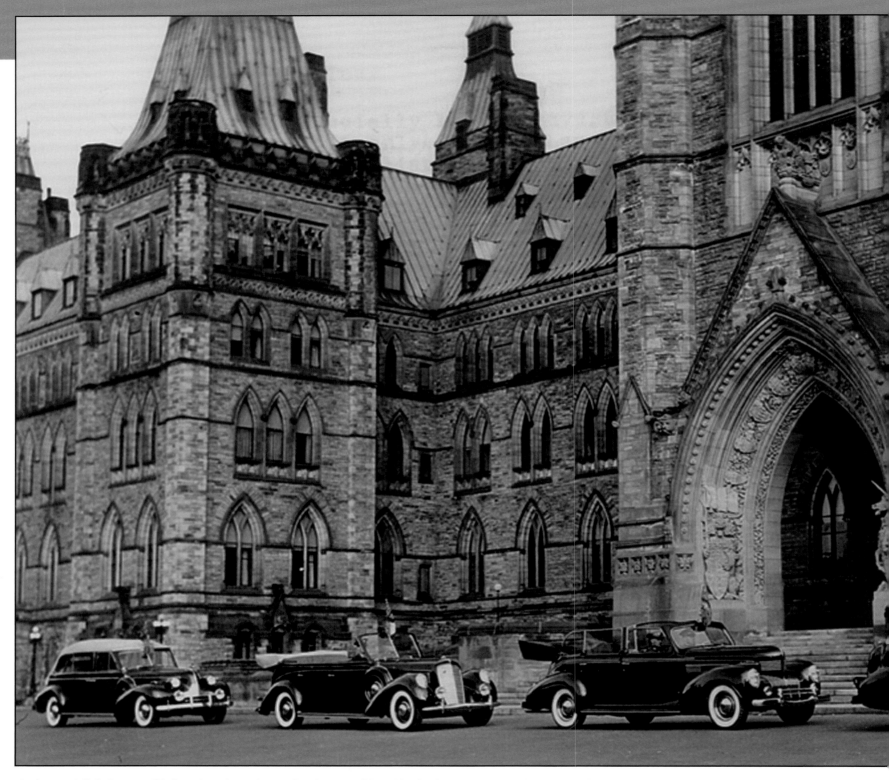

The four specially built convertible limousines, for use in Canada only: McLaughlin-Buick, Chrysler,, Lincoln, McLaughlin-Buick. Parliament Hill, Ottawa, May 1939.

installed in the folding armrests of each car. These centre folding armrests also contained a white kid-lined compartment with notebooks, and flasks for liquid refreshment.

When the Royal Tour Buicks were built, General Motors of Canada said they cost $15,000 for each vehicle. The Canadian government paid GM $5,000 for each, with the stipulation that, should the cars be sold after the event, the proceeds were to be handed over to the government.

Car No. I (Serial #9-4929-02501) was upholstered in maroon broadcloth, while car No.2 (Serial #9-4929-02502) was finished in beige broadcloth. A white sheepskin rug lined the floor of the car with the maroon interior. The beige interior had a matching beige sheepskin rug. The front compartments of both were upholstered in leather. The dividing wall between passenger and chauffeur was faced in walnut with two built-in cabinets and an electric clock. The chauffeurs were in constant touch with the rear compartment by an electrical communication system that the GM Press release called "dictographs" — one in each corner of the rear seat panels. A signal light flashed on the instrument panel when the device was picked up, and special amplification was provided for us when the top was down. Rear-facing auxiliary seats were installed to accommodate members of the royal party riding with the King and Queen. The cars were outfitted with six Safety Tube tires (which included two spares), special driving lamps, an auxiliary battery, and a blue light at the top centre of the windshield. The significant difference between the exteriors of the two Buicks was that No. 2 had the royal crest on the trunk lid between the handle and the Buick emblem/turn signal and No. 1 didn't.

On April 28, the *Toronto Star* scooped its rivals by publishing the first pictures of the McLaughlin-Buick, but only as an artist's rendering. Photos of all four Royal Tour cars were published on May 9, the day that they were formed into a convoy to travel from Oshawa to Ottawa. A uniformed motorcycle rider led the way, followed by the cars, each driven by a pair of drivers from the Royal Canadian Air Force or the

Their Majesties alight from the McLaughlin-Buick at the Parliament Buildings, May 19, 1939.

C-065499

One of the two McLaughlin-Buicks used in the 1939 Royal Tour.

Vern Bethel photo

Royal Canadian Army Services Corps. They had no licence plates, but the royal crest mounted above the windshield with Royal Standards flying from short staffs behind made them distinctive. After dark, as in Britain, a mounted blue light lit the standard. Following the convoy was a sedan with additional team members, and finally an army truck with fuel, oil, and spares. To prevent gawking crowds, the convoy was prohibited from stopping in built-up areas and was to be serviced on the road. Finally, all aircraft were directed to maintain a distance of at least three miles from any car (or train or ship) being used by Their Majesties on the tour. While the RCAF and Army maintained the cars, they were not allowed to drive them while Their Majesties were sitting in them. With rare exception, whatever car the King and Queen were in was driven by Tom Southgate, the Governor General's chauffeur.

The logistics of getting the cars to convenient points along the tour were worked out. There were to be two teams: Group A would consist of one of the Buicks, the Chrysler, and eight motorcycle escorts. Group B would have the other Buick, the Lincoln, and eight motorcycle escorts. As it was impossible to have either team in place in Portage la Prairie, Manitoba, and in Banff, Alberta, in these two cities the King and Queen used privately owned open cars. In Portage la Prairie, the King and Queen rode in a 1939 non-Classic McLaughlin-Buick "Special" convertible. In Banff, they were driven in a Packard V-I 2 custom-bodied convertible sedan. These cars, although used by the royal couple, were not considered Royal Tour cars, because they were not used throughout the tour.

The memories of Their Majesties passing through their hometowns have remained with a generation of Canadians forever. After the austerity of the Depression, for car-crazy boys and young men, the resplendent McLaughlin-Buicks were as magical as the royal couple themselves. Arthur James (who had been car crazy, he wrote, since the age of three) recalled the day they came to Toronto:

> Only the senior kids from our school were allowed to go … we were loaded onto a … smelly bus, taken seven miles along Danforth Avenue to Broadview Avenue. Unloaded, we were each given a small Union Jack and taken to the designated spots. Once there, we were told to wait.
>
> And wait we did. The motorcade wasn't due for some three hours yet. Thousands and thousands of school children stood and waited. We knew they were coming but when? Lunchtime came and went and still we waited. Just after one o'clock we could hear cheering in the distance. They were coming. The cheers grew louder and then two motorcycles came into sight ridden by RCMP officers. It was now our turn to cheer. Two more motorcycles and then, the gleaming maroon convertible limousine moved slowly, majestically, towards us at 5 mph. The Queen with her frozen smile, waving; the King with his solemn look, waving. The crowd roared its approval. The mighty Buick moved slowly into the crowd followed by the maroon Chrysler, four more RCMP motorcycles and on horseback, Toronto's mounted police. And that was it. It was all over. I had seen the King and Queen, I had seen the big McLaughlin-Buick.[51]

For the American part of the tour only the Chrysler Derham built especially for the King and Queen was used, although several convertible limousines including a Cadillac, a Lincoln, and a Packard were also in service. Amazingly, at Hyde Park, away from the pomp and ceremony, President Roosevelt and Eleanor drove the King and Queen in a mundane 1936 Ford Touring car, with special controls for the President's disability. But the four cars were always in the public eye, except once, when at the Glenlea Golf Club in Aylmer, Quebec, Their Majesties managed to snatch a few hours of privacy, taking one to pick wildflowers.

On the final portion of the trip from Newcastle to Fredericton, New Brunswick, the McLaughlin Buick No.2 was used on the hundred-mile drive. The Lincoln took them onward to Saint John and from there to Moncton. It was waiting for them at Charlottetown, and finally at Halifax, where the *Empress of Britain* waited. The greatest Royal Tour ever undertaken covered a total distance of 9,150 miles; after a month in North America, the royal couple boarded the liner for home. All of the cars had performed flawlessly and, during a private audience, His Majesty complimented Mr. Hudson personally.

The four Royal Tour cars were then returned to their respective makers. The Lincoln was owned by the Edison Institute and was placed in the Ford Museum at Dearborn, Michigan. It was used in 1959 for Queen Elizabeth's tour and on October 19, 1985, was sold at auction for US$210,000 to Carail, the privately owned museum of Richard Kughn, the CEO of Lionel Trains. On September 21, 2003, when it was auctioned off once more, it had been driven only a remarkable 8,300 miles. No one knows what happened to the Chrysler. The two Buicks were sent back to the plant at Oshawa to await disposal. In the late summer of 1939, they were displayed at the Canadian National

Vern Bethel photo

Shown here in 1986 with Prince Charles and Princess Diana, the 1939 Royal Tour McLaughlin-Buick has carried royalty and VIPs many times,

Exhibition in Toronto. An attempt was made to take the cars to the New York World's Fair, but the duty was found to be so high that the idea was discarded.

By May 1940, both Buicks had found new homes. Car No. 1 was sold through a dealer in Windsor to Mrs. Helen Ross Palmer of Victoria, British Columbia. Even before the Royal Tour, she had been negotiating for the purchase of one of the cars through a family friend who worked for General Motors. Car No. 2 was offered by Colonel R.S. McLaughlin to the Governor General, the Earl of Athlone. But before McLaughlin could give it away, the government had to be consulted. On May 28, 1940, Colonel McLaughlin received the following letter from the Under-Secretary of State for External Affairs, O.D. Skelton:

> Dear Mr. McLaughlin:
>
> I have been instructed by the Prime Minister to inform you that the government of Canada approves the presentation of one of the Buick cars, built for the King's visit, to the Earl of Athlone, as Governor General, for use at Government House. I am also instructed to express the Prime Minister's appreciation of your initiative in this matter.

The colonel replied immediately:

Dear Mr. Skelton:

We are very happy to learn by yours of the 28th inst., that the government approves the presentation of one of the King's cars to the Earl of Athlone. May I ask if you will kindly suggest how the matter should be handled from here on. The car would be available on a day or two's notice. Thank you for your further advice.

I am

Sincerely yours, R.S. McLaughlin

Before it was sent to Ottawa, the former royal car was modified. The top was reworked to fold over the rear seat only and the forward section was made removable as a unit with rigid frames. The rear-facing auxiliary seats were replaced by conventional front-facing jump seats. Used throughout the war by the Governor General, it was returned to General Motors in Oshawa in 1946 to be converted into a Brougham. Later, it was sold to Calvin Norton, a foreman at General Motors, and it returned to Ottawa when the National Science Museum purchased it on November 11, 1984. The former Royal Buick was still in working order five years later, as Her Majesty the Queen Mother rode in it on July 5, 1989, from the Westin Hotel to Parliament Hill — a journey that must have brought back for her many memories.

As for the second Buick, Mrs. Palmer picked it up at Oshawa on May 20, 1940, and drove it back to British Columbia. In 1941, George, Duke of Kent, the King's younger brother, visited Canada in connection with the British Commonwealth Air Force Training Plan. As an RAF Air Commodore, he toured many of the plan's air bases, one of which was at Patricia Bay in Victoria. Mrs. Palmer loaned her car to Air Commodore A.E. Godfrey, Western Air Command, for the Duke's visit to Victoria. In a letter to Mrs. Palmer, Godfrey expressed his thanks, adding that through her kindness the public were afforded a much greater opportunity to see the Duke as he drove through the streets of Victoria and that the car contributed in no small measure to the success of the visit. He noted that the Duke himself drove the car from the Patricia Bay Station into Victoria, and personally expressed his delight at the splendid performance of the Buick. After all, His Royal Highness owned a similar model McLaughlin-Buick at home. In 1946–47, Mrs. Palmer's Buick was again loaned to the government when Viscount Alexander of Tunis, the new Governor General, toured through British Columbia. Later, on a trip to the province, Viscount Lord Montgomery ("Monty") also rode in it, preferring the Buick to his usual Jeep. As the newspapers reported, "Monty was boyishly pleased with its performance." Mrs. Palmer died on November 30, 1970, and two years later the car was bought by Vern Bethel, its present owner. This Buick has served royalty many times since, and more recently it was used by the Prince and Princess of Wales in their 1986 tour of Vancouver. Convertibles of many makes would be used by members of the royal family when they toured Canada in the post-war years; when security became a concern from the 1970s onward, closed limousines would take their place, but none would possess the allure and history of the 1939 cars.

The Prince and Princess of Wales during their 1983 tour of Australia. The car is one of the Daimlers bought for previous Royal Tours.

In Britain during the Second World War, the royal Daimlers continued in use. When His Majesty visited the British Expeditionary Force in France on December 5, 1940, one was taken to the headquarters of the Commander-in-Chief of the British Army in France, Viscount Gort.

A reporter described the tour and car by noting:

> Its immaculate paintwork streaked with mud, the only colour on the Daimler the Royal Standard, flapping in the wintry stormy weather. His Majesty, in the uniform of a field marshal and bundled in a trench coat, not only acknowledged the Highland troops and French children waving hastily made Union Jacks but also the Great War veterans that lined the roads. On many occasions, he had the car stopped to step out and salute.

Camouflage was rudimentary: "On its roof was a net covered with rags coloured to resemble leaves." The Daimler was driven by Lord Gort's personal chauffeur, who for fifteen years had been a driver for the royal family. With the King was Major General the Duke of Gloucester, his brother and principal liaison officer. The object of the visit, reported the media, was to symbolize Anglo-French unity and to stress to the French that the British troops already in France "were only the vanguard of thousands more to come from the Dominions."

The war affected the royal Daimlers in an unexpected way. As with all vehicles in Britain, their headlights were cowled and all driving at night was done by sidelights only. Because of wartime censorship, there are few photos of the Daimlers in wartime livery, but two of them were also armoured with 2-mm steel and thick glass.[52] On December 19, 1940, three of the Daimlers were damaged, not by the Luftwaffe but by an anti-aircraft shell that burst outside the Royal Mews. Little harm was done, but the King was informed that the insurance company would not pay because of the war risks.

Throughout the war, the royal family visited squadrons, ships, and army bases in England. His Majesty was caused great amusement whenever sentries quite properly halted the royal car and asked to see his identity card, for like all his subjects, the King carried one throughout the war.

At one Canadian air base, identified as "somewhere in England" by the censor, His Majesty was once more driven by a Canadian chauffeur in a Canadian-made vehicle. Accompanied by Major General Victor Odlum, on March 27, 1941, the King and Queen paid a visit to the Second Canadian Division. The King was in his field marshal uniform with whipcord breeches and high leather boots, and Her Majesty was dressed in a three-quarter-length coat of Regina blue with an off-the-face hat to match. The Canadian troops were delighted to note that she wore a silver maple leaf in the hat. Their Majesties reportedly so enjoyed the informality of the visit, walking freely among the ranks and chatting with the men, that it should have come as no surprise when the King climbed aboard a Canadian-built Brengun carrier. Lieutenant W.D. (Denis) Whitaker of Hamilton, a former Hamilton Tigers quarterback, was chosen to drive His Majesty a half-mile over rugged country. To the consternation of the watching general staff, the carrier rocked violently and plunged in and out of ravines, but the King was unruffled and amused to note that it had the nickname "Hell's Angel" painted on its side.

In 1973, Daimler brought out its last landaulette. It was used by Queen Elizabeth II on a visit to Jamaica.

After the war, for the Royal Tour of South Africa, seven Daimlers were completed in November 1946. Specially built by Hooper, they were to be shipped out before the tour began. On January 31, 1947, they left Buckingham Palace for the Royal Albert docks, where they were put on board the *City of Madras*. Sir Dermot Kavanagh, then the Crown Equerry in the Royal Mews, ensured that the King's private requests were met with regard to the cars. The armrests in each had ashtrays, and there were containers built into the walnut division with cigarettes and pipe tobacco. The King also asked that the transparent roof panel have an electric roller blind that could cover it from the hot African sun. Besides the four limousines, two laudaulettes,[53] and one all-weather version, there were other cars lent by the local governor or wealthy owners. Daimlers, both convertible and closed, were also shipped out to Australia for the Royal Tours, Her Majesty and the Duke of Edinburgh using them in 1954 and 1956. One survived to be used by Prince Charles and Princess Diana during their visit to Sydney in 1983.

In 1947, when Queen Mary was nearly eighty years old, she ordered what was to be her last Daimler. She gave instructions that it was to be in all respects practical and as nearly as possible follow the design of her previous motors. A six-cylinder model, was considered to be quite adequate and suitable. The Queen was shown drawings of Hooper's standard coachwork, but she considered the driver's compartment to be far too wide, and insisted that the width be reduced. In consequence, a special dashboard had to be fabricated and the steering modified, with the column inclined 2.5 inches towards the centre, and finally special front wings had to be made up by hand.

Because the Queen experienced difficulty in bending her head, special care had to be taken in the design to ensure that between the step and the underside of the door cantrail there was a space of 62.75 inches and that the overall interior headroom measured 57 inches, which made this vehicle the tallest Hooper-bodied car built post-war. In King George V's day, the state cars had been built, according to convention, with precisely 60 inches floor to interior roof height; George VI's new cars were reduced from 57 to only 54 inches high.

Instructions were given that the windscreen surround, deflector window surrounds, and radiator were to be chromium-plated and not finished black as hitherto. The boot lid was designed to fold down in the pre-war fashion to create a platform for extra luggage, and to go within the boot Hooper made a picnic case (31 inches by 9 inches by 12 inches). Queen Mary's favourite colour of green[54] was used for the paintwork, as she intended it for use on private occasions and to avoid the attention that a car in the traditional royal maroon livery might attract by its presence outside a shop or gallery in and around London. For this reason, Queen Mary used to refer to the car as "the shopping Daimler." Her monogram in gold was painted on the rear doors and back panel. The car was finished in green and black, dark-green leather was used for the trim, and the headlining was carried out in a matching colour. The front seat cushions were fitted with loose green cloth covers and similar washable linen covers were made up for the rear cushions and squabs.

The wood finishes were of straight-figured walnut, and armrests were built into the quarters. In the nearside one there was a leather-lined open tray and the corresponding companion on the other side contained a notebook and pencil, ashtray, and matchbox; in addition to these there was also a walnut-veneered cabinet erected between the occasional seats and the backing on the division. There were no folding armrests. All the windows had spring-loaded silk roller blinds. Like the other royal cars, a headlamp flasher switch was added. An interior heater was installed in the nearside front, with an outlet in the rear compartment. There was a DWS jacking system built into the frame, so that the car could be raised quickly with minimum effort.

Just before delivery , Queen Mary's new Daimler was weighed, and the record showed "2 tonnes 12 cwt 0 lb." The registration number of the Daimler Twenty-Seven Limousine was A3179; the price for the standard model was £5,904. The car was delivered to Hooper on July 26, 1947, and was sent by them to the Royal Mews on November 7 that year.

Her Majesty was highly delighted with the new car and the usual letters of appreciation were despatched. The car was used until the Queen's death on March 24, 1953. By this time, she was the first and perhaps the only queen to have owned Daimler motor cars for nearly half a century. When Queen Mary died, the car was bought back again by the original vendors (Stratstone Ltd.) and later sold to the Nigerian Produce Marketing Co. Ltd. in London, which used it as the board's official car. It was purchased from the NPM Company by Henry Maxwell in the latter part of 1963 and presented to the National Trust. The car is now exactly as it was when Queen Mary owned it and, by permission of Queen Elizabeth, it once again bears the original number plates.

In 1949, King George VI purchased a final Daimler for his personal use. But his new Ford V-8 Pilot shooting brake, ordered in 1951, was more unusual. Registered as VUL 3, this is known as the

Her Majesty's Rolls-Royce Phantom followed by the Queen Mother's Daimler.

REC94-1734-6

"Woody shooting brake," and was the last new car King George VI owned. Several modifications were made, and it was a "special" from stem to stern. For example, the gear lever on the steering column was removed and converted into a floor change, for, much as King George liked Pilots, he did not care for the column gear change. The seats were eventually all made facing forward, and the two rear seats were removable. It was built on a chassis twelve inches longer than normal, with commercial running gear and with parts that would normally be chromium-plated painted black. Even the Garner shooting brake body was much larger than usual, with increased headroom; the windscreen was sixteen inches high against the normal thirteen inches, and gun racks were built on the roof.

Sadly, the King died in 1952 before he could really enjoy his new Pilot, but the royal family retained the car for sentimental reasons. The car was still in use in the 1960s, although the number plate was changed with the change of ownership in 1953.

Like any other driver, Her Majesty and members of the royal family have driving licences. The story that Her Majesty drove in the Auxiliary Territorial Service (ATS) during the Second World War is true, but she had already taken driving lessons in 1943-44 from a Mr. Cracknell of Stratstone, practising around Windsor Great Park. On her eighteenth birthday in 1944, Princess Elizabeth was given, by her father, a Daimler DB 18 saloon with the registration number JGY 280, which she has kept for all her personal cars since. As part of the ATS, she took a driving and vehicle-maintenance course at No. 1 Mechanical Transport Training Centre, near Camberley, in 1945.[55] Her Royal Highness was taken over each day by a royal car to work on vehicle maintenance, read maps, drive in convoys, and learn how to strip and service an engine. When her proud parents came to see her on graduation day, she was found under an army truck, wearing dirty overalls and with black hands. As a final driving test, Her Royal Highness drove her company commander all the way from Aldershot to Buckingham Palace, in London's traffic, going twice around Piccadilly Circus on the way. When she was later posted to Malta with Prince Philip, the Daimler was shipped out to the island.

In 1949, Rolls-Royce Ltd. received an order from Princess Elizabeth and the Duke of Edinburgh for a Rolls-Royce limousine. Aware that Daimler had always enjoyed royal patronage, the company was very keen to ensure that they made the best car possible. The largest model they had was the 1947 Silver Wraith, with its ten-foot-seven-inch wheelbase, but this was more of an owner-driver model than a limousine. The company directors had considered manufacturing a replacement for the larger Phantom III, but with the post-war economic climate, they didn't think that such a large and expensive car would sell. Then General Franco of Spain ordered two armour-plated limousines and a cabriolet. Rather than build these on the Silver Wraith chassis, Rolls-Royce decided to make a limited number of long-wheelbase Phantom IVs for royalty and heads of state. The Silver Wraith wheelbase was stretched to twelve feet, one inch wide and nineteen feet, one inch long. The coachwork for a run of eighteen cars was distributed out to H.J. Mulliner, Hooper, and Franay in France, the Saudi royal family's preferred coachbuilders. Under the code name "Nabha," the royal Rolls-Royce was painstakingly hand-built at Clan Foundry, Belper, near the Derby works, rather than at Crewe. When No. 7162 was completed in July 1950, a public announcement accompanied its delivery,

Princess Elizabeth and the Duke of Edinburgh visit an Air Force squadron using the Rolls-Royce Phantom IV.

UNN photo

saying that the Phantom IV had been "designed to the special order of Their Royal Highnesses, the Princess Elizabeth and the Duke of Edinburgh." With it, Rolls-Royce could only hope that the first crack in the Daimler royal monopoly had been made. As the car was privately owned when delivered to the young couple, it was painted Valentine green, and only when it replaced the Daimlers in the Royal Mews and became a state car was it repainted in claret and black. An interesting feature of Her Royal Highness's Phantom IV was that the rear compartment featured a seat that could be wound forward by a handle above the heel board. Besides the transparent panel in the roof with an electrically operated sliding cover like those in the South African Daimlers, it also had an electrically operated rear-window blind and division behind the chauffeur — the first royal car to use electricity for such a purpose.

Naturally, as Her Majesty did not pay tax, her car did not have a number plate (or the disc on the windshield that indicates the owner has paid British road tax), and it may have been in this Rolls-Royce, when she had just become queen, that a delightful incident took place. Her Majesty and the Duke of Edinburgh were being driven home from a dinner one night without the usual police escort. As the car was entering a small village, the local bobby thought it was exceeding the speed limit and stepped out on his bicycle to pull it over. Then he noticed that it had no licence plate or road-tax disc and asked the chauffeur for his driver's licence. At that point the bodyguard sitting next to the chauffeur said, "Do you realize that we have the Queen and Prince Philip in the back?" Whereupon the policeman, who had heard this before, said, "Yes and I'm Roy Rogers and this is my horse Trigger," pointing to his bicycle. Then Her Majesty put her head out of the window and said, "Well, you and Trigger had better let us get on our way."[56]

The other seventeen Phantom IVs did eventually find royal owners as well; among them were the Shah of Persia (Iran); the Sultan of Kuwait H.H. Aga Khan; the Duke of Gloucester; King Feisal II; and the Prince Regent of Iraq. One was also delivered to Princess Margaret in July 1954 as her first car. This Rolls-Royce was a seven-passenger limousine, the coachwork built by Mulliner with elegant lines. For Princess Margaret, instead of the "Spirit of Ecstasy," its mascot was the winged horse Pegasus.

For the Royal Tour of Canada in 1959, the Big Three auto manufacturers, General Motors, Ford and Chrysler, competed once more for the honour of transporting royalty, Her Majesty the Queen and Prince Philip. On June 13, 1959, a Lincoln, a Chrysler, and a Cadillac — all to be used on the tour — were displayed before the Peace Tower at the Parliament Buildings. At first the government had considered using fourteen limousines and fourteen convertibles, stationing two in each of the cities to be visited. Then the decision was made to use only three and to fly them ahead of the royal couple in RCAF C-119 freighters appropriately called "Flying Boxcars." The Chrysler and Cadillac had removable glass tops over the rear passenger compartment and only the Lincoln was a convertible. "Her Majesty and Prince Philip will have every conceivable luxury … the flooring material looks like dyed mink. There is a button that enables the Queen to shift the seating arrangement in any one of six ways," the *Ottawa Citizen* wrote. "Prince Philip gets to move his two ways, forwards and back. The cars cost about $150,000 and look every dollar of it. The spare tires are covered in special cloth, which somebody recalled as mohair…. There is no armour plate or bulletproof glass," concluded the *Citizen* reporter. "The royal couple have nothing to fear but too much affection from Canadians."

"Very handsome," said Prime Minister John Diefenbaker, who left a cabinet meeting to be photographed with the three cars. After the tour, the cars were auctioned off to the highest bidder.

In October 1965, Rolls-Royce announced that its Silver Shadow was the most radically new model the company had made in fifty-nine years. The first Rolls-Royce to employ unitary or monocoque (i.e chassis-less) construction, the Silver Shadow was equipped with modern features such as disc brakes, electrically operated seat adjustment, and gear-range selection, all aimed at owner-drivers and the export market. Remaining in production for fifteen years, 37,000 Silver Shadows were built, setting a record for Rolls-Royce. A long wheelbase variant was built for Princess Margaret and her husband, the Earl of Snowdon in 1967, its coachwork finished in dark green with upholstery in special green leather with

1959 Canadian visit: Her Majesty alights from a Cadillac landau.

pale grey-green carpets. The fascia was made of oiled teak, and the stainless-steel and chromium fittings had a stain finish. To give Margaret maximum visibility for ceremonial occasions, the rear seat was adjustable for height and forward movement, and extra night illumination was installed. The special royal Silver Shadow eventually became the forerunner of the long-wheelbase Saloon that was introduced in mid-1969. If, even in the hard economic times of post-war Britain, there were those clientele who were prepared to pay well and wait long months for the coachwork of their new car to be a "one off" that was leisurely built, they were not enough to support the coachbuilding industry. Coach-built bodies invariably began as sketches and watercolour wash drawings that were shown to the customer and to the motor car manufacturer. If both approved, wooden jigs were used to form the wings and doors as the body framing took shape. By 1950, with most of the cars aimed at the export market, seasoned ash, which suffered overseas, was abandoned, and composite bodies with steel and aluminium alloys were adopted. The chassis, rear bulkhead, side panels, bonnet, radiator shell, instruments, boot platform, and engine now came from Rolls-Royce or Daimler, which had to sanction the design, but given the number

UNN photo

With Royal Standard flying, the Rolls-Royce Phantom VI conveys Her Majesty in all the grandeur befitting a state occasion.

and variety of deviations that were crafted onto their cars, permission must have been liberally given. The coachbuilders began to close even before Rolls-Royce adopted monocoque for the Silver Shadow in 1965. Mulliner had already merged with Park Ward in 1959, and Hooper closed its doors that same year.

For the Queen's Silver Jubilee in 1977, the Society of Motor Manufacturers and Traders asked if they could present Her Majesty with another Rolls-Royce, the medium-priced Silver Shadow II, for her personal use. Her Majesty is supposed to have said that it was too expensive a car for her private enjoyment and that perhaps it could be more widely appreciated if used publicly. The Society got the hint, and a Rolls-Royce Phantom VI, which was three times more expensive, was delivered to Buckingham Palace instead. The construction of this car, code-named "Oil Barrel," began in 1976, but an industrial dispute at coachbuilders Mulliner Park Ward prevented delivery to Her Majesty until March 29, 1978.[57]

UNN photo

A rare glimpse at the interior of the royal Phantom VI — a folding mirror and cassette recorder.

Another of the earliest modern estate cars used by the royal household was a 1961 Vauxhall Cresta 2262 CC. This Royal Mews vehicle was used to convey staff and luggage to stations and airports. Its modern successors in the Royal Mews are a number of Vauxhall Sintra "people carriers" (mini-vans). In the 1960s, on private occasions, the Queen found it very useful to get through traffic in London in a 1963 Rover 3.5-litre Saloon. Her Majesty would sit beside the driver, with the detective in the back. It was one of her two royal Rovers: the second was the 1971 Rover P5B 3.5-litre Saloon. As these were not state cars, like all the private cars owned by the royal family they had number plates — JGY 280 and JGY 280K, exactly as her first car had. The Rover was a solid, comfortable motor car painted Edinburgh green, a special dark-green colour chosen by Her Majesty. Today it is displayed in the Royal Motor Museum at Sandringham. At present, Her Majesty drives a Daimler Jaguar Saloon or a Vauxhall estate car, and like all the private royal cars, they are also painted green.

As a midshipman in the Royal Navy, Prince Philip was too poorly paid to own a car. The first time he is known to have driven one (either rented or borrowed), was in Cairo in 1941 when he was serving on HMS *Valiant*. The next time was when he made his way back to Britain from the Middle East via South Africa on the Canadian Pacific liner *Empress of Scotland*. As it docked at Newport News, Virginia, Philip rented a car and drove off to see Washington. During the war, perhaps due to youthful hijinks or to the blackout, he and a friend crashed his Uncle Dickey's (Lord Mountbatten's) Vauxhall in London. In May 1946, he borrowed a Canadian Army vehicle and drove across Europe to Germany for his sister Princess Sophie's wedding to Prince George of Hanover. On his return, Philip bought a black MG sports car that took all of his naval salary to run.

With his rise to international attention while courting Princess Elizabeth, Philip's driving came under public scrutiny. He was on occasion admonished by the press for speeding (once after their marriage when he hit a taxi), especially when the Princess was his passenger. The Duke of Edinburgh is credited with ordering the Rolls-Royce in 1949 and ending Daimler's monopoly on furnishing royals with cars. The reason given was an embarrassing gearbox failure with a Daimler. On a personal level, one of Prince Philip's first cars was a 1956 Ford Zephyr estate car. No longer called a shooting brake, this car was one of the first modern estate cars to be acquired by the royal family. Over the last few years, the Ford has undergone a complete refurbishment carried out by students from Manchester College of Arts and Technology.

In 1961, an Alvis TD 21 3-litre Series II Drophead Coupe was specially built for Prince Philip to specifications drawn up by Mulliner Park Ward Ltd. It had a taller screen and higher roof-line than usual (raised by three inches), with an electric folding hood in Everflex and the fascia was leather-covered rather than the standard walnut veneer. The two-door saloon first appeared as a special Graber-bodied TD 21-100 at the 1955 Geneva Show and, in 1958, Park Ward adopted this design and modified it to provide greater head- and leg-room, coupled with better visibility, while still retaining the main lines. Its 2993-cc, six-cylinder pushrod engine was smooth and quiet, and the slender roof pillars and deep windows allowed a splendid view all round. Everything, it was said about the Prince's Alvis, served a useful purpose, rather than simply being flamboyant.

In November 1977, when Prince Philip toured the Lucas factory in Birmingham, he was shown examples of an electric vehicle. Always interested in new technology, the Prince was keen to try out his own model. His 1980 Lucas Bedford CF electric limousine is a Bedford van used by the Post Office for city deliveries in the 1970s. It was fitted with a Lucas forty-kilowatt traction motor and was able to reach fifty miles per hour with a range of seventy miles. It was used for driving around London and for the journey between Buckingham Palace and Windsor Castle. Unfortunately, the inconvenience of electrical charging and its quietness in operation — other drivers couldn't hear it come up behind them — meant the Bedford was given up. More unusual is his present Metrocab, a London taxi, which the Duke of Edinburgh still uses to travel unobtrusively to his engagements.

In March 1972, a 1969 Austin Princess Vanden Plas Limousine registered NGN 1 was delivered to the Royal Mews. This car was one of the last to be produced by the Austin Company, as Princesses went out of production about 1969, but two were kept aside for the Royal Mews since the alternative at the time was a Daimler Limousine, which was considered to serve no better purpose and was substantially more expensive. This car was painted in the royal colours (royal claret over black) unlike its predecessors, which were black all over. It could then be used for junior members of the royal family on official engagements.

This was also the car that was involved in the incident in the Mall while carrying out an official engagement with Princess Anne. This happened in March 1974, when Princess Anne and her husband, Captain Mark Phillips, had just left a charity film show and were heading back to Buckingham Palace. A man in a white Ford Escort overtook the royal car and then stopped in front, forcing the chauffeur to brake hard. The Princess's bodyguard got out to see what was wrong, only to be faced with a revolver. The would-be kidnapper shot and wounded the bodyguard and chauffeur and then forced open the door and grabbed Princess Anne by the arm. After much struggling and a number of gunshots, the man was arrested and Princess Anne was unharmed. However, it brought to light the lack of security, as, in common with other royal cars, NGN 1 had neither bulletproof windows nor a radio for use in emergency.[58] The Austin continued in use until recently for official purposes, providing a useful accompanying car behind the main Rolls-Royces. The body is coach-built — probably the last truly coach-built production body in manufacture. It has a timber framework panelled in aluminum. The most modern methods were applied to this form of construction, such as the use of synthetic adhesives. The result was an extremely durable body and by 1967,

Prince Philip's London taxi is refuelled with environmentally friendly LPG (liquid petroleum gas).

out of over four thousand Princess Limousines built, there were only two known cases of complete write-off due to accident or old age.

Princess Anne, like her brothers, learned to drive on the estates, and at eighteen, in 1968, was given her own car, a Rover 2000. A champion rider and fearless driver (with the speeding tickets to prove it), she has even driven a London double-decker in the police skid-pan.

Until 1973, Queen Elizabeth the Queen Mother used a 1955 Jaguar Mark VII finished in royal claret for her private transport. She then took delivery of a Daimler DS420 and her Jaguar was sent to the Jaguar Daimler Heritage Trust Museum. The DS420 was replaced in 1978 and again in 1992 by identical models, the last being the final car acquired before her death in 2002. However, the Queen Mother is better remembered for having used a converted golf buggy in the late 1990s to assist at her many public appearances at events and race meetings all over Britain. By Her Majesty's one-hundredth birthday in 2000, the buggy was well-known, allowing many more people to meet the Queen Mother at Sandringham Flower Show and outside Sandringham Church after morning service. Now in the Sandringham Museum, the buggy is painted in the late Queen Mother's racing colours: buff and pale blue, with a black racing cap with gold tassels on the roof, made especially by Bob Rowlands, stud groom at the Royal Stud in Sandringham.

As a little boy, Prince Charles drove an American Style Imperial 1 Midget Racing car, circa 1955. This electric car was purpose-built for him and was a gift from an American organization at a time when miniature racers were very popular in California in the 1950s. It was powered by a two-stroke engine capable of forty miles per hour and has since been used by a wide variety of children of the royal families. The Prince of Wales's first road car was a 1968 MGC GT under the registration number SGY 776F. Designed to replace the ageing Austin Healey 3000, the MGC was based on the contemporary MGB GT, but with the larger 3-litre engine from the Austin Healey. Prince Charles drove this car for many years, and then he presented it to the Queen's head chauffeur, Harry Purvey, who used the MGC for four years more before it then passed into the collection at Sandringham. It was refurbished by students from Manchester College of Arts and Technology and was presented back to the Prince of Wales in 1999.

In April 1966, when Her Majesty visited the Aston Martin factory in Buckinghamshire, she was presented with the James Bond Aston Martin. This replica was produced for His Royal Highness Prince Andrew, age six, and had taken two and a half months to be built by a specialist team of over thirty people. With steel bodywork, it is electrically powered by two twelve-volt batteries and does about ten miles per hour. An almost perfect reproduction of the James Bond car used in the movies *Goldfinger* and *Thunderball*, it includes electrically operated revolving front and rear number plates (so that English, French, or Swiss registrations could be selected), extending overriders, concealed dummy machine guns, a bulletproof shield (concealed in the trunk), and electrically operated water jets hidden in the rear light reflectors. The car also has a special ground radar system, a smoke discharger, a Luger pistol with silencer, and two transistorized two-way radio units. With a fibreglass body, the car rides on a steel chassis. Its scale is to four-sevenths, and it is powered by a Honda GXV 160 vertical-shaft engine with an automatic clutch. The transmission has five forward gears and one reverse gear. There are two pedals, one for the

Prince Charles driving his Aston Martin with his bodyguard Tony Parker at his side.

acceleration control and the other to apply a single brake to the rear wheels. Suspension is by simple shock absorbers and coil springs. Steering is of the rack-and-pinion type. A battery supplies power for electric starting, lights, and radio cassette. The interior has leather seats and Wilton carpets, and the paint finish is to the same specification as the full-scale Aston Martin cars.

Prince Charles has always favoured Aston Martins and owned a number of the sports cars. When His Royal Highness made an official visit to the company at Newport Pagnell on February 23, 1988, the Chairman of Aston Martin Lagonda Limited presented him with a Volante Junior in four-seventh scale. From the limited edition of twenty-five cars built of this model, it was finished in Balmoral Green with tan Connolly leather trim piped in dark green, with Wilton Green carpet. The car was the same specification as the Prince of Wales's own Aston Martin V8 Volante. His Royal Highness took his Volante on a two-hundred-mile trip from Balmoral to the Castle of Mey in Caithness, near John O'Groats, his beloved grandmother's favourite Scottish home, just before it was due to be opened to the public for the first time. In March 2004, during another tour of the Aston Martin headquarters, the Prince of Wales enjoyed seeing some of the movie world's most famous cars. Like his father, who has owned Aston Martin Lagondas, Prince Charles remains a lifelong fan and owner of the firm's luxury cars.[59]

Although every movie buff knows Aston Martins, few could trace their origins. Designed to compete with Italian sports cars like Bugatti, the first Martin car was built by Robert Bamford and Lionel Martin in 1913. After the First World War, their cars earned a reputation for performance, especially in the Aston Clintozi Hill Climb race in Italy. In one of those moments of genius, Martin (rather than Bamford) combined his name with the hill climb, and "Aston Martin" was born. In 1947, David Brown, a wealthy Yorkshire industrialist, bought the company and merged it with the faltering Lagonda company. W.O. Bentley himself designed the DB2 two-seater's 6-cylinder engine making it an exceptional post-war sports car, and in 1953 the addition of two small rear seats made the DB2 into a 2+2 version and a hatchback model far ahead of its time. Mark II and III versions followed and, when author Ian Fleming wrote *Goldfinger* in 1959, he put his hero James Bond in a DB Mark III. But when Eon Productions was shooting the movie in 1963, Aston Martin no longer made that model, and offered instead its latest, the Silver Birch DB5, making it attractive to the most discerning of secret agents — and princes.[60]

Less exotic are the Queen's Land Rovers, which she has used as her personal transport for many years, particularly when off duty, travelling around her country home estates in Scotland and Norfolk. The first such SUV, as they would now be called, was a 1954 Land Rover Royal Review Vehicle, specially adapted for royal occasions from a basic 86-inch wheelbase Land Rover. The body was custom designed, with a rear platform from which the Queen could acknowledge the crowds. As one of a fleet, it accompanied the Queen and Prince Philip on a six-month Commonwealth tour soon after her coronation. It covered fifty thousand miles over a route from London to New Zealand and Australia, then Ceylon (Sri Lanka), Aden (Yemen), and Africa, returning to Europe via Gibraltar. Donated by Her Majesty to the royal collection at Sandringham, is a 1983 Land Rover 110 Station Wagon. It was in service until recently on the private Crown estates of Sandringham and Balmoral as rural transport for royal pursuits. The vehicle is fitted with some equipment to special order, including leather seats and security

Not as exotic as the Rolls, Land Rovers have served Her Majesty since 1954, sometimes on tours.

radio system and is finished in unique green paint of Her Majesty's personal choice. At present, a 2001 Land Rover Defender 110 County Station Wagon is used for the same purpose.

As for the makers of the traditional royal car, Daimler floundered about through the late 1950s, losing ground to Rolls-Royce. As the late Andrew Pastouna, Rolls-Royce owner and author summed it up: "To acquire the Royal Warrant of Appointment is a notable achievement, but in most cases it does little for sales. However, to lose the honour usually conveys to the general public an impression of a lowering of standards by the concern involved which can be immeasurably bad for business." Daimler tried to enter the sports-car field in 1954 with the Conquest Roadster, which also had a saloon version, the Century, then followed them with the equally unpopular Daimler Dart sports car and the six-seater Majestic Major. All were commercial disasters and, in 1960, Jaguar bought the Daimler name, with the 1961 Majestic Major Limousine built as the last complete, purely Daimler car. In a throwback to an earlier era, in 1973 Daimler converted two of its DS420 models to landaulettes. They were then the most expensive car ever to be built by government-owned British Leyland, costing £15,000, the same price as a Rolls-Royce Corniche, and twice that of a standard DS420 model. The press calculated that an equivalent amount of money that year would buy sixteen Ford Escorts. The first of the landaulettes

DND photo

The number plate on this Royal Phantom V demonstrates that it belongs to the Duke of Kent, who has kept "YRII" for all his Rolls-Royces since before the Second World War.

was ordered by the Governor General of Jamaica for a visit by Her Majesty in April 1975. The second was delivered to an unknown African buyer. The Daimler name and fluted radiator live on in the large Jaguar models, like the Sovereign and XJ6, and when Ford acquired Jaguar in 1989, it continued the marque. In 1996, Daimler's one-hundred-year anniversary was celebrated with a special called "The Daimler Century." The greatest fan of the old marque was the Queen Mother, and with her death in 2002, it looked doubtful that more Daimlers would be acquired by the royal household.

Responsibility for the Queen's state and private motor cars in the Royal Mews rests, as it always has, with the Master of the Horse. The late Duke of Beaufort had this position for forty-two years, serving three sovereigns before his death in 1978, when the Earl of Westmoreland took over. In charge of the fleet is a team of eight chauffeurs, whose task is to drive members of the royal family, senior royal-household employees, and official visitors from one place to another. Each chauffeur is allocated one or two motor cars, and it is their responsibility to keep them clean, polished, and valeted. While there are no petrol pumps at Buckingham Palace, filling pumps at Windsor Castle and other royal residences allow the motor cars to be refuelled. Four royal cars — a 1960 Rolls-Royce Phantom IV, a Daimler Limousine, a Rover 400, and Prince Philip's Metrocab — have so far been converted to run on liquid petroleum gas, a more environmentally friendly fuel than petrol or diesel.

For official duties like providing transport for state and other visitors, as well as the Queen herself, there are nine state Limousines, two Bentleys, four Rolls-Royces, and three Daimlers, all in royal-maroon livery. Two Rolls-Royces were always kept at the Royal Mews and, in 1994 they were transported to Russia for use during the state visit by the Queen and the Duke of Edinburgh. The shield displaying the royal arms and the Royal Standard flagpole can be fixed to and taken down from the roof from inside by the chauffeur while on the move. This model has a removable rear roof section, exposing an inner Perspex lining, and allowing spectators a clearer view of the royal passengers.

A Rolls-Royce Phantom VI was presented to the Queen in 1978 for her Silver Jubilee by the Society of Motor Manufacturers and Traders. The oldest motor car in the fleet is still the 1949 Phantom IV, made especially for Her Majesty when she was a princess and sometimes seen in the royal car procession at Ascot. All state motor cars have certain features which make them instantly recognizable. All wear an illuminated shield bearing the Royal Coat of Arms, and the Royal Standard when the Queen is being driven. Also fixed above the grille of the motor car that Her Majesty is in is her official mascot. Designed for her by the artist Edward Seago in the form of St. George on a horse poised victorious over a slain dragon, it is made of silver and can be transferred from motor car to motor car. Driving in Scotland, the Queen uses the lion mascot formerly used by Queen Elizabeth the Queen Mother. The Duke of Edinburgh's mascot, a heraldic lion wearing a crown, is adapted from his coat of arms. The late Queen Mother's mascot featured a figure of Britannia on top of the globe, which was originally made for King George V's Daimlers; it is now in use by the Prince of Wales. In 2005, when His Royal Highness Prince Charles married Camilla Parker-Bowles, they left Windsor Castle for the Guildhall in a 1962 Rolls-Royce Phantom V that had once been the Queen Mother's, and it took a sharp eye to notice that her mascot was still in place.

Her Majesty was so taken with the Perspex canopies used by her cars on the Canadian tour in 1951 that on her return she had Hooper make a tranparent top for one of the Royal Daimlers. The British media dubbed it the "goldfish bowl."

The royal mascots are the only exceptions that Rolls-Royce will allow to replace their own Spirit of Ecstasy on the hoods of their cars. For while it has always been acceptable for royalty to have their own mascots, as long ago as 1910 Rolls-Royce looked for an elegantly styled mascot by which it would be known. The pioneer motorist Lord Montagu of Beaulieu, who had introduced Edward VII to motoring, was also the editor of the illustrated magazine *The Car*. He commissioned Charles Sykes, a leading sculptor of the day, to design a mascot for one of his cars. Sykes used as his model Montagu's secretary, Miss Eleanor Velasco Thornton. He created a small statue of a young woman whose robes fluttered in the breeze behind her and who held one finger placed to her lips. He called the mascot "The Whisper." It denoted speed and quiet, exactly what Montagu wanted. With Montagu's standing in the motor-car world — and his royal connections — other motorists were persuaded, as was Rolls-Royce. They approached Sykes for a similar mascot, and once more he used Miss Thornton as his model, basing the design on "The Whisper." This time he produced a figure of a girl with arms outstretched to hold the folds of her gown, which were being blown by the breeze. He called it "The

Spirit of Ecstasy," and from February 6, 1911, onward, every Rolls-Royce ever made would carry it — except the Queen's and her immediate family's.[61]

Princess Margaret has owned more Rolls-Royces than any other member of today's royal family, and made certain that very positive ideas of her own were included in their specification. Prince Henry, Duke of Gloucester; Princess Marina, Duchess of Kent; and her son and daughter, Prince Michael of Kent and Princess Alexandra of Kent, have all owned and used Rolls-Royce cars on official duties.

The most recently acquired state motor cars, used for most of the Queen's present engagements, are two state Bentleys, one of which was presented to Her Majesty on June 4, 2002, as a gift to mark her Golden Jubilee.

Born in 1888, Walter Owen Bentley was a railway apprentice from a middle-class family in St. John's Wood, in London. The young Bentley loved cricket as much as he did racing a motorcycle at Brooklands. With his brother, W.O. began designing and building racing cars that became well known for breaking speed records at Brooklands and doing "a flying mile" in 89.7 miles per hour. In August 1919, he formed Bentley Motors Ltd, which was undercapitalized from its birth, the brothers having to take out a personal mortgage to finance the building of a factory at Cricklewood in North West London. Whatever their financial woes, they made the best touring cars, and when Bentleys were entered for the twenty-four-hour races at Le Mans, they were first across the finish line in 1927, 1928, 1929, and 1930 — a record unequalled until the 1950s by Jaguar, and not beaten until the 1960s by Ferrari. Success on the track meant fame for Bentley as expensive sports cars, and soon the younger members of the royal family, and celebrities Gertrude Lawrence and Beatrice Lillie were among their customers.

But the Depression so badly affected sales that, in 1931, the Bentley Company was forced into liquidation and taken over by Rolls-Royce Limited. The production of

Buckingham Palace photo

Her Majesty's personal mascot — St. George poised over a slain dragon — can be transferred from car to car.

The first Bentley to be used for state occasions, it broke the tradition that Rolls-Royce and Daimler had held for almost a century.

BCA photo

Bentley cars moved to Derby and later to Crewe in 1946. W.O. stayed with Rolls-Royce for a while as an advisor, leaving in 1935 to join another sports-car manufacturer, Lagonda, and his designs would ultimately go into the Aston Martin DB2. There would soon be no difference between Bentley and Rolls-Royce versions except for the latter's traditional radiator, for which customers paid an additional £130. This similarity did not appeal to most owners, who felt that, as they had paid for a Rolls-Royce, that was what they should get. W.O Bentley died in 1971, too soon to see his cars used by the Queen. He would also have been pleased to know that Rolls-Royce revived his original racing concept when it brought out the faster Mulsanne model, naming it after the Mulsanne Straight at Le Mans where so many of the Bentley brothers' cars had been driven to victory.

Her Majesty's new Bentleys were specially designed from conception. Company chief designer Dirk van Braeckel and exterior stylist Crispin Marshfield began work on them in February 2000. As the Queen's first new limousines for state and ceremonial occasions in fifteen years, the cars were planned with input from the Queen, the Duke of Edinburgh, and Her Majesty's Head Chauffeur and developed by a collaboration of fifty firms. The major partners joining Bentley Motors in the consortium to build them were Mayflower Vehicle Systems (bodywork), Leoni Wiring Systems (electrics), TWR Group (trim packaging), Radshape (brightware), Rimotor cardo PLC (powertrain), Intier (interior trim substrates), and MSX International (structural analysis and validation). Bentley's responsibilities extended to the design, styling, chassis, and construction of the motor car. Although their design was derived from the latest Series Two Bentley Arnage, the engineering challenges they posed often bore no relation to those of any conventional motor car. Designed for a minimum lifespan of twenty-five years and 125,000 miles, the limousines are expected to be the Queen's principal (perhaps final) transport at state and ceremonial occasions.

Their monocoque construction enables greater use to be made of the vehicle's interior space. This means the transmission tunnel now runs underneath the floor, without encroaching on the cabin. This allowed the stylists to work with a lowered roofline while preserving the required interior height. The rear doors were redesigned, permitting the Queen to stand up straight before stepping down to the ground. The rear seats are upholstered in Hield Lambswool Sateen cloth while all remaining upholstery is in light grey Connolly hide. Motor carpets are pale blue in the rear and dark blue in the front.

The glasshouse design of the rear cabin were a problem was the design team. With such a large rear cabin and so much glass, the motor car would potentially be subject to huge solar loadings or, in other words, the build up of heat from the sun, which, left unchecked, would swiftly cause intolerable interior cabin temperatures. Normally, this would be addressed by fitting heavily tinted glass, but the Queen was insistent that visibility both into and out of the motor car was not to be compromised. The solution was fitting laminated glass in all windows with a reflective coating sandwiched between the two layers. This allowed a tint of 15 percent, and is barely noticeable inside or out. The tint on the roof panels is 40 percent. Air conditioning is also fitted to ensure the vast rear cabin stays cool in the hottest weather. The average speed at which the Bentley travels in processional occasions is nine miles per hour and sometimes as slowly as four miles per hour. As a result of thorough computer modelling and testing at the Motor Industry Research Association (MIRA), a system was devised that produced a large and slow-moving mass of cool air to be distributed silently about the motor car.

One monumental problem was conserving sufficient rigidity within such a heavy motor car without employing unattractively thick pillars. This is the first royal limousine to use monocoque construction rather than the body-on-chassis method of the Phantom series of Rolls-Royces, and the pillars are stressed members and are required to do a lot more than just support the roof. Powering the Bentley limousine is a modified version of Bentley's new 400 bhp, twin-turbo 6.75-litre V8 engine that later made its debut in the Bentley Arnage R. With 616 lb ft/835 nm of torque, it gives the royal limousine with an imposing turn of speed up to its electronically limited top speed of 120 miles per hour. Modifications have been made to the air boxes to allow them to be fitted under the bonnet, while a larger alternator is fitted to cope with the added demands of the electrical system. Running on liquid petroleum gas (LPG) will not only extend the range of the motor car but will also dramatically reduce its output of emissions.

Her Majesty was delighted with the new Bentley state limousine presented to her as a Golden Jubilee gift. The Queen's is the only car permitted to be on British roads without a licence plate.

Tim Graham/CORBIS

Contrary to expectation, the limousine is not filled with every electronic toy available. In fact, Her Majesty asked that it should not contain such items. Nevertheless, the highly specialized role the motor car plays has necessitated the fitment of a large number of components vital to the execution of the head of state's duties. Inside there is a glass division between the front and rear compartments that can be lowered by its passengers from a console mounted between the seats. An intercom is also fitted. Both rear seats are height adjustable, so passengers are seen at the same level and squarely within the rear side window. Both rear windows can also be operated from either rear seat. Naturally, all security equipment is classified.

To be able to carry royal passengers securely, smoothly, and swiftly is not enough. For a royal car, maximum visibility of its passengers is paramount. The Bentleys are fitted with a removable exterior roof covering, which exposes a clear inner lining, giving an all-round view of their royal passengers. Hinged at the back rather than the front, the doors also allow bystanders and photographers to see the Queen as she leaves the motor car, while allowing easier entry and egress.

Yet despite their special form and purpose, in many ways royal cars are just like any others. Subject to normal speed restrictions, they are liable to the London Congestion Charge, payable by all motor cars which drive within central London. Except for the Queen, they also need road tax, regular MOTs, and insurance. Their chauffeurs must also follow all the rules of the road. Even a police escort can't prevent the Queen's motor car from being held up in traffic. And then there are those inexplicable first dents. Less than a week after the Golden Jubilee celebrations and the new Bentley's first public use, Her Majesty was at the Epsom racecourse to watch the Vodafone Derby when it was noted that there was a nick on the hood of her Bentley.

A motor car may be a means by which one is transported from A to B powered by an internal-combustion engine. But for the incurably romantic (and motor car buffs everywhere) a car designed, built for and used by Her Majesty, maintains the glamour, mystique, and history of the Gold Coach, the Bentley of yesteryear.

AIRCRAFT

Detail of photo from page 173.

The first British monarch interested in aviation was King George III. In September 1784, Vincenzo Lunardi wrote to the King giving details of his successful balloon flight (the first to be made in Britain), the start of which was watched by the Prince of Wales. The connection between actual flying and the royal family can be traced almost to the dawn of aviation. In 1909, during a visit to Paris, King Edward VII met with Orville and Wilbur Wright and watched them demonstrate their Flyer aircraft.

The Prince of Wales (left), later King Edward VIII, about to fly in 1918.

Prince Albert (the future King George VI) with Major Louis Greig, about to make a flight to northern France during the First World War.

Royal flight itself dates back to the First World War when Edward, the Prince of Wales (later Edward VIII) flew in an aircraft while at the front. He wrote to his father on July 24, 1917: "It was kind of you to give me leave to fly — which permission I took advantage of last Tuesday (exactly a week ago) and had a hour in the air above Abeele and Cassel with General Longcroft (GOC 5th Bde RFC) in a R.E. 8. I must say I enjoyed my first trip very much indeed as such flying is extraordinarily safe nowadays."[62] Only after the war would His Majesty hear that the heir to the throne had made other flights. On April 16, 1918, when visiting 139 Squadron on the Italian Front His Royal Highness flew with the Canadian air ace, Major William Barker VC. When the Armistice was declared, the Prince of Wales, now attached to the Canadian Corps, visited American army units in Germany. At one, he met Brigadier General William "Billy" Mitchell and, from a field near Koblenz, Mitchell flew him over the Rhine. Immediately after the war, the Prince flew with Barker once more, this time in a Sopwith Dove, and, as if that was not bad enough, Barker would pilot the aircraft with one arm in a sling. At a time when flying was considered extremely dangerous and those who trusted their lives to the wood and wire contraptions foolhardy, His Majesty could be forgiven, when hearing of this, for immediately prohibiting his son from ever going up in an aircraft again. It took almost ten years for the ban to be officially lifted for the Prince of Wales, and by then, flying was the least of his peccadilloes.

His brother Prince Albert (later George VI) was taken for his first flight by Lieutenant R.E.C. Peirse[63] on March 4, 1918, at RN Air Station Sleaford, the present RAF Cranwell. Demonstrating the difference between the two brothers, Prince Albert would write to his mother: "It is a curious sensation and one which takes a lot of getting used to." His Highness qualified for his licence by flying solo in a peculiar way. An instructor

PA-006333

The Prince of Wales (left) and Lieutenant Colonel W.G. Barker, VC, preparing for flight in Sopwith Gnu.

did accompany him, but never touched the controls. When Prince Albert received his pilot's wings on July 31, 1919 (the first member of the royal family to become a fully qualified pilot), two Avro 504Js from a communications flight were allotted to him. Prince Albert would also be the first member of the royal family to serve in the Royal Air Force, doing so between 1918 and 1919. In the summer of 1921, he even attended the Royal Air Force ball at London's Ritz Hotel, where His Highness danced for the very first time with a certain Elizabeth Bowes-Lyon. The Duke of Windsor wrote:

> By 1929, aviation had made such spectacular progress that I approached my father again. My airmen friends encouraged me to believe that if I travelled around Britain in my own aeroplane the example would give much-needed impetus to the struggling aircraft industry. My father offered no objection my buying a De Havilland Gypsy Moth — a surprising concession in view of his ban on steeplechasing only a few months before.[64]

Royal Air Marshals: King George V (centre) with his two eldest sons, Edward, Prince of Wales, and Albert, Duke of York. The photograph is signed by all three men and was taken at the RAF review.

Wartime royal visit to RCAF 420 Squadon with Halifax Mk III in background; Their Majesties chat with RCAF personnel.

Although King George V never flew, he is closely associated with the Royal Flying Corps and later the Royal Air Force and the Royal Canadian Air Force. It was His Majesty who, after the First World War, gave Canada the Imperial Gift of surplus fighter and bomber aircraft that began the Canadian Air Force and then on April 1, 1924, bestowed the title "Royal" upon it, the date marking the birth of the RCAF. His sons Prince Henry (later the Duke of Gloucester) and Prince George (later the Duke of Kent) also obtained their pilots' licences in the 1920s. A Bristol Fighter J8340, the first aircraft officially built for royal engagements was assigned to the Prince of Wales in April 1928 for his personal use, and maintained at 24 Squadron. The following year it was exchanged for a faster Westland Wapiti. In September 1929, the Prince of Wales would buy for his private use the first of several aircraft, a Gypsy Moth G-AALG. It was painted in the red and blue colours of the Brigade of Guards, the regiment he had served in during the Great War.[65] With his father's permission, he learned to fly, making his first solo from RAF Northolt on November 17, 1929. As he later recalled:

> I had already to my credit many hours of dual instruction, and that summer evening I had made a number of successful practice landings. Suddenly without explanation, my instructor jumped from the front cockpit and I noticed with surprise that he had his control stick in his hand [the sticks were removable]. "With a dramatic gesture, he waved me into the air alone. Taking off, I completed two extremely lonely circuits of the field and landed twice without cracking up the machine. Once out of the aeroplane, my first act was to telephone my two younger brothers. "I've beaten you to it," I announced triumphantly to each in turn.[66]

Given that official records state G-AALG crashed on November 16, 1929, the Duke's memory was faulty, but not his enthusiasm for aviation. Even in the very throes of his abdication problems in 1936, he would entertain Charles Lindbergh at his home, Fort Belvedere.

A young RAF Flight Lieutenant E.H. Fielden was appointed as the Prince's personal pilot in 1929 and then would be made Captain of the King's Flight when it was formed. A perfectionist in everything he did, incorporating his exacting standards into the Flight, "Mouse" Fielden would retire in December 1961 as Air Vice-Marshal Sir Edward Fielden and was decorated by four monarchs: George V (1929), Edward VIII (1936), George VI (1943, and 1946), and Elizabeth II (1952 and 1968). He would die in 1976 at the age of seventy-two, having served the royal family for forty years.

In 1930, the Prince of Wales and Prince George entered their own aircraft, a Hawker Tomtit G-AALL and a DH Hawk Moth G-AAUZ respectively, for the King's Cup Air Race. Now based at Hendon airfield in north London, the Prince's aircraft would be unofficially called the "royal flight." In April 1931, when the Prince was on a tour of South America to open the British Empire Trade Exposition at Buenos Aires, he had his own Puss Moth G-ABFV crated and shipped out on the aircraft carrier HMS *Eagle*. Whether he personally used it is not known, but off Rio de Janeiro, witnessed by Prince George and Fielden, who were in the Puss Moth, he would land a Fairey III on the aircraft carrier's deck.

With room only for an aide-de-camp and a valet but no luggage, the Moths were too small for functions, both official and unofficial, and in July 1931, His Royal Highness would hire a large Westland Wessex for a holiday in France. His G-AALG would be sold to Jean Batten in February 1933,[67] and in May, His Royal Highness had a twin-engine Vickers Viastra X, G-ACCC, specially built for him. It was rarely flown, and in 1935 the Prince of Wales bought his own Dragon Rapide G-ADDD, using it for some royal engagements.

With the death of King George V on January 20, 1936, the Prince of Wales, now Edward VIII, flew in the Rapide to attend the Accession Council in London, the first time that a British monarch had ever flown. As Marshal of the Royal Air Force, he was now entitled to an air force communications aircraft and on June 21, 1936, the King's Flight was officially formed at Hendon. His own Rapide was replaced with an Airspeed Envoy II in civil registration G-AEXX — the first royal aircraft to be publicly financed. Although many considered the Envoy too small for official use, as a civil version of the common Oxford trainer, it had the advantage of

PL-32411

Wartime royal visit to RCAF 420 Squadron. W/C J.D. MacIntosh is being presented to the King.

Royal trainer: the forgiving Avro 504. Note skid under nose to prevent tipping during landing.

The Lockheed Hudson, the only aircraft in the King's Flight to be armed.

King George VI about to leave RAF Northolt in 1938.

being readily available. Serviced by the RAF, the Envoy was officially placed on the inventory as part of No. 24 Communications Squadron. It was also in red and blue, the King's regimental colours, the first time that they would be used on an official aircraft. Setting a precedent in royal travel, His Majesty flew everywhere in it: on July 26, 1936, after unveiling the monument of Canada's war dead at Vimy Ridge, he had Fielden pick him up in the Envoy and take him home. In August, he would do the same after the public relations disaster of his *Nahlin* cruise.

To have their aircraft chosen for the King was quite a coup for the relatively new and unknown aircraft manufacturer like Airspeed. Established in 1931, it was a Portsmouth, Hampshire, company with little prospect of competing with the larger aircraft manufacturers. But the great long-distance pioneer Sir Alan Cobham was one of its founders, and perhaps it was the publicity from his efforts that caught the eye of the Prince. All wood, with control surfaces fabric covered, the Envoy appeared in 1934. Powered by two 350 hp Armstrong Siddeley Cheetah radial engines, its retractable landing gear, speed of 180 miles per hour, and seven seats made it a steady — if unimaginative — aircraft. Bought by the RAF, the Royal Navy, and the air forces of China, France, South Africa, Japan, and India, it would also compete in the England-Australia Air Race. Both of the Prince of Wales's former aircraft, the Puss Moth and Dragon Rapide, were sold to Western Airways, which operated out of Weston Airport. In an unusual coincidence, in 1946, Western Airways would also buy a Percival Petrel G-AHTB, another aircraft originally from the King's Flight.[68] When, as the Duke of Windsor, Edward VIII went into exile, there would be no private aircraft in his life and few aircraft at all, for the Duchess of Windsor was afraid of flying.[69]

Upon Edward's abdication, Prince Albert, the Duke of York, became King George VI, and, if less enamoured with aviation than his brother, he continued to enlarge the King's Flight. As the Envoy was too limited for the staff and luggage that a royal flight now required, Fielden had been looking for a larger replacement and was considering a Bristol Bombay 142 (owned by Lord Rothermere) and an American Lockheed Super Electra airliner. This last was operated by British Airways on its European routes, and was made famous when Prime Minister Neville Chamberlain emerged from one on September 30, 1938, after meeting with Adolf Hitler. But with the onset of the war, it was decided that the

King's Flight should now be armed, and Fielden made the controversial choice of buying the military version of the Super Electra, called the Hudson patrol bomber. This was controversial because the royal family flew only in British-built aircraft, but there was nothing domestically to compare with the Hudson. Fitted with the Atlantic ferry tanks, it had a range of three thousand miles, a Boulton-Paul turret with twin machine guns (becoming the only aircraft of the Flight to ever be armed), and could carry more passengers. The Hudson was repainted in camouflage and, to escape the bombing, the Flight was moved away from Hendon in the London suburbs to RAF Benson in Oxfordshire. Fielden, now Wing Commander, was the King's pilot, and the crew now included dorsal and front-turret gunners and a steward who also acted as side-gunner. In the desperate days after the fall of France, the King's Flight Hudson also carried royalty into exile from other countries, such as the King of Norway and the Belgian royal family. On August 9, 1941, His Majesty flew in it from Inverness to Hatston in the Orkney Islands. As the Luftwaffe had just bombed shipping along the Orkney coast, the Royal Navy was "trigger happy" about anything in the air and, to Fielden's annoyance, fired on the King's aircraft. Later, as they overflew a British convoy, the royal Hudson was once again fired upon. Fortunately, it was not hit. As the pilot said, "Thank God, the Navy cannot shoot."

A De Havilland Flamingo, G-AGCC, was added to the fleet on September 7, 1940, but does not seem to have been used. That month, at the height of the Battle of Britain, the King visited as many RAF bases as possible in the Hudson. One was RAF Northolt. He had toured the base once before and now, in the midst of the Battle, arrived to watch the squadrons in action from the Sector Operations Room. The day was an extremely busy one for the station, as recorded by Group Captain Vincent:

> The visit of the King was a most inspiring day. The squadrons took off to intercept a raid on Southampton while he was there. He watched the interception from the Sector Operations Room and heard the leader's "Tally Ho" and subsequent orders ... pilots from Northolt had destroyed sixteen aeroplane for no loss to us ... [the King] overstayed his programmed time by about two hours.[70]

As the unarmed Flamingo would have required a fighter escort whenever His Majesty flew in it, the King felt that both aircraft in the King's Flight could be better used elsewhere. As a result, on February 14, 1942, the Flight was disbanded, with the Flamingo going to 24 Squadron and the Hudson to 161 Squadron, where Fielden happened to be Station Commander. The former royal Hudson would be used in Special Operations for dropping and picking up agents behind enemy lines, and would be destroyed by enemy action at St. Luc, France, on May 29, 1942.

That summer, on August 25, 1942, the King lost his younger brother, Prince George, Duke of Kent. Flying in dense fog to Iceland to inspect the RAF bases there, his Sunderland flying boat crashed against a Scottish mountainside and all on board were killed. Prince George was the first member of the House of Windsor to be killed in active service in war and in the air. Thirty years later, his nephew, Prince William of Gloucester, also lost his life in a flying accident, when his plane crashed at Halfpenny Green Airfield in August 1972.

George, Duke of Kent, the fourth son of King George V, served in the Royal Air Force. He toured air training bases in Canada in 1941 and was killed in an air crash on August 25, 1942.

MOD photo

MOD photo

Avro York: VIP transport for His Majesty during the Second World War.

Realizing that the post-war aircraft market would be dominated by American designs, (and in contravention of the Anglo-American agreement that all transport aircraft would be made in the United States), in 1941, Avro designer Roy Chadwick began to sketch out a long-range, four-engined transport based on the Lancaster bomber. His design married the wings, tail assembly, engines, and landing gear of the bomber to a square fuselage. The prototype Avro Type 685 flew on July 5, 1942, and production of the York (as it was called) began in 1943.

Prime Minister Churchill used a York as a flying conference room for overseas flights, as did General Bernard Montgomery, Field-Marshal Smuts, and Lord Mountbatten. These VIP Yorks had a private cabin, a dining room that could be used for conferences, and bunks to sleep eight. In May 1943, Churchill's personal York *Ascalon*, LV633, the second prototype, was delivered to RAF Northolt, and from there was flown to Gibraltar to pick up the prime minister, who was returning from Washington by flying boat. If transporting Churchill wasn't historic enough, the York was to have another such passenger.

When the last of the German forces had surrendered in North Africa that month, the Cabinet thought that a visit from His Majesty to Allied troops there would be good for their morale, especially to recognize the efforts of the Free French. Mr. Churchill was very pleased that His Majesty was going to "borrow" the York from him, perhaps forgetting that all RAF aircraft belonged to the King. The Queen was distraught: eight days earlier, actor Leslie Howard had been killed on the same route when his aircraft had been shot down. But His Majesty, who had fought at Jutland, frustrated at not being able to do, in his opinion, "anything military" for the war effort besides target-shooting at Windsor, was adamant. He called in his lawyers and checked his will. Then, his identity disguised as General Lyon, on June 11, 1943, King George VI left RAF Northolt at 2107 hours, the York flying far out into the Atlantic and then south, keeping out of range of the Luftwaffe's Ju 88 fighters based at Brest. Making for Gibraltar, it flew to Lisbon at 0418 on June 12 but because that city was fogbound, the York was diverted to a tiny air force staging airfield of Ras El Ma, outside Fez, Morocco, much to the poor station CO's consternation. From there, it continued on to Algiers, where the King met with General Dwight Eisenhower, and then flew on to Oran where he reviewed the U.S. Fifth Army under General Mark Clark. On June 17, His Majesty continued on to Tunis and then Tripoli, where he boarded the cruiser HMS *Aurora* for Malta. The homeward journey was begun on June 24, the York once more going through Ras El Ma — this time with sufficient warning — to arrive back at Northolt and to be met by the Prime Minister. Her Majesty later wrote to her mother-in-law, Queen Mary, that while he was away she had walked up and down her room staring at the phone, expecting the worst. But the King came back safely, tanned and well pleased with himself.

In 1944, His Majesty "borrowed" Churchill's aircraft again to fly to North Africa and Italy. His departure from Northolt on July 22 was not without some drama, for the Queen and Princess Elizabeth were inspecting the York when a German V-1 buzz bomb flew over the base. On this flight, a Mosquito flew ahead of the York to check out the weather and, after an uneventful eight hours, His Majesty landed once more at Ras El Ma. After a three-hour rest, escorted by Beaufighters and Spitfires, he flew onward to Naples. With him were his secretary Sir Eric Melville, his equerry Colonel the Honourable Sir Piers Leigh, Group Captain E.H. Fielden, Captain of the King's Flight, a Scotland Yard bodyguard, and two valets. The pilot of the York, Wing Commander Henry Collins, said that the King spent about twenty minutes in the cockpit before retiring. As a former pilot, he was particularly interested in the automatic pilot.[71] The York remained in Naples while His Majesty flew to the front lines in a general's C-47. Ten days later they returned to Northolt, landing just as another V-1 passed overhead.

At war's end, as His Majesty had been so impressed by the flight in the C-47 in Italy that he asked that one be allocated to 24 Squadron for his use in June 1945. The King's Flight was re-formed on May 1, 1946, at RAF Benson in preparation for the Royal Tour of South Africa. The York was now retained for royal duties exclusively — Churchill was no longer prime minister — and was scheduled to be used on a Royal Tour to New Zealand in 1948. However, because of the King's failing health, this trip was cancelled. Instead, the first of three specially built Vickers Vikings (one each for Their Majesties and one for the ground crew) were to be sent to South Africa and pre-positioned and there. Civil versions of the Vickers Wellington bomber, the Vikings were cramped, unpressurized, and noisy. But at a time when the British aviation industry was trying to catch up with the American, the airliner was all that was available. The Royal Vikings sat eight passengers, in two saloons each with four large armchairs, two forward and two aft. Each armchair had a parachute in the upholstery. Between the seats was a white telephone that connected with one at the seat used by the Captain of the King's Flight. In the rear of the Viking was a small toilet and wardrobe and behind them, a very cramped cabin with a divan bed. The decor for the whole aircraft's interior was royal blue in the carpets, curtains, and upholstery, with the walls, ceilings, and door in cream.[72]

They were put to good use in South Africa during the Royal Tour, but when one crashed on return at Aberdeen in September 1947, critics of the King's Flight thought that, in the austerity of post-war Britain, money could be saved if it were disbanded and its duties taken over by the two state airlines BOAC and British European Airways, with the RAF on standby.

Her Majesty the Queen's first official flight was from RAF Northolt in July 1945, when she accompanied her parents on a visit to Northern Ireland. If her uncle, the former Prince of Wales, had been a keen aviation enthusiast, the young Princess Elizabeth proved no less so, and although she never took flying lessons, she was the first member of the royal family to fly across the Atlantic, in a British Overseas Airways Corporation Stratocruiser to Montreal. The Royal Tour of Canada in 1951 was the first time that aircraft would be extensively used. As the Princess Elizabeth's first overseas tour, it was to be of modest size: three Canadian cities in ten days, an almost leisurely pace. But then,

Princess Elizabeth about to embark on the Canadair C-5 on the 1951 tour.

DND photo

between the politicians in London and Ottawa, it grew to fifteen thousand miles in thirty-five days, and worse was to come. The Edinburghs, as they were known then, were to travel on September 25, 1951, on the Canadian Pacific liner *Empress of Britain*, but the news that His Majesty was in hospital gravely ill with cancer threw all the plans into chaos. The Princess refused to leave her family, and the tour was to be abandoned. Two days before the *Empress* sailed, the King was operated on, and his affected lung was removed. As always, duty came first for His Majesty, and he insisted that the tour proceed, but by then it was too late to go by ship. The time factor prevented the couple from taking another liner, and when a transatlantic flight was considered, the politicians, especially Churchill, thought it too dangerous for the heir to the throne.

PL-52800

1951 Royal Tour: Princess Elizabeth signs the visitor's book on C-5.

It was Philip who stepped in and took charge, meeting with Prime Minister Clement Attlee to work out a means by which the government had to allow the Princess to fly or abandon the tour completely. The tour was to be a training exercise for Princess Elizabeth, abroad for the first time without her parents and, as the future consort, he pointed out that he too was on trial. But so threatening was the King's illness that, when the young couple boarded the BOAC Stratocruiser from Heathrow Airport for Montreal on October 8, 1951, they carried with them a sealed envelope containing a message to both Houses of Parliament in the event of the King's death.

In Canada, the Royal Canadian Air Force put its only VIP aircraft, 412 (Falcon) Squadron's Canadair C-5 at their disposal. *Promptus Ad Vindictam* ("Swift to avenge") is a strange motto for a

Prince Charles with 412 Squadron personnel and Challenger.

Duke and Duchess of York with 412 Squadron, who flew them from Charlottetown to Regina in July 1989.

Prince Edward poses with 412 Squadron personnel during 1990 visit.

transport squadron that ferried VIPs about, but 412's history can be traced back to the merger of two units after the Second World War. On September 10, 1939, Number 12 Communications Flight was formed at RCAF Station Ottawa while on June 30, 1941, 412 Spitfire Fighter Squadron — also an RCAF squadron — was similarly formed at Digby, England. The pilot-poet Flight Lieutenant John Magee was a member of the squadron, and through the war it had earned an impressive list of battle honours.[73] In the post-war reorganization of the RCAF, it was decided that 412 should not disappear and, on April 1 1947, Number 12 Communications Flight was re-designated as 412 (Composite) Squadron. In 1949, 412, now a transport squadron, assumed its present VIP transport role, operating initially from CFB Rockcliffe in Ottawa. In January 1950, a Squadron North Star carried Lester Pearson, the Minister of External Affairs, to the Commonwealth Foreign Ministers' Conference in Ceylon, making it the first around-the-world flight by 412. In May 1953 in its post-war VIP role, it would receive the first of two De Havilland Comet 1As, becoming the first squadron to operate jet transport, not only in the RCAF but in any air force in the world. The squadron would move to Uplands, Ottawa, in June 1955, and in its VIP role, flew to every corner of the world.

The C-5 that the Princess and Prince were to use had come to 412 Squadron on June 21, 1950. A larger version of the civil Canadair North Star then operated by Trans-Canada Airlines (and as the Argonaut with British Overseas Airways Corporation) it was a one-off hybrid. But so desperately did the RCAF need an aircraft for the Prime Minister and visiting VIPs that the C-5 was pressed into service as soon as it was taken on strength. On July 7, 1950, it carried Prime Minister Louis St. Laurent to Calgary to open the Calgary Stampede, although not till July 29 was it to be officially accepted by the RCAF.

The C-5 was the most luxurious of any aircraft in Canada, if not the world. A slightly larger version of the Canadair North Star, it had a DC-6 undercarriage and Pratt and Whitney radial engines that were quieter than the North Star's Merlins. The cabin was pressurized to 8,500 feet and divided into two compartments. The main portion had room for twenty-four passengers, with seating that could be converted into double beds. Thick carpets and insulation reduced outside noise. Behind this section was the galley, with washroom and cloakroom for these passengers. Major M. Joost, Office of Air Force Heritage and History 1 CAD, wrote:

It is in the rear compartment that luxury was the byword. Here there was seating for thirteen. It had its own private washroom with hot and cold water. The furniture consisted of two divans, a semi-circular lounge, an executive desk with swivel chair, a filing cabinet, and a telephone to talk to the captain. The divans could be converted to 3/4 size beds.

The aircraft had no regular flight commitments. Each flight was a special case, although some runs, such as Ottawa to London and Ottawa to Paris were more frequent. There were trips of longer duration, such as Prime Minister St. Laurent's eleven-country trip around the world in 1954, and the repeat for Prime Minister Diefenbaker in 1958. For many of its flights, the C-5 had to arrive at a specified time as there were often guards of honour or dignitaries at the ramp. It is a testament to the crew and aircraft, and with some help from air traffic controllers, that they invariably arrived on time.

There was no crew exclusively assigned to the C-5: there was a fair degree of competition within 412 Squadron to be a member and all VIP personnel were eligible. The standards required to be a member of the VIP personnel contingent were high. Just to qualify as a First Officer, a pilot had to have two years experience in a transport squadron with experience on transatlantic and trans-continental flights, plus a minimum of 3,000 hours, of which 1,000 had to be on four-engined aircraft. Over the years, besides carrying Princess Elizabeth and Prince Philip, the C-5 also flew Queen Juliana and Prince Bernhard of the Netherlands, Emperor Haile Selassie of Ethiopia, and Prince (now Emperor) Akihito of Japan. Then there were Prime Ministers, Cabinet Ministers, foreign dignitaries, and senior military officers.

PL-52754

1951 Royal Tour: Royal Standard erected on C-5 by S/L Stuart Cowan.

The C-5 was retired on August 28, 1966, after logging 9,600 hours, more than 3 million miles, and having visited 150 different countries. For sixteen years, she ferried dignitaries to all continents except Antarctica, logging over 2,500,000 miles in 9,500 hours in the air. All who flew her or in her appreciated her, yet in her final moments, she suffered an indignity undeserved of such a fine aircraft. The one blot on her record occurred at that time with no fault on the part of the aircraft!

Major Joost concluded:

In typical Canadian fashion, the C-5 had been refurbished that year at a cost of over $383,000, including $40,000 to overhaul three spare engines. Yet, the C-5 was sold for $49,000. Needless to say, the *Globe and Mail* newspaper had a field day and the Auditor-General was not amused. The new American owner failed to get U.S. certification for the C-5, and she was stripped of useful parts and scrapped.

The last word on the C-5 should go to His Royal Highness, Prince Philip. His comments are illustrative of the aircraft's and crews' efforts. While approaching Vancouver during the Prince's tour of Canada in 1955, the hydraulic system failed. The co-pilot and flight engineer took turns hand-pumping the landing gear and flaps all the way to the ramp. Exhausted after an otherwise ordinary landing, they breathed a sigh of relief, hoping the Prince had not noticed anything. To their chagrin, he was standing in the doorway and quipped: "Nicely rowed, chaps!"[74]

Canadian C-5, the RCAF royal transport for the 1951 Royal Tour.

The 1951 North American Tour a success, the British government then asked that Princess Elizabeth and Prince Philip visit Kenya, Ceylon, Australia, and New Zealand the following year. Concerned about her father's rapidly declining health, Her Royal Highness did not want to be away for so long, but the dedication to duty above all that her father had taught her predominated. On the bitterly cold day of January 31, 1952, the couple embarked from Heathrow for Nairobi on a BOAC Canadair Argonaut. At the airport, the King, bareheaded, tired, and ill, bade them farewell with the words "Look out for yourselves." He died on February 6, and the Argonaut that had taken a princess away returned with Her Majesty Queen Elizabeth II.

That May, Queen Elizabeth, now the Queen Mother, and Princess Margaret toured the De Havilland plant at Hatfield, England, where the Comet I, the world's first jet airliner, was being built. At a time when jet travel for civilians was unknown and the Comet itself largely untried, the royal party boarded one and flew over France, Italy, and Switzerland on a four-hour flight, their bravery putting the seal of approval on the aircraft. It was later learned that Her Majesty had even taken the controls while in flight, and had actually flown the Comet. On return to Hatfield, she sent a telegram to the RAF's No. 600 (City of London) Squadron, of which she was the Honorary Air Commodore: "I am delighted to tell you that today I took over as first pilot of a Comet aeroplane. We exceeded a reading of 0.8 Mach at 40,000 feet. What the passengers thought, I really wouldn't like to say. Elizabeth R, Hon. Air Commodore, 600 Squadron."

Squadron Leader J. Meadows replied, "Your squadron is overwhelmingly proud that their honorary Air Commodore piloted a jet as high and as fast as any of her squadrons."

In 1952, with the succession of Her Majesty Queen Elizabeth to the throne, the Flight was renamed the Queen's Flight.

"I wanted to fly," the Duke of Edinburgh once revealed, "like all small boys who want to drive railway engines." The exercise of piloting an aircraft was to Philip "an intellectual challenge." His biographer, Douglas Liversedge, wrote that, if it had been left to him, Prince Philip would have embarked on a career in the Royal Air Force, rather than the Royal Navy. In 1952, his status as Consort to Her Majesty meant that he had to adopt titles like Admiral of the Fleet, Field Marshal, and Marshal of the Royal Air Force. To accept the last without earning his pilot's wings was morally repugnant to Prince Philip, although the government of the day (in the person once again of Prime Minister Sir Winston Churchill) were reluctant to allow him to pilot an aircraft. The effect that an accident would have on Her Majesty — and Churchill's government — was just too awful to contemplate. But Prince Philip was to have none of that, and as an individualist (and former pilot) himself, Churchill admired that quality in the young man; permission to learn how to fly was granted. Both the Royal Navy and the Royal Air Force competed to train the Prince, but he chose the RAF, arriving for his medical examination at the central medical establishment at Hallam Street, London, in October 1952. Flight-Lieutenant Carol Gordon, an instructor at the RAF Central Flying School was selected to teach him. "If you kill him," warned his commanding officer, "you realize what this will do to the Queen." This was repeated to Gordon by no less than an Air Marshal, two Vice-Air Marshals, an Air Commodore, and the Secretary of State for Air himself.

Besides the Duke of Edinburgh, Prince Charles and Prince Andrew learnt to fly on the De Havilland Chipmunk.

The Prince began his training in a De Havilland Chipmunk on October 29, 1952. He was so determined to earn his pilot's wings before Christmas that he made his first solo flight on December 20. A windsock was set up on Smith's Lawn in Windsor Great Park that month, and the cricket pavilion remade into a briefing room. Because the young couple were then living at Sandringham, the advanced training continued at the closer airfield of Bircham Newton, where Philip also designed an instrument to make landing approaches. On February 15, 1953, he bade the Chipmunk goodbye and transferred to the more advanced North American Harvard trainer and finally the twin-engined Oxford. Permission for these transfers had to come from no less than the Chief of Air Staff himself, and only after long consultations with the Prime Minister and Cabinet. His instructors admired the young man's spirit, but sometimes Prince Philip ignored their instructions. He flew across the country, practised aerobatics, and even flew at night, all in contravention of the restrictions set down by the government. Rumours were soon reaching Downing Street that he was even flying in helicopters, at that time still in an elementary stage of development. Churchill understood that the press, ever vigilant, were waiting to see if Philip would overreach himself, resulting in an accident. The Prince's private secretary was asked to call in at 10 Downing Street, where Churchill remonstrated with him. "Is it your intention to wipe out the royal family in the shortest possible time?" But a month before the Queen's coronation, on May 4, 1953, Prince Philip had enough hours to be awarded his RAF wings at Buckingham Palace.[75] The other members of the royal family who also learned to fly on the Chipmunk were Prince Michael, the Duke of Kent; Prince Richard; and, much later, Her Majesty's sons, Prince Charles and Prince Andrew.

The Chipmunk was a suitable successor to De Havilland's classic, their famous Tiger Moth, except that it was Canadian. Designed and produced in Downsview, Ontario, by De Havilland Canada, the Chipmunk had been adopted as the Royal Air Force's primary trainer — the first foreign aircraft to be so honoured. The first RAF units to receive them were the University Air Squadrons, shortly followed by the Reserve Flying Schools. With increased orders to meet these expanded needs, eventually totalling 735 aircraft, the Chipmunk came close to repeating the success of its celebrated predecessor. Because of the Duke of Edinburgh's flights, it had received the royal seal of approval and the Chipmunk that His Royal Highness used can today be seen at the RAF Museum at Cosford. Even when new trainers like the Scottish Aviation Bulldog entered service with the RAF in the 1960s, they did not completely replace the beloved "Chippie," and many RAF Air Experience Flights continued to operate it well into the mid-1990s.

With his wings, Philip had won this his first battle with the government and press, and established a precedent that other members of the royal family would follow. But when it was learned that he now wanted to fly a jet aircraft, the calls to check his enthusiasm began once more. After all, Philip reasoned, he had looked after himself in the Navy during the war, why should it be any different now? He ignored them and had Gordon take him up in a Gloster Meteor VIII jet fighter. When he flew one himself, Prince Philip's royal call sign, "Rainbow," gave him special attention; it alerted control towers as to who was on the airway and, to the displeasure of all other pilots, all private aircraft were grounded while he flew over. Typically, it was a precaution that the Prince himself disliked.

Prince Phillip always championed the use of aircraft for royal travel, especially helicopters. As early as 1947, the Royal Mail had been delivered from Aberdeen to Balmoral while the royal family was on holiday there by an RAF Sikorsky R-4 Hoverfly helicopter flown by Flight-Lieutenants A.J. Lee and B. Trubshaw. The latter remembered landing the Hoverfly at the cricket grounds at Balmoral, where they were met by the Court Postmaster (who was always upset at being called just Postmaster). The two pilots took their breakfast in the servants' hall until Her Majesty heard of this and was so upset that henceforth they were told to eat in the royal dining room. With the cancellation of the use of the York for the South African Royal Tour, Trubshaw, who was to fly it, was posted out of the Queen's Flight and, with Fielden's help, got a job as a test pilot at Vickers.[76]

The first operational helicopter to be developed by the Allies, the Hoverfly saw limited use in the closing months of the war in the Pacific. Although only 133 were built, as the first practical helicopter, it holds a significant place in the history of the United States Army Air Force, the Royal Air Force, and the Royal Flight. On display today at the RAF Museum, Hendon, the Hoverfly 1 was taken on strength in 1947 at the Helicopter Training School at Andover and carried the Royal Mail — but no royal passengers. But with Prince Phillip encouraging the use of helicopters for intercity travel, in September

1954, a Westland WS-51 Dragonfly, the licence-built version of the American Sikorsky S-51, was loaned to the Royal Flight by the Central Flying School. The Prince himself took a helicopter course the following year with the Royal Navy, qualifying as a pilot in 1956.

But it was Her Royal Highness Princess Margaret who was the first female member of the royal family to fly in a helicopter. In July 1954, she made a tour of the British forces in Germany, visiting six Army units, three RAF stations, and a Royal Navy centre, all in four days. The only way this was possible was to use a military helicopter — a machine that had not yet been added to the Queen's Flight. "It will be something my mother and sister haven't done," the Princess said. Unluckily, she attempted her inaugural flight in poor weather and although her helicopter made five attempts to take off before finally getting into the air, two miles from their destination, they had to turn back as the mist rolled in. "Pity!" said Margaret succinctly. "I've never had such a thrill in an aircraft before."

Although now Marshal of the Royal Air Force, a qualified jet and helicopter pilot, and patron of the British Gliding Association, Prince Philip had never experienced powerless flight. Perhaps it was the self-sufficiency of the sport that appealed to him. In May 1957, at the Bristol Gliding Club, he was taken aloft in a T42 Slingsby glider by the instructor. At two thousand feet, he took over the controls himself and learned so quickly that two months later at the gliding championships at Lasham, His Royal Highness was able to fly a Slingsby from take-off to touchdown by himself.

The first member of the royal family to be flown by helicopter out of the Buckingham Palace garden, the Duke of Edinburgh who in more than fifty years has achieved 5,986 hours in fifty-nine types of aircraft would in February 1983 even fly the twin-engined Westland W30, an enlarged version of the Lynx helicopter. His Royal Highness's final flight was on August 11, 1997, from Carlisle to Islay, following which he stopped piloting aircraft.

A replacement for the pre-war Dragon Rapide had occupied De Havilland, both in Britain and Canada, since 1944. In response, its chief engineer R.E. Bishop, designed a low-wing monoplane of all-metal construction powered by two De Havilland Gipsy Queen 400-horsepower engines. As with all De Havilland products, the Dove was a handsome design. With retractable tricycle landing gear and seating between eight and eleven passengers, it was the first British aircraft to use reversible pitch engines for better braking. It proved reliable and popular. Between 1945 and 1968, 542 Doves were built, with the RAF version called the Devon. A single Devon was taken on by the Queen's Flight to supplement the aging Vikings.

The Dragonfly helicopter would be exchanged for two S-55 Westland Whirlwind HCC-8s in 1958, although it would continue in the Flight to deliver mail to the HMY *Britannia*, the mail flights to the ship ending in August 1976. The HCC-8s were themselves replaced in 1964 with two Westland Whirlwind HCC.12s (XR486 and XR487). In 1967, Whirlwind XR487 crashed with loss of all crew, but XR486 would be retired in 1969 and is on display today at the Helicopter Museum in Weston-super-Mare on the Bristol Channel.

As for longer flights, there had been discussions of buying British-built airliners like the Airspeed Ambassador or Vickers Viscount, but the De Havilland Heron was chosen instead and, in April 1958,

Chris Hallewell, Helicopter Museum, Weston-super-Mare

Royal Squadron crest on former Queen's Flight helicopter.

the Devon and the last remaining Viking were replaced by four Herons. The DeHavilland Heron was a scaled-up version of the Devon, with four Gipsy Queen engines, longer fuselage, and accommodation for fourteen passengers. From May 1955 to September 1964, a Heron C3 was made Prince Philip's personal aircraft. That November, the Duke and Duchess of Gloucester used two Herons to tour Ethiopia, British Somaliland, and Aden. In 1960, all aircraft of The Flight were painted a fluorescent red.

As the Queen's Flight has only ever operated small aircraft that are sent ahead of a Royal Tour, a long-range airliner has always been chartered from BOAC/British Airways or loaned by the Royal Air Force. But if Her Majesty is flying to Canada, Australia, or New Zealand, she is offered an aircraft from their air forces or national airlines. With the exception of the United States, where the President has allowed her use of Air Force One, in all other countries, a Queen's Flight aircraft is always used.

But even when an aircraft from a friendly foreign air force is used, the Captain of the Queen's Flight is closely involved with the planning of the flight and always accompanies Her Majesty on it, for a royal flight is an exercise that requires the best in military, diplomatic, and personal planning. Long before Her Majesty steps off the aircraft in another country and onto the red carpet, an in-depth reconnaissance visit

The corgis go on holiday with Her Majesty and a young Prince Andrew. The Andover is in the background.

has taken place, the Royal Flight crew has been made familiar with local maps, flight guides, air traffic control, search and rescue, fire cover, fuelling facilities, and even the local catering. Should fuel be pre-positioned there for the royal aircraft? With the expected rains, heat, or sandstorms next month, will the chosen airstrips still be viable? Given the volatility of the area, would bottled water, airport security, or decent hotel rooms still be available? Are the spares for the Andovers' Rolls-Royce Dart engines packed and the crew's visa applications processed? Are there enough U.S. dollars and American Express cards for wherever the Royal Flight is bound (for the royal crest on the aircraft carries no weight in most of the Third World)? Then there is the political aspect. The Queen's Flight is registered as a military aircraft and diplomatic clearances have to be obtained from all countries that they overfly, refuel, and land at. Everyone involved in such an operation is aware that royalty has to be flown safely and (given the usual exhausting program ahead) in as much comfort as possible — and on exact time. Commercial aircraft can be late or diverted, and their passengers can disembark rumpled, jet-lagged, tired, and sulky but never the Royal Flight or its passengers.

To take a single example: in 1985, when Princess Anne, as president of Save the Children Fund, travelled to Africa, the Queen's Flight Andover had to land in areas of the continent that even the local pilots refused to. To meet the welcoming party of the host nation exactly where and when they were supposed to, her pilots had to taxi the Andover precisely to where the red carpet ended or the line of dignitaries began, so that Her Royal Highness could emerge, pristine, relaxed, and well-briefed. Once the royal passenger was off and away, the crew's work, no matter the local environment or temperature, continued — for the aircraft had to be refuelled, checked over mechanically, cleaned, and prepared for the next leg.

Contrary to accusations in the media, because every flight is planned far in advance, short-notice flights are rare, and the

Royal Flight is never used as a taxi service to play golf or go shopping. With all the special engineering rules, clearances, and time-consuming checks that have to be made on the aircraft, it was never possible for a member of the royal family to show up at the airport and ask for an aircraft at short notice. And over the years, the Royal Flight has been a photographer's dream — if only because, within Britain, Her Majesty's corgis also flew to Balmoral and photos of a member of the household escorting them off an aircraft was sure to sell newspapers.

MOD photo

In 1964, the Hakwer Siddeley Andover (in foreground) replaced the De Havilland Heron.

Her Majesty and other members of the royal family have flown in British Airways Concordes and Boeing 747s, but if any one aircraft would become fixed in the public's mind as the Royal Aeroplane it was the humble Andover. A short/medium-range turboprop airliner, the Hawker Siddeley 748 (called Andovers in the RAF) first flew on June 24, 1960. The low-wing monoplane is powered by two Rolls-Royce Dart engines and, aimed at the regional market, is designed to accommodate between forty and fifty-eight passengers in paired seats along a central gangway with galley and toilet aft. Its range with maximum payload (and reserves for 230 miles) is, on an average, 1,000 miles. In July 1964, two Andover CC Mk 2s were modified for use in Her Majesty's Flight, and both XS789 and XS790 would see more than twenty-five years of service, either pre-positioned for a tour or flown directly. As the first royal aircraft to have a proper galley on board, with a small grille, a hotplate, and a boiler, it allowed the stewards to (somehow) prepare meals of several courses for the passengers. The Andovers would first be used for a state visit in February 1965 to Africa, with one carrying the Duke of Edinburgh onward to a tour to Saudi Arabia, India, Nepal, Singapore, and Borneo. Princess Margaret would tour Uganda and later the United States in one of the Andovers in March 1965, with the Duke of Edinburgh doing the same in Canada and the United States the following year with the other. Throughout the next two decades, the Andovers would carry members of the royal family to South America, Austria, the Pacific, Canada, Cambodia, Thailand, Iran, Swaziland, and Nepal. The Queen and the Duke of Edinburgh would fly in an Andover in February 1974 on a tour of Papua New Guinea, the Solomon Islands, Indonesia, and later in the year to Canada and the United States, while Princess Alexandra would use one on a visit to Poland and Berlin. In July 1977, both Andovers took the royal family to RAF Finningley for the Queen's Review of the Royal Air Force. By May 1983, the Andovers had completed ten thousand hours each and the government was considering replacing them with a small jet airliner, the BAE 146. The busiest year for them would be 1984, when they would carry members of the royal family to the far corners of the world.

In 1959, when Her Majesty and the Duke of Edinburgh visited Newfoundland, they flew into Gander on June 19 in a BOAC Comet 4B, for, as with the Concorde, flying the new Comet was good advertising for British-built aircraft. But while the British government was to entrust the monarch's safety to a non-national aircraft, air force, or airline, such has not been the case for the lesser royals. Princess Margaret, for example, had flown on Trans-Canada Airlines in 1955 from Toronto to Victoria and back.[77] The Queen

BAe 146 of 32 (The Royal) Squadron. The 146 was the first jet aircraft to be operated by the Royal Flight.

MOD photo

Mother had flown to Australia on Qantas in 1958 and, to the embarrassment of the Australians, the airliner had broken down on the tour.

Perhaps because of this it took the British government a few years before they consented to allow a foreign commercial airline to transport royalty again. As a result, in 1962, the employees of Trans-Canada Airlines were delighted to hear that Her Majesty the Queen Mother would be taking a scheduled TCA flight (Flight 857) from London to Montreal, where she would present the colours to the Black Watch Regiment of which she was Colonel-in-Chief. The royal passenger was just what the airline's employees needed: the previous year, TCA had suffered the largest deficit in its history, and that June the Conservatives had been re-elected and were promising to give rival Canadian Pacific Airlines more transcontinental routes. Besides, most TCA employees were of the pre-war generation who had cheered Her Majesty in 1939 and held her in deep affection. The airline's president Gordon McGregor (one of "the few" during the Battle of Britain), had been presented to the King and Queen when they visited his squadron during the Battle, and had been decorated by His Majesty at Buckingham Palace.

Mindful of the Qantas disaster, the airline ensured that their latest aircraft, a brand new DC-8, would be used for Flight 857. On June 7, at Heathrow Airport, Canadian High Commissioner George Drew escorted Her Majesty to the TCA DC-8 (not wanting to take a chance, TCA had a second DC-8 in readiness in the hangar) and for the first time in the airline's history, the Royal Standard fluttered from a cockpit window of one of its aircraft. The DC-8 took off at 2:45 p.m., with arrival at Montreal's Dorval Airport expected for 5:00 p.m. local time. At Dorval, the airline had been in two days of frenzied preparations, with the base freshly painted, the Black Watch regiment practising march-pasts, and airline staff rehearsing their curtsies and bows. Stewardess Joyce Potruff got to play Her Majesty for two days, even reviewing the Black Watch ranks. The only member of the airline missing was McGregor himself who, as chairman of the International Air Transport Association that year, had to preside over their convention then being held at St. Jovite in the Laurentians, north of Montreal.

Author's photo

On October 13, 1964, Her Majesty took an Air Canada DC-8 from Ottawa to London — it was tha first for both the Queen and the airline.

On board the TCA flight, the Queen Mother and her retinue naturally occupied all of first class, and the passengers in economy were elated to hear that Queen Elizabeth the Queen Mother was sitting ahead of them. They were thus agog when, in mid-flight, she suddenly appeared from behind the curtain. Curious to see what economy class looked like, and typically ready for a walkabout, Her Majesty came down the aisle and chatted with the mainly speechless passengers. Encountering a crying baby among them, the Queen Mother leaned down to speak to its mother, as she had done many times on the 1939 Royal Tour, and even gave the baby a gentle poke in its ribs. The baby stopped crying but grabbed the royal digit and then wouldn't let go. The Queen Mother was put in the quandary of either continuing the remainder of the flight in this position or removing the finger, subjecting the aircraft to the baby's screams. In the end she chose the latter.

At St. Jovite's tiny airport, at 3:30 p.m. a car driven by Gordon McGregor pulled up before a waiting Cessna 310. The TCA president got out wearing a morning suit and squeezed into the Cessna's cockpit and the aircraft took off for Dorval Airport. The president landed at Dorval just as Prime Minister Diefenbaker and Governor General and Mrs. Georges Vanier arrived to take their places. McGregor quickly joined them beside the red carpet and noted three very small white rectangles painted on the apron in front of the mobile stairs. "At four minutes to five, the tenth or fifteenth quick look over my shoulder revealed a DC-8 low on approach to Runway 24L. Precisely on the hour, the aircraft stopped at the edge of the carpet, the mobile stairs squarely lined up with the First Class door," he later wrote. "Later examination determined that no part of the main undercarriage bogies or the nose wheel overflowed any part of the small painted rectangles. It was a 3,000 mile shot which had precisely hit the bullseye, both as to time and place."[78]

McGregor's airline was soon to change its name to Air Canada, an initiative sponsored by a young MP called Jean Chrétien, and this too had a royal connection. On October 5, 1964, Her Majesty Queen Elizabeth attended the Centennial commemoration of the Charlottetown Conference. She was flown home from Ottawa on October 13 in an Air Canada DC-8, the first time flying as Queen in a non-national airline. But what elicited media attention was not only her visit. Although Trans-Canada Airlines would not legally become Air Canada until January 1, 1965, the aircraft sported the new name and colours.

Although the Queen and Prince Philip arrived in Canada to celebrate the country's centenary in July 1967 on the royal yacht, because of the pace of the tour, an Andover piloted by Air Commodore John Blount DFC the Captain of the Queen's Flight was flown over, via Iceland.[79] At the tour's conclusion when they left Ottawa on July 5, a chartered BOAC Super VC-10 was used. The VC-10 had been modified with the addition of two sleeping berths. Presumably, wrote the *Globe and Mail* reporter, the remainder of the royal party were going to sit up all the way home. It had been a triumphant centennial visit and the royal couple arrived at the airport directly from a dinner at Government House. To the fascination of the crowd of onlookers at Ottawa Airport, Her Majesty exited the limousine that night wearing a white gown with a wide band of gold brocade at the hem, an ermine stole, and a tiara. Prince Philip was in a dinner jacket with his tie crooked. Her Majesty was escorted along the red carpet to the waiting aircraft by Governor General Roland Michener, Prince Philip followed with Mrs. Michener, and they were followed by Prime Minister Lester Pearson and Mrs. Pearson. The group

The Vickers VC-10, long-range RAF transport sometimes used by the royal family.

Prince Charles arrives in Ottawa on a RAF VC-10 on his way to Texas, February 17, 1986.

chatted at the bottom of the aircraft stairs, and the *Globe and Mail* noted that the Queen laughed heartily "as in the way of one who has had a thoroughly enjoyable evening." When interviewed, New Zealander Captain Ronald Hartley, who commanded the BOAC flight, said he was going to take the aircraft up to 33,000 feet immediately. About 200 miles east of Gander he expected to pick up a 60-knot tailwind and then fly at 37,000 feet the rest of the way to Heathrow. The 5,000-mile flight he thought would take a little more than six hours. At exactly 11:14 p.m., the doors of the royal jet closed and the aircraft pulled out for takeoff. The trip was Elizabeth's fourth as Queen of Canada and the only one that she would make during the Centennial year. Prince Philip would return twice more that year to officiate at the Pan American Games in Winnipeg and the Royal Winter Fair ceremonies in Toronto.

Like his father, Prince Charles, the Prince of Wales, would also learn to fly on a DeHavilland Chipmunk, and in July 1968, the little aircraft was returned to the Flight. On January 14, 1969, His Royal Highness would make his first solo flight from Bassingbourn airfield. While at Cambridge, Prince Charles would continue his air experience, completing it on February 6, 1970, in a twin-engined Beagle Basset, the aircraft to be retained by the Flight to train the Duke of Kent. Given permission by the Prime Minister to qualify as a jet pilot, the Prince took a four-month course at the Royal Air Force School at Cranwell before he entered the Royal Naval College at Dartmouth in the autumn. He landed at Cranwell on March 8, 1971, at the controls of the Basset, where, after a fortnight of ground school, he was taken up in a BAC Jet Provost. The college itself was honoured that Prince Charles had joined, and there was the hope that he might make the RAF his career. As with the Queen's Flight, with the heir to the throne on campus, all the security precautions came into effect. His instructor was Squadron Leader Richard Johns (later to be Air Marshal) and two aircraft were assigned to the Prince, both under continuous guard and scrupulously maintained. As his father had similarly experienced, and to His Royal Highness's impatience, no flying exercise involving him, however mundane, was possible without permission from the Secretary of State for Defence.

After one hundred hours on the Provost, His Royal Highness soloed on March 31, and on August 20, 1971, he was awarded his RAF Wings at Cranwell, where his grandfather had taken his first flight in 1918. Then he was, in his own words, "let loose in my own jet" and, like his father, even went on to surreptitiously perform aerobatics. Poor at navigation, the Prince later wrote that he was amazed he had made a cross-country flight by himself and found his way back. Prince Charles left the RAF and Cranwell after five months with some regret. In contrast with his Cambridge years, this was the first time he had been in the company of military men, and he felt completely at home boarding at Cranwell. But his father, Prince Philip, who had lost his own career in the Navy, was keen that his eldest join the Senior Service.

At Dartmouth he was refused permission to fly the tiny college Wasp helicopter, and after entering the Navy, the only connection he would have with aviation was in 1974 when he qualified as a helicopter pilot. He joined 845 Naval Air Squadron, which operated from the Commando carrier HMS *Hermes*. On the carrier, two Wessex 5 helicopters were reserved for the Prince and maintained to the exacting standards of the Queen's Flight. This made flying as crew with His Royal Highness very popular. Other pilots judged

MOD photo

Like his father, HRH Prince Charles also learned to fly on a De Havilland Chipmunk. On January 14, 1969, he flew solo.

him competent, and he flew instinctively and with skill. On his return home, Prince Charles even took up hot-air ballooning and the media began calling him "Action Man."

Other members of the royal family also took to aviation. Prince Andrew joined the Royal Navy in 1979 and after graduating from the Royal Naval College, Dartmouth, he went on to elementary flying training at RAF Leeming, Yorkshire, later learning to fly the Gazelle helicopter at Royal Naval Air Station Culdrose, Cornwall. After conversion to the Sea King helicopter, he joined 820 Naval Air Squadron (NAS) on the aircraft carrier HMS *Invincible*. In 1982, Prince Andrew sailed with his squadron on HMS *Invincible* to the South Atlantic as part of the Task Force that was despatched to regain the Falkland Islands. Throughout the conflict, he flew Sea Kings on various missions, including Anti-Submarine Warfare (ASW), casualty evacuation, and Search and Air Rescue (SAR), the first member of the royal family to be in a battle zone since his grandfather had served at Jutland. The Prince was subsequently appointed to 703 NAS at Portland for conversion to the Lynx helicopter and, on completion in May 1984, served on HMS *Brazen* as the Flight Pilot.[80]

That October, the next generation of royals would take to flying, with Prince William — albeit as a passenger — making his first helicopter flight. The Duchess of York began her pilot's training in a Piper Warrior G-BLVL, flying solo in November 1986, becoming the first female member of the royal family to gain her Private Pilot's Licence.

In July 1966, like BOAC, the RAF acquired the Vickers Corporation VC-10 airliner. Initially a long-range troop and freight transport based at RAF Benson, with the retirement of the Victor tankers in the early and mid 1970s, the VC-10 would begin a dual role of transport and air-to-air tanker aircraft for the next three decades. Although an old design, the VC-10 is equipped with a modern flight-management navigation system and avionics to allow worldwide operations. The crew comprises two pilots, flight engineer, navigator, and an air-load master. Up to three air stewards are carried, depending on the number of passengers on board. Today, the bulk of the RAF's air-to-air refuelling fleet of VC-10 K3 and K4 aircraft are flown by No. 101 Squadron based at RAF Brize Norton. In the transportation role, it accommodates 150 passengers, freight, and also has an aero-medical evacuation capability and as it has done since the 1970s, continues to be used for Royal Tours.

It was an RAF VC-10 that brought the Duke of Windsor's body home to England from Paris on May 31, 1972. The founder of the King's Flight and the first member of the royal family to fly, in death the former King received all the pomp and circumstance that he had given up in life. The VC-10 landed at RAF Benson (then home of the Queen's Flight) and was met by a Royal Guard of Honour, the Duke and Duchess of Kent, and the French Ambassador. As the coffin was taken from the aircraft to the station's chapel, the guard of honour from The Queen's Colour Squadron of the RAF presented arms and the Central Band played the first six bars of the national anthem. The Duchess of Windsor did not accompany His Royal Highness's body as she was said to be unwell. The coffin lay overnight in the station chapel and officers of the RAF kept a vigil. On the following morning it was taken by road to Frogmore House, where today both the Duke and Duchess are interred. The Duchess arrived by the Queen's Flight at Heathrow two days later and was met by Admiral of the Fleet Earl Mountbatten of Burma.[81]

In 1982, the Royal Flight (its motto is *Adeste Comites*, or "Rally round, comrades") received the first of its Hawker Siddeley 125 executive jets. The British Aerospace 125 CC3 is a swept, low-wing monoplane, with twin engines mounted on its rear fuselage. It can maintain a cruising speed of between 415 and 485 miles per hour at an altitude of up to 41,000 feet over a range of 2,000 miles. It can carry up to seven passengers, is crewed by two pilots, and carries a steward/stewardess. The first versions of this VIP aircraft were built by the former Hawker Siddeley Company and known as HS125 CC1s. They were delivered to the RAF between April 1971 and 1972, and two improved aircraft CC2s followed in April 1973. Six more BAe 125 CC3s joined No 32 Squadron in 1982-83, and it is these aircraft that remain in service today, the CC1s and CC2s having been retired during the 1990s.

For longer flights, the BAe 146 was selected. A four-turbo-fan short-range regional/feeder airliner with a distinctive cantilever high wing, the BAe 146 Whisper jet had its beginnings in 1973 as a Hawker Siddeley design. In 1978, British Aerospace, having taken over several of the local aviation companies like Hawker Siddeley, committed itself to building it. To keep all the aircraft firms in business and decrease the financial risk, aircraft production was allocated to several BAe plants: Hatfield built the forward fuselage and was responsible for final assembly, Brough the fin, Filton the central fuselage, Manchester the rear fuselage, and Prestwick the engine pylons. Participation also

MOD photo

Two BAe 125s with BAe 146 of 32 (The Royal) Squadron.

stretched overseas, as Saab Scania (Sweden) made the tail planes and Avco (United States) the turbofan engines and wing boxes. The first four-engined jet airliner to be built in Britain since the VC-10, the BAe 146 Whisper jet flew on September 3, 1981. It came in two series: the 100, with a seating capacity of between seventy-one and ninety-three passengers and designed to operate from short, rough airstrips, and the 200, for operation from paved runways, with seating capacity for eighty-two to one hundred and nine passengers. Among its first customers was the Ministry of Defence (MOD), which ordered two Series 100 for the Royal Flight, with an option to purchase two more. In April 1986, the first BAe 146 CC Mk 2 ZE701 was handed over, arriving just in time to celebrate the fiftieth anniversary of the Royal Flight. Though they were flown around the world, perhaps the strangest flight that the Royal BAe146s ever took part in was in October 1994, when Her Majesty became the first British monarch to visit Russia. As her BAe 146 entered Russian airspace, it was escorted by a formation of five businesslike SU 27 fighters that kept with it until it landed at Moscow.

In June 2002, His Royal Highness Prince Andrew, who flew Sea Kings in the Falklands conflict, flew himself to the Helicopter Museum.

Helicopters would continue to play an important part in the Royal Flight. During the 1960s, gas-turbine-powered Whirlwind HAR10 and HC10 helicopters became the backbone of the RAF's search-and-rescue and tactical transport helicopter force. Their new turboshaft engines were lighter and more powerful than the piston engine they superseded and offered improved performance and reliability. Sixty-eight new air-sea rescue HAR10 and transport HC10s were manufactured by Westland and a number of Whirlwind HAR2 and HAR4 piston-engined helicopters were subsequently re-engined. The royal Dragonfly helicopters had been replaced with two S-55 Westland Whirlwind HCC-8s in 1958, although the Dragonfly would continue in the Flight to deliver mail to the Royal Yacht *Britannia*. In turn, the HCC-8s were replaced in 1964 with two Whirlwind HCC.12s (XR486 and XR487). In September 1966, in Whirlwind XR486, the Queen Mother would make her first helicopter flight (to an aircraft carrier at sea!) but her more cautious daughter, the Queen — who has always disliked this means of travel — waited until August 1977 to make her first helicopter flight. In 1967, Whirlwind XR487 crashed with loss of all crew, but XR486 would survive to retire in 1969, and is today also on display at the Helicopter Museum, Weston-super-Mare.

The Wessex was a turbine-powered development by Westland of the American Sikorsky S-58. The initial production version was for the Royal Navy, but in the early 1960s the RAF required a powerful general-purpose helicopter capable of troop-motor-carrying, air-ambulance, and ground-attack roles. Westland responded with the Wessex HC2, which first entered RAF service in January 1964. Four years later Westland Helicopters received an order for two Wessex aircraft to equip the Queen's Flight. Designated

HCC4, they were built to HC2 standards but with the main cabin in a VIP interior finish, furnishings, and soundproofing, plus an external folding step below the cabin door. Additional Decca navigation equipment was also installed on the flight deck. The first flight took place on March 17, 1969, with the first official flight on July 1, 1969, in support of the Investiture of the Prince of Wales at Caernarvon Castle, Wales. In their distinctive red-and-dark-blue paint scheme, the two Wessex helicopters were an institution at RAF Benson for, like the Andover, the Wessex was to be the workhorse of the Royal Flight as it was of the British military.

Chris Hallewell, Helicopter Museum, Weston-super-Mare

Wessex — former Queen's Flight helicopter.

Whirlwind — former Queen's Flight helicopter.

PL-113527

RCAF helicopter lands at Cartier Park, Ottawa, to take Princess Margaret to Harrington Lake, 1958.

Built at Yeovil and nicknamed the "Junglies" because of the dark green camouflage used, the Wessex helicopters flew commandos, Special Air Services, and forward troops off carriers and assault ships, lifting off from hemmed-in Sek Kong airfield in Hong Kong, from North Sea oil rigs, and in search-and-rescue roles. Characterized by the large intake grille, the Wessex was powered by two Rolls-Royce Gnome turbo shaft engines in the nose, the engines exhausting through a large duct on the starboard side of the aircraft. Although they were fitted for two pilots, the standard operating procedure for all RAF Wessexes was one pilot, except in Northern Ireland and the Queen's Flight. The original design for the S-51 was for shipboard operations, and as a result the main landing wheels were heavily stressed, making it ideal for tactical as well as royal transport, which sets down in terrain not usually used by helicopters. By March 1983, the two royal Wessex helicopters had completed 10,000 hours, and in July alone one flew 135.5 hours. Today, XV732 is on display at the RAF Museum, Hendon and XV733 at the Helicopter Museum joining the Whirlwind that it replaced, delivered there by the Royal Navy on November 15, 2001. The two Queen's Flight Wessex helicopters were rarely used by Her Majesty and more by the younger royals, although the Queen flew in XV733 during tours of Northern Ireland in 1991 and 1993.

For the royal family to take a helicopter flight involved much preparation. Nothing was left to chance or done spontaneously. Once the itinerary was agreed upon, the royal household contacted the secretary to the Queen's Flight as far in advance as possible and a proving flight was carried out. Local authorities where the royal passenger was to land — the Lord Lieutenant's office of the local county, the police, and the organizers of the event — were briefed. The police would identify the best site for a landing and the crew would carry out a proving flight to it, checking its size, surface, approach, and departure flight paths. Once there, the Flight's crew would meet with all interested parties, discussing the arrival and departure times, security, crowd control, car-park access, and medical coverage. The event's organizers had to be reassured that the helicopter would arrive on time or as close as possible and that, if it was late, to not to panic. An integral if lesser-known part of the Queen's Flight was the helicopter support crew with their HSVs (helicopter support vehicles) pre-positioned at the landing site and at potential landing sites along the way. Besides ensuring that the mandatory fire engine and ambulance were in place, this team ensured that fuel was on hand for the return trip and jerry cans of aviation fuel were brought along. Was the landing ground firm enough? Would the rubber matting and the canvas marker "H" be needed? If it was a night operation, a complete lighting system had be carried and installed. The HSVs arrived with everything from spare parts (and even a whole engine-change unit for the helicopter) to a water-boiling unit to fill the helicopter crew's vacuum flasks.

Even without the royal visitor, helicopters descending in the neighbourhood are magnets for crowds of local children, and in their distinctive livery, more so those in the colours of the Queen's Flight. For the advance crew, crowd control would always be a problem. It had to be repeated to the local organizers that six tonnes of helicopter downdraft would lift all the freshly cut grass, clouds of dust, and everyone's hats — and skirts. The selection of a royal flight route was not as simple as it might be: as helicopters fly at low altitude, the worst weather conditions were always assumed, and a route was sought that would avoid high ground, tall buildings, and low hydro wires. This sometimes meant weaving through twisting valleys and over populated areas. Airports on the way were also to be avoided, so that their activities would not be jeopardized by a royal flight. The Queen's Flight had no control over the weather on the day itself, so IFR (Instrument Flight Rules) were always assumed, with the possibility of let-downs to airfields en route if the weather was socked in. Then the royal passenger could continue the journey by car or train—both modes of transport that were kept ready for such an event. Royal helicopter flights also rarely started and finished at airfields, as the pick-up points were mainly in central London or at one of the royal residences. This meant that, since the crew had to maintain visual contact with the ground on the final stages of the flight, fog, very low cloud, or icing could cancel a flight. It took three crews to operate the two helicopters, and as both Prince Philip and Prince Charles were qualified pilots, when they flew the Wessex, each had personal pilots allocated to them. Since Her Majesty dislikes helicopters, she will only do so when security is thought to be a problem, as in her trip to Northern Ireland in 1977 or to commemorate the D-Day landings at Normandy in June 1984. But no one enjoyed the Wessex's capabilities more than Her Royal Highness Diana the Princess of Wales. With her crowded engagement calendar, she appreciated their speed and convenience.

Chris Hallewell, Helicopter Museum, Weston-super-Mare

Seating within a royal helicopter.

Their Royal Highnesses Prince Charles and Princess Diana depart on Canadian Forces CC-137.

MOD photo

The Queen Mother departs on Canadian Forces 707 after 120th running of the Queen's Plate.

SWC79-1395

In 1995, when the Queen's Flight was combined with No. 32 Squadron at RAF Northolt, the two Wessex helicopters had been in service for thirty years. They were replaced on April 1, 1998, by a single, privately leased Sikorsky S-76. After her last flight aboard a Wessex, the Queen wrote a personal note of thanks to the crew.

With the retirement of its Yukons in 1971, the Canadian Forces chose the Boeing 707 for its long-range transport role. First flown on July 15, 1954, this airliner changed commercial aviation. The 707 was operated by almost every major airline in the world (except Air Canada and Canadian Pacific Airlines) as their first jet transport. In Canada, it was flown by the second-tier airlines like Wardair, Quebecair, and Pacific Western Airlines — and the Canadian Forces, who purchased five Boeing 707s (13701—13705), the first three delivered to 437 Husky Squadron at Trenton, Ontario, on April 10, 1970. Designated in the Canadian Forces as CC-137, these were configured to carry either 172 passengers, cargo, or a combination of both. The military made heavy use out of the CC-137s since, besides twice weekly scheduled flights between Comox, British Columbia, and Shearwater, Nova Scotia, and on across the Atlantic to the Canadian Forces base at Lahr, Germany, the airliners were also used for VIP transport, taking Prime Minister Pierre Trudeau on a historic trip to China in 1973 and bringing the Pope to Canada in 1984. It came in two VIP configurations: either a specially fitted stateroom for Heads of State that seated eight in luxury with 115 seats aft or a "mini-capsule" for senior officials that accommodated six passengers with 155 high-density seats. Beginning in 1993, the CC-137s were gradually retired, with the last two maintained in an air-refuelling configuration until 1997. "I have been a transport pilot since my graduation from flying training in 1969, when I chose to fly the 'heavies,'" remembers Canadian Forces Major Al Mornan. He continues:

My first royal trip was flying Lord Mountbatten in the Cosmopolitan Convair 580 during his visit to the Montreal area in March 1976. I flew Her Majesty the Queen and Prince Phillip in the same aircraft around the Montreal area during the '76 Olympics.

But my most memorable royal was Her Majesty, the Queen Mum when I had the privilege of flying her on the CC-137 from London Heathrow to Ottawa and back in June 1987. She was most gracious and actually took the time to invite each of the pilots into her stateroom for a private audience, where she showed genuine interest in hearing about our personal lives. I couldn't believe that it was happening to me and I was caught somewhat unprepared, to say the least. My moment of glory was somewhat subdued, as my mind was, believe it or not, preoccupied with what was going on in the cockpit during my absence. The other pilot was very senior and, by the very nature of his job, didn't fly as much as the line pilots, and we were at a particularly busy and demanding phase of our flight. We were just beginning descent into the horrifically busy airspace in the London area, and I had to leave him alone up there when I was summoned to have a chat with Her Majesty! You can imagine how that went. I can hardly remember the conversation but found myself trying to find an excuse to leave and get back to the flight deck.

IXC87-166

Her Majesty Queen Elizabeth arrives on a Canadian Forces 707, 1987.

Through the 1970s, former bush pilot Max Ward pioneered charter flights in Canada, and by 1987, he had parlayed Wardair into becoming Canada's third-largest airline That year, responding to what promised to be limitless traffic growth, as Air Canada and Canadian Airlines purchased fleets of Boeing 767s and Airbus A320s-200s, Ward decided to reform his airline into a scheduled carrier. He sold off his giant 747s for aircraft that were more adaptable to a domestic/cross-border market and ordered twelve A-310 Airbuses at a bargain price of $42 million each. But with Air Canada and Canadian Airlines controlling 90 percent of the domestic market, Ward discovered few passengers were going to connect on an airline that had no local carrier. Losing $1 million a day, he was soon $700 million in debt and forced to sell Wardair to Canadian Airlines. They needed the routes, but not the extra aircraft (or employees) and soon in financial trouble themselves, were considering a proposed merger with AMR, the giant parent company of American Airlines. State-owned Air Canada appealed to the federal government for help. In response, Marcel Masse, the Minister of National Defence, suggested that, if Canadian Airlines could break off the merger discussions, his department would take off its hands the former Wardair A-310s. The merger talks ended (temporarily) and on August 25, 1992, DND bought three of the A-310s for $150 million, with two more later.

Modified to military standards, renamed Polaris, and designated CC-150, the five-plane fleet's primary role was long-range transport of military personnel and equipment, carrying up to 194 passengers or 32,000 kg of cargo. Now equipped with a large cargo door plus a strengthened floor and fuselage, four of the aircraft were configured in the combination role of both passenger and freight carriers. But one later Polaris (CC150-001) was permanently configured for VIP transportation duties, costing the

One of 437 Squadron's five hard-working CC-137 Boeing 707s, royal transport from 1970 to 1997.

Canadian taxpayer $ 53 million to purchase and an additional $35 million to outfit for a VIP role, with a conference room and shower the size of a phone booth installed. The executive suite had a bedroom, living room, and office space, which included a satellite telephone, computer workstations, and a small refrigerator. As the Conservatives under Prime Minister Brian Mulroney were in power, the press nicknamed it "Air Force 1," and it was derided by Opposition leader Jean Chrétien as the "flying Taj Mahal." Those who have been on board 001 claim that it is no more luxurious than a good motor home but, sensitive to criticism, Mulroney never flew in it, and when he became prime minister, Chrétien refused to come near the "flying Taj Mahal" and tried to sell it off. Prospective buyers that were approached like the Toronto Blue Jays and stars like Madonna and Kenny Rogers did not think it luxurious enough, the media comparing the aircraft's wood veneer panelling decor to that of a finished basement or a low-cost mobile home.[82] Tacky or not, 001 was ideal for transporting foreign dignitaries, including members of the royal family, to and from Canada and taking the Governor General around the world.

When Her Majesty the Queen and His Royal Highness the Duke of Edinburgh visited Canada in 1987, this historic visit began on October 4 with Her Majesty's arrival in Iqaluit and continue with stops in Victoria, Vancouver, Winnipeg, Toronto, Fredericton, Moncton, and ending in Ottawa from where she returned home on October 15. The responsibility for the royal couple's travel to Canada and between each of the cities fell to the Huskies of 437 Squadron and its VIP Polaris. As the Commanding Officer of 437 Squadron, Lieutenant Colonel D.C. Murphy was assigned as Mission Commander for the Royal Flight; a duty he considers to be one of the highlights of his military and flying career. He wrote:

> 437 Squadron has provided airlift for many very important persons throughout its long history but the privilege of flying Her Majesty Queen Elizabeth is considered by us to be the greatest of honours bestowed this squadron. Her Majesty's presence affects all crew members on board the Royal Flight. I met Her Majesty on her arrival at the aircraft at London's Heathrow airport during the morning hours of 14 October. Ever gracious, she immediately offered her hand to greet me once I was officially introduced by Group Captain Tim Hewlett, RAF (Ret'd), the officer in charge of royal travel at Buckingham Palace. Accompanied by His Royal Highness the Duke of Edinburgh, I led Her Majesty to the special VIP compartment on board aircraft 001 to show her some of the features of the suite. VIP flying is relatively straightforward with the focus primarily on two areas — comfort and punctuality. The absence of clear air turbulence on every leg of the twelve-day visit satisfied the first requirement, the experience of the Aircraft Commander, Major Carl Kap, and the First Officer, Captain Steve Rundle, easily satisfied the second. Comfort of our passengers cannot be expressed solely in terms of the turbulence encountered at altitude. The cabin crew led by Master Warrant Officer Claude Bolduc did an outstanding job of catering to the comfort of the royal couple and members of the entourage.

DND photo

437 "Husky" Squadron crest, Trenton, Ontario.

Buckingham Palace vets all menus on tour. Her Majesty does not like heavy meals or exotic foods while flying.

On board a VIP Polaris: the decor and standard of service provided far exceed that expected from first-class travel with any airline.

The standard of service provided far exceeded that expected from first-class travel with any airline. Other than the two very short flights in British Columbia and New Brunswick, meals with several courses were prepared and served to Her Majesty and all passengers. Whether a Cabinet Minister in the Canadian delegation or a passenger of noble birth in the Queen's party, those standing in the aisles during the serving of meals stood a serious chance of being unceremoniously cast aside if caught in the path of a sprinting flight attendant given forty minutes to serve sixty meals accompanied by a full beverage service. Those members of the crew looking after the care and comfort of the Royal entourage worked tirelessly and never let their good humour and charm fade in the face of fatigue. Of particular note are, Leading Seaman Al Brown, Leading Seaman Denis Gautreau, and Corporal Angie Wilson, who were assigned to the Royal suite at the front of the aircraft and focused solely on the needs of the royal couple. Judging by the comments by both the Queen and the Duke as they left the aircraft in London, they were highly impressed.

The paying of compliments at the embarkation and disembarkation of VIPs is how a Mission Commander is best remembered after flights such as these. This is due primarily to the media coverage of both the VIPs' arrival and departure. Having been proudly at my post at the top of the aircraft stairs for each arrival/departure of Her Majesty at/from the aircraft, I managed to perfect my salute for Her Majesty and the

CBC. However, once the door to the aircraft was closed on that last departure from Ottawa on October 15, I was delighted to learn that the crispness of my salute was to be recognized by an invitation to lunch on board the aircraft with Her Majesty, the Duke, and five other selected guests. I was honoured to receive an invitation to dine with the Queen and shall never forget the protocols adhered to nor the intimacy of the meal shared with the Queen and the Duke in the limited confines of the Polaris at 35,000 feet over Newfoundland. The meal served by the front flight stewards was superb and the conversation with the Queen promises to be a lasting memory. Later, approaching London on that final leg of the royal flight, I was called to the VIP suite for a private audience with Her Majesty and His Royal Highness. The Queen, ever gracious with that warm smile, thanked the squadron for supporting their visit to Canada. After a short conversation, Her Majesty and His Royal Highness signed the 437 Squadron Book of Honour, taking time to look through each page bearing their own earlier signatures, their children's, and those of several other VIPs that we have flown over the years.

The final leg of their journey was as comfortable and punctual as the first, with the aircraft touching down on time, late in the evening of 15 October. As they slipped into their limousine for the short drive to Windsor Castle, I could not help but think how fortunate we all were to have been part of such a historic visit to Canada.

DND photo

The Canadian equivalent of the Queen's Flight.

For 437 Transport Squadron, from towing gliders filled with troops over the bloodbath of Arnhem to looking after the royal family on a VIP flight was a long stretch, but it justified their motto *Omnia Passim* ("Anything, anywhere"). The Canadian equivalent to the Queen's Flight, the Husky Squadron is so named because it adopted as its badge a husky's head, indicative of its function of towing the gliders during the war. On June 16, 1946, 437 Squadron had been disbanded at Odiham, England, and was not reformed until October 1, 1961, at RCAF Station Trenton, where it remains today. Flying royalty requires a cadre of specially trained squadron personnel, and flight attendants are selected from across the Canadian Forces and from any number of professions. They are all volunteers who have undergone an intensive training period. They serve in the air for two years and may be extended for a third. "We need people who can think on their feet," said the squadron's flight-attendant leader. "There are often media on the flights, and you have to be able to field questions politely while guarding the privacy of your passengers. We also have to be extra alert, and we work with airport security officers, military police, checking baggage, and everything that comes aboard, even flowers."

DND photo

The CC-150 Polaris symbolizes the 437 Squadron motto.

Major Al Mornan's favourite flight on the Polaris was with the Earl and Countess of Wessex, Edward and Sophie.

I had the honour of being their personal pilot on the Polaris for the entire visit to Canada in July, 2000. We picked them up at Heathrow and flew them to Charlottetown, Montreal, Halifax, and St John's, before returning them home to London. I think that they enjoyed their trip immensely. During many VIP missions, someone in my position certainly has the opportunity to see many sides of individual personalities, and these two certainly showed their ability to put on the show and then turn into human beings when they disappeared inside the sanctuary of their own aircraft. They would put you at ease and you couldn't help but feel like you could chat about anything just like you would with long-lost best friends at a reunion. I even invited them to join the crew for a beer at the Legion![83]

The Queen pays an official visit to RAF Northolt in May 1997, as her father and grandfather did.

In 1993, the Queen's Flight must have been looking around for support. That year, the three BAe 146s and the two Wessex helicopters had cost the Ministry of Defence £12.43 million to operate, and the government was determined to reduce this. As part of the cost-cutting measures imposed on his department by the Treasury, on June 23, 1994, the Secretary of State for Defence, Malcolm Rifkind announced that the Queen's Flight was to be moved from RAF Benson to RAF Northolt and amalgamated with No. 32 Squadron to become No. 32 (The Royal) Squadron. He also announced that Her Majesty had volunteered to reimburse the government for private use of the aircraft. The disbandment of the Queen's Flight took place on April 1, 1995, when the aircraft and personnel left for Northolt. The captain and deputy captains of the Flight would henceforth be Air Equerries with responsibility for ensuring the royal family's needs for aircraft.

In May 1997, the Queen, as her father, uncle, and grandfather had done so many years ago, paid an official visit to RAF Northolt to visit the newly formed squadron. Later that year, the Flight and RAF Northolt featured in the aftermath of the tragic death of Diana, Princess of Wales. The BAe 146 that brought her body home from Paris was captained by Squadron Leader Graeme Laurie, with the Prince of Wales on board. The plane was met by, among others, the Lord Chamberlain, the Prime Minister, the Lord-Lieutenant of London, the Secretary of State for Defence, and the RAF Chaplain-in-Chief. The world watched with grief as The Queen's Colour Squadron of the RAF provided the bearer party to carry the coffin, draped in a Royal Standard, from the plane. It was a sombre moment in the history of the Flight.

On March 31, 1998, when the two Wessex HC Mk 4s were retired, the Ministry of Defence gave up the task of providing helicopters for the royal family. The royal household awarded a ten-year contract to Sikorsky Aircraft Corporation and Hanson Helicopters to provide the Queen with an S-76 and crew. The personnel of the Queen's Helicopter Flight (TQHF) would be almost exclusively ex-armed service. In 2004, the Operations Officer was ex-Queen's Flight and, of the four pilots, two were RAF and two RN, with the landing site personnel also all ex-RAF. The hope was, said a spokesperson, that, while the equipment may have changed, the style and standards had not. The new TQHF began operations with a Sikorsky 576B, loaned to them as part of the purchase contract, and in January 1999, they received their own brand-new S-76C. The Sikorsky was a well-proved machine and the C version ideal for the TQHF. It had a comprehensive avionics suite centred around a UNS1D Flight Management System, providing all the navigation, time, fuel, and weight management that the pilot needs. The all-glass cockpit has an eleven-screen display with Electronic Flight Instrument System, Integrated Instrument Display System (all RPMs and temperatures and pressures were on two screens), Traffic Alert and Collision Avoidance (a digitized map with scanned-in half- and quarter-million-scale charts to the U.K., plus ordinance survey maps of London), and a weather radar with good coastal mapping performance that also displays the checklist. The workload reduction is provided by the dual digital fully coupled autopilot. The Queen's helicopter flies mainly on the Instrument Landing System, and speed can be reduced from 145 knots to 70 knots while the aircraft arrives at fifty feet right over the H landing pad. "TQHF destinations are often field locations, and therefore the task is planned VFR at an altitude between 1,500 and 2,500 feet. Unlike operations with the Wessex, when the en-route weather deteriorates, we prefer to operate FR [Flight Rules] rather than go low level," Lieutenant Commander Christopher Pittaway RN (retired), the manager of the TQHF in 2005, said. "At the initial set-up stage it was thought that this would be a great disadvantage, but it hasn't proved to be the case. Civil rules allow FR below 3,000 feet as long as Minimum Safety Standards are maintained. The S-76 achieves best SFO [fuel burn] at around 6,000 feet and this is the preferred level for longer-range tasks."

When Prince Charles toured the Yukon in 2001, the CC-138 Twin Otter aircraft was not as sophisticated as the S-76, but more appropriate for the needs of the tour. In February 2001, Canadian Forces 440 Transport Squadron was tasked to fly His Royal Highness from Whitehorse to Mayo in Yukon Territory, where the Prince was to open the new Prince of Wales Trail in Mayo. Captain Steve Thompson takes up the story:

> The two aircraft departed Yellowknife on February 26 for Whitehorse, where they were screened intensely by a special group of military and RCMP security personnel. This screening included sealing all access panels and doors with a special sticker that would show if anyone had tampered with them. The day prior, the aircraft was placed under twenty-four-hour armed guard. Normally these aircraft are in a utility transport configuration, which includes seating for a total of ten passengers. For this flight the aircraft was configured in what was called a VVIP configuration, which included carpet on the floor and airline-style seats on the left side for a total seating capacity of eight. The day before the flight, each aircraft also received a wash from each crew.

On February 29, Prince Charles arrived via a CC-150 Polaris aircraft.[84] Thompson continued:

> My co-pilot, Major Andrew Tissot van Patot, along with our Flight Engineer, Master Corporal Scott Beeston, met the Prince at the door, while I completed last-minute pre-flight checks in the cockpit. Within minutes we had His Royal Highness airborne and en route to Mayo, bearing the call sign "Royal 1." The second aircraft, piloted by Captains Bryan Sullivan and Gavin Crouch and Flight Engineered by Corporal Brian Doll, departed around five minutes before us with the advanced party. A third Twin Otter, from the RCMP, carrying security personnel departed before that. On board the aircraft, the Prince was very quiet and hard at work. For the entire flight His Royal Highness studied his itinerary and speeches for his next leg of the multi-city visit day. Both on the transit to Mayo and return to Whitehorse, we were in contact with a CC-115 Buffalo aircraft which was tasked to fly top cover with search-and-rescue technicians ready to jump out should the need arise. The weather on arrival in Mayo was not exactly the best, but we were able to pick up a valley and safely follow it into Mayo. There were scattered snow showers in the area for the remainder of the day. While the Prince went into town, the two crews remained at the airport to prepare for the flight back to Whitehorse. After about three hours, the entourage returned, and we were back at it again. Prince Charles could see that the weather had not improved significantly. He came to the

In February 2001, Canadian Forces 440 Transport Squadron was asked to fly HRH Prince Charles in their CC-138 Twin Otters from Whitehorse to Mayo in the Yukon.

"You guys are doing a great job. Keep it up." HRH Prince Charles poses with the Twin Otter pilots.

CC-138 Twin Otter used by 440 Squadron to fly the Prince of Wales.

front of the aircraft, patted me on the back, and said, "Looks like it may be a rough one," to which I answered, "Yes, sir, but we will do our best to keep you out of the bumps." He smiled and stated, "You guys are doing a great job. Keep it up."

On the flight back, it was more of the same, light to moderate turbulence and a lot of convective clouds. We diverted around some clouds and finally made it back to Whitehorse. This time the entire crew met the Prince as he stepped off the aircraft. After a few more encouraging words from His Royal Highness, Prince Charles presented everyone on the crew with a leather wallet bearing the Royal Emblem. Both our crew, the second crew, and the RCMP pilot posed for pictures with the Prince, and he was off to do more speeches in town. All in all, we flew thirty hours in support of HRH and it was easily my most memorable flight as an aircraft captain on the CC-138.

What was exceptional for 440 Squadron was all in a day's work for 412 Squadron. When the Comet transports were retired on October 10, 1963, 412 operated two Canadair CL44 Yukons in VIP configuration. With their retirement five years later, the squadron became exclusively North American–oriented and acquired seven Falcon executive jets to complement the Cosmopolitan fleet it acquired in 1960. The overseas role would not resume until 1983. The origins of the Canadair (now Bombardier) Challenger lie with the aeronautical genius William P. Lear. In April 1976, hoping to diversify from manufacturing fighters and trainers, Canadair acquired the rights to build and market Lear's LearStar 600, an executive jet that incorporated the use of an advanced technology wing and two high bypass ratio turbofan engines. By the time it flew on November 8, 1978, as the CL-600 powered by Avco Lycoming engines, it had become better known as the Challenger. A second version, called the CL-601 with General Electric engines, flew on April 10, 1982, and was distinguished by its winglets. The first military order for it came from the Canadian Forces for two CL-600s, the first of which was delivered to 412 Squadron at CFB Uplands on May 3, 1983.

In 1985, as the old Cosmo marked its silver anniversary, the Challenger fleet grew to eight. The squadron was also downsized from 120 persons to its current strength of sixteen pilots, eight flight stewards, and eight civilians. The Cosmopolitan fleet was finally retired in 1994 and the squadron relocated to

UP83-1142

Their Royal Highnesses the Prince and Princess of Wales arrive on the Cosmopolitan in 1983.

DND photo

412 (Falcon) Squadron's Challenger in D-Day commemorative colours.

the Transport Canada hangar on the civilian side of the Ottawa International Airport. The squadron's current home, the Pilot Officer John Gillespie Magee Jr. Annex, was officially opened on January 11, 1995, as Transport Canada assumed responsibility for the maintenance of 412 (T) Squadron's remaining four 601 Challengers. Besides their VIP role, the Utility Challengers are used for military transport and can be configured for medical evacuation for CF personnel on duty anywhere in the world.

In Britain today, the Royal Air Force's No. 32 (The Royal) Squadron remains primarily a communications flying squadron, and royal flying accounts for less than 20 percent of the combined tasking of both the BAe 146 and the HS125, which are more commonly used by non-royals, such as senior military officers and government ministers. Three of the Royal Flight's HS125s were deployed in Operation Veritas in Afghanistan and Operation Telic in Iraq, where their cruising speed of between 360 and 420 knots and 2,000-mile range were ideal for shuttling between the coalition bases in the region. They weren't just moving high-ranking officers around the theatre either, said the squadron spokesman; sometimes they carried relatively junior officers with specialist skills and, because they could be ready in thirty minutes, "compassionate cases" as well.

Despite flying into war zones, the aircraft of No. 32 Squadron still sport the distinctive red, blue, and white livery, including the privately contracted royal household S-76, the colours of the Brigade of Guards, keeping in the tradition of the early days of royal flying. Today, RAF Northolt and No. 32 (The Royal) Squadron, provide the royal family with the means of getting to and from various official engagements around the country and the world. The close relationship developed between the royal family and the Station seems set to continue for many years to come, a relationship that began seventy-five years ago. In 2005, official flying for members of the royal family was provided by the Squadron's BAe 146 and Hawker 125 aircraft and the Sikorsky S-76 helicopter operated by the royal household from Blackbushe Aerodrome in Hampshire. Commercial helicopters are also used either alone for other members of the royal

DND photo

CC-144 Challenger and its predecessor, CC-109 Cosmopolitan.

CLC90-484-5

Her Majesty departs on the Cosmopolitan.

For royal flights, all royal china and reading material are supplied by Buckingham Palace. Her Majesty's favourite *Racing Post* is in evidence.

family or as back-up or to ferry the necessary entourage with Her Majesty's S-76. "In all cases, charter companies operating on our behalf have to meet strict operating requirements set out by the TQHF," says Lieutenant Commmander Christopher Pittaway.

> The helicopter uses its own registration or company call sign when empty [without the royal person on board] and adopts the royal call sign only when in task. The call signs are laid down in Royal Flight Procedures, as issued by the Directorate of Airspace Policy. Basically, if it's a TQHF task in either our own machine or the leased S-76 the call sign is "Rainbow" and if it is a commercial charter the call sign is "Sparrowhawk."

In recent years, the royal household has become a model of good governance. Air travel costs have decreased from an initial budget of £17.2m in 1997-98 to £7.5m in 1999-2000. Charges for royal flights by the RAFs 32 (The Royal) Squadron are based only on variable costs, and exclude Ministry of Defence overheads. A switch to variable cost charging allows the royal household to use the squadron when the variable cost is lower than the cost of a charter. As full-size airliners like Boeing 747s still have to be chartered, overseas flights involve the largest single expense.

As with the helicopter flights, before any foreign tour is undertaken, the airline (usually British Airways) works closely with the Director of Royal Travel. A reconnaissance flight is made along the route, and facilities at stopovers thoroughly checked. The flight crew is always chosen from the most experienced in the airline. They are briefed as to what the royal passengers expect: for instance, Prince Philip likes to visit the cockpit and chat. Flight crews are also made to stay at an airport hotel the night before the flight, rather than reporting for duty three hours before departure. In case something goes wrong, a backup crew is also in standby.

The details of the royal family's personal requirements are never divulged, with those who serve on the royal flights insisting that such matters are private, but it is understood that each member has a list of things which they cannot live without (or with, in some cases) when they are travelling. It is safe to say that they do not go anywhere without being cocooned by a small piece of England.

While a security team supervises the loading (and unloading) of all royal clothing, the Controller Aircraft Catering, the Route Catering Manager, and the Manager Menu Development all ensure that the food and drink served on board is suitable and safe. It would not do for a royal visitor to cancel a tour because of Delhi Belly or Montezuma's Revenge. Buckingham Palace supplies all Royal Flight china and cutlery to the airline or air force, as it does all menus and reading material: Her Majesty's favourite is the *Racing Post*. Buckingham Palace also vets all menus for the tour. For whether it is British Airways, Air Canada, or the Canadian Forces, they receive from Buckingham Palace a six-page instruction list, exhaustive in detail as to what and what not to do. Womens' magazines report that she does not like shellfish or lobster — more a precaution against an upset stomach than personal preference. As a result, on the flight over and back, the aircraft pantry is stocked with what the Queen is used to eating at home. Her monogrammed electric kettle always accompanies her for a

Chris Hallewell, Helicopter Museum, Weston-super-Mare

Royal crest on former Queen's Flight helicopter.

Courtesy Chris Hallewell, Helicopter Museum

In February 2004, Her Royal Highness Princess Anne arrived by helicopter to renew her acquaintance with the ex-Royal Flight aircraft at the Helicopter Museum, Weston-super-Mare.

cup of China tea. In the spirits selection, Bollinger is not in evidence as neither the Queen or Prince Philip drink champagne (and only pretend to sip it at toasts). Prince Philip likes German wines and Double Diamond beer, and the stewards are taught to pour the beer from the bottle so that a perfect head is obtained every time. Famously, Her Majesty only drinks Malvern water. Comfort foods such as Dundee cake, shortbread, and Tiptree raspberry and Chivers strawberry jam are loaded on board. Prescription and spare reading glasses are carried for both Her Majesty and Prince Philip. Barley sugar for Her Majesty to suck between speeches, a favourite hot-water bottle,[85] and special feather pillows are all a must. And most importantly, whenever a member of the royal family travels, a supply of their blood type accompanies them.

And forget cramming everything into the overhead bins. The royal passengers on tour sometimes change clothes several times in a single day, from whites to mess kits to full uniform, depending on the program, the weather, and the rank of the host. All of these outfits have to be chosen, stored, made ready for wear, and later cleaned, sometimes within the cabin of a small aircraft.[86] Seat allocation on a royal flight is done by the Master of the Household himself, and everyone flying with Her Majesty arrives at the airport — a special area of Heathrow — well-dressed. Once on board they are allowed to change into more comfortable attire, such as tracksuits. As there is always a red carpet and welcoming party of dignitaries at the other end, preparations for arrival have to begin hours before final approach, taking into account the weather and national dress, so that Her Majesty can exit the aircraft in correct style.

But as Major Al Mornan cautions, it is not the royal passengers who are the problem. "The one thing that everybody fears in dealing with VIPs was that they were some kind of inhuman monsters who will bring down the wrath of God if you can't read their mind and get things right," he says. "I've found that the opposite, in most cases, is true and that they realize that we are professional pilots chosen for this job because of our skills, and that we are doing our best. The trouble is dealing with the panicky people between you and 'them.'"

Following the Al-Qaeda terrorist attacks on September 11, 2001, the security services advised the Queen to stop using international scheduled flights. This could put up the cost of royal travel, as going first class on scheduled flights is cheaper than hiring a private plane or using a military aircraft. It remains to be seen how the British government will take this into account.

But at present and into the foreseeable future, for short flights, Her Majesty Queen Elizabeth will continue to arrive at her destination in the maroon S-76. From the same design stable as the Hoverfly, Whirlwind, and Wessex, it has another link to tradition. The De Havilland Gypsy Moth that her uncle the Prince of Wales first flew in the King's Flight had the registration G-AEXX. While it was not possible to have the same registration for the S-76, the reverse was chosen: G-XXEA. Lieutenant Commander Pittaway, RN, concludes, "TQHF may on the face of it be a new organization, but I hope we can continue the long-established traditions of high quality and service to the royal family."

MOD photo

Her Majesty's helicopter G-XXEA landing on aircraft carrier HMS *Invincible*.

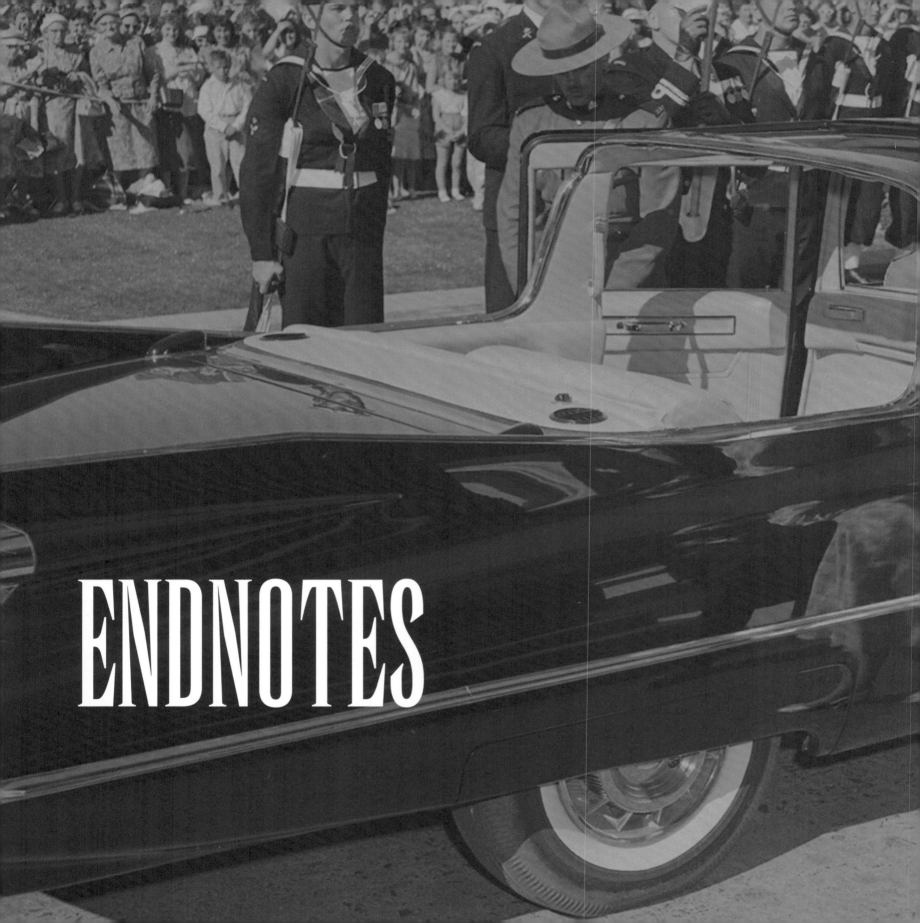

ENDNOTES

Detail of photo from page 128.

1   When, during the First World War, George V changed the family name to Windsor, his cousin the Kaiser said he was looking forward to seeing *The Merry Wives of Saxe-Coburg-Gotha*.

2   The grant-in-aid for the year to March 31, 2004, was £5.9 million (£5.4 million in 2002-03). Actual expenditure during the year was £4.7 million (£4.2 million in 2002-03). This represents a reduction of 76 percent in absolute terms and 79 percent in real terms during the seven years since the royal household assumed responsibility for royal travel expenditure.

3   Preserved at the National Railway Museum, York, are Queen Adelaide's 1842 carriage and Queen Victoria's 1869 LNWR saloon.

4   Only the Duke of Sutherland had his own private railway and also ran his own private train.

5   Since 1967 the station buildings were privately owned, and in 1977 they were reopened as a museum.

6   The consummate "boulevardier," no one loved Paris and its pleasures more than the portly Edward, as Prince of Wales and King. Yet Parisians would name one of their main streets after his very staid son King George V, someone who the Duke of Windsor once said hadn't been in a nightclub in his life and hated jazz and flappers.

7   Unfortunately, when King George VI died suddenly in February 1952, number 4082 was in the Swindon works for repairs, and the number 4082, together with the name of "Windsor Castle" and the commemorative plaques, was transferred to number 7013 "Bristol Castle" to haul the funeral train to Windsor.

8   His sleeping car was confiscated after the Fall of France and used by Nazi leaders, eventually becoming a target for the French Resistance and being blown up.

9   In Washington, the expatriate British community in Hollywood — David Niven, Errol Flynn, Lawrence Olivier, Vivien Leigh, Cary Grant, and C. Aubrey Smith — broadcast a special show for Their Majesties.

10   The only one of its class is preserved at the Canada Museum of Science and Technology in Ottawa.

11   No. 2850, the actual "Royal Hudson" that pulled the train, is preserved at the Canadian Railway Museum in Saint Constant, Quebec.

12   Her Majesty came into her own on the tour. In Washington, as entranced as all who met her, a grizzled old senator grabbed the King's hand and exclaimed, "My, you're a great Queen-picker!"

13 Tom MacDonnell, *Daylight Upon Magic: The Royal Tour of Canada, 1939* (Toronto: Macmillan of Canada, 1989), 268.

14 Donald Zec, *The Queen Mother* (London: Sidgwick & Jackson, 1990), 237.

15 Although he won, the Kaiser took exception to the system of handicapping at Cowes and sent a telegram to the Prince, who was Commodore of the Royal Yacht Squadron, complaining how appalling they were. The telegram was framed in the squadron hall for many years.

16 His Royal Highness always retained his romantic memories of Canada and, when King, his favourite musical was *Rose Marie*. When it was playing in London, he took the Queen to see it a few times.

17 The Prince of Wales's younger brother Prince Arthur (the Duke of Connaught) would be named Governor General and would, more than half a century later, relay the stone for the new Parliament Buildings.

18 On April 3, 1987, when the Duchess of Windsor's jewellery was auctioned at Sotheby's, one of the items was a Royal Naval officer's sword, dated 1913, inscribed "To Edward Prince of Wales, Lieutenant RN, from his affectionate father George, March, 1913."

19 And never was it more in fashion. One morning, David came down to breakfast wearing the latest (i.e. American) style in men's trousers, which had cuffs. He was immensely proud of them. His father looked at them and suddenly asked, "Is it raining in here?" To His Majesty, why else would one turn up one's trousers if not to jump puddles?

20 His sons would have preferred to tour the world in a more comfortable passenger ship, as he had with the *Ophir*, but George V thought a formidable battleship like the *Renown* displayed more power and prestige and it was his choice that the old dreadnaught became home to them. In 1927, Bertie's young wife, Elizabeth (the future Queen Mother), who had just left her nine-month-old daughter, also had to do so. On that tour, its boilers blew up and stranded the royal party alone in the middle of the Indian Ocean.

21 When the Prince of Wales returned from his North American tour, the King thrust clippings from the American newspapers at him and asked him to explain the headlines: "Prince Gets in with Milkman" and "Here He Is, Girls — Who'll Ask His Royal Highness What He Wears Asleep?" Impossible as it is for us to grasp, at this time, the British media abstained from commenting on the private lives of the royal family.

22 There is a story (probably fictitious) that when Queen Mary was going to launch the liner, she commented to her lady-in-waiting, "Oh dear, I'm sure I'm not going to remember the name."

23 Edward, like his mother, Queen Mary, spoke excellent German, which further endeared him to the Nazis. On the other hand, Queen Mary, a true aristocrat, despised Adolf Hitler, because she said his German was atrociously poor.

24 The *Nahlin* survived the war, Nazis, and Communists — and even worse, tacky modernization. Discovered after the fall of Communism working as a floating restaurant, she was purchased by a British consortium and returned to her home port of Glasgow in 1999, where she is being restored.

25 What was constructed in 1938 was the royal barge. Built by the Vosper yard as the tender to the *Victoria and Albert III*, the triple-screw vessel was well tested by Vosper for royal use. Stored during the war, when it ended she was refitted with more modern engines and an automatic fire-extinguisher system. In 1947, the Vosper barge would be taken aboard HMS *Vanguard* for the Royal Tour to South Africa, and when HMY *Britannia* was launched, she was carried on her as well. Today, she is again in storage.

26 P. Ziegler, *Mountbatten* (Fontana/Collins, 1985), 95.

27 The Post Office had to cancel hundreds of royal family First Day covers dating the start of their Canadian visit as May 15, 1939.

28 The last time that Lapointe had met the British royal family was when he stood with Edward VIII at Vimy Ridge on July 26, 1936.

29 Gustave Lanctôt, *The Royal Tour of King George VI and Queen Elizabeth in Canada and the United States of America, 1939* (Toronto, E.P. Taylor Foundation, 1964), 53.

30 Tom MacDonnell, *Daylight Upon Magic: The Royal Tour of Canada, 1939* (Toronto: Macmillan of Canada, 1989), 267

31 After escorting Their Majesties home from Canada in 1939, HMS *Glasgow* also took another quantity of gold to Fort Knox as an emergency reserve. In the spring of 1940, she again carried treasure and gold, this time being transferred from Norway when the King and Queen of Norway were given passage to the north of their country. She, like HMCS *Saguenay*, would survive the war.

32 Philip was the son of Mountbatten's sister Alice and Prince Andrew of Greece, both parents now exiled from Greece.

33 To Princess Margaret Rose's delight, the ten-year-old heard that some of the Canadian forestry corps at Windsor were "Red Indians."

34   Lascelles would be made a viscount and later Earl of Harewood, returning to Canada as the aide-de-camp to the Governor General.

35   At the time the sad story of the Townsend–Princess Margaret romance was in the news, the Duke and Duchess of Windsor were photographed in their Bois de Boulogne home with their pugs, Trooper, Disraeli, Imp, and Davy Crockett. "We did have one called Peter Townsend," said the Duchess, "but we gave the Group Captain away."

36   Once more, Her Majesty the Queen Mother shone: when the diehard Boers confronted her by saying that they could never forgive the British for conquering their country, without batting an eye, she replied, "I understand that perfectly. We feel very much the same in Scotland."

37   This was gunboat diplomacy at its best. The rebels were ready to execute Prince Andrew when someone rushed in and pointed to the cruiser in the bay. The captive was speedily driven to the dock.

38   The wreck of HMS *Calypso* can be visited today, as she was torpedoed on June 12, 1940, by an Italian submarine and lies fifty miles off the coast of Crete.

39   The signals that passed between the ships, like *Surprise* to *Magpie*: "Princess full of beans," or *Magpie* to *Surprise*: "Is that the best you can give her for breakfast?" have since become family jokes.

40   Unfortunately, unlike her husband and daughter, Her Majesty does not like sailing.

41   For Diana, a royal honeymoon on HMY *Britannia*, with its full complement of two hundred men, must not have been easy. Intimate dinner conversations would have been impossible in the loud fellowship of the Officers' Mess and the Royal Marine Band in full swing. The Prince would write that he spent the days alone on the veranda deck immersed in one of Laurens van der Post's books.

42   It even has a royal Rolls-Royce in the original garage on board. Visitors to *Britannia* are able to view the £150,000 car in the original garage on the shelter deck through a glass screen. The 1964 Phantom V was found several years ago in poor condition in a barn in the United States and re-imported to Britain. Having previously been used by Princess Alexandra, it was a royal vehicle, and now, repainted in claret, it is complete with the original blue royal roof light. Until its arrival, the garage had been used as a beer store.

43   In 1902, His Majesty Edward VIII went for another drive with Montagu and the Daimler stopped at a Lymington railway tollgate. The keeper was furious about another motorist who had gone through and not paid the toll and, not recognizing His Majesty, he was surly and rude to the party: "King or no King, 'oo was it 'oo rushed my gate?" he kept repeating. Even then, motoring could bring out the worst in people.

44 Another connection made then was that all royal Daimlers would be bought from the firm of Stratstone in Pall Mall.

45 It was only during the reign of George V that the Ministry of Transport directed that vehicles used by the royal family for more private occasions be licensed. As today, the personal vehicles of the monarch carry neither identification plates nor licences.

46 Even the chauffeurs' travelling costumes had a history. The black coats with red lanyards had once secured pistols with which to defend the royal personage from highwaymen or footpads en route.

47 It was the same when he visited Australia in 1920, where shouts of "Digger" accompanied him everywhere — the ultimate Aussie compliment. Like their Canadian comrades, the ANZAC veterans loved the Prince of Wales because he had served at the front.

48 The Duchess of Windsor, *The Heart Has Its Reasons* (London: Michael Joseph, 1956), 224–25.

49 In 1924, Queen Mary was presented with a doll's house designed by the great imperial architect Sir Edwin Lutyens. Patterned after the great English country houses, it was eight and a half feet long by five feet wide, and in its garage were a pair of tiny, perfectly made Daimlers.

50 As famous as the second car were the two dolls, France and Marianne, that had been designed for it. The dolls and their collection of 350 outfits were given to the Princesses Elizabeth and Margaret Rose in 1938 to mark the state visit to France by King George VI and Queen Elizabeth. France and Marianne's miniature Citroën 7B Traction Avant cabriolet was a symbol of French innovation, being a two-seater version of the first front-wheel-drive car invented by Citroën in 1934. Once kept on show at Sandringham, the Citroën has joined the two dolls and a selection from their wardrobe on display at Windsor Castle. France and Marianne were commissioned by the Société Française de Fabrication de Bébés et Jouets, and their bisque heads were modelled by Jumeau, one of the most famous of French doll-makers. The princesses were formally presented with France and Marianne by the French Ambassador, M. Charles Corbin, at Buckingham Palace.

51 Arthur James, "If a Buick is a Grand Classic, Then That's the King of England's" (*Torque*, September-October, 1980), 32.

52 Queen Mary used her ancient Daimler to forage in the countryside for scrap metal, and often it would return to Windsor Castle with rusty bits of metal tied to its roof. Unfortunately, neither she nor her chauffeur could distinguish between what was discarded or simply left out in the fields by the farmers, and a few of the agricultural implements brought home on the Daimler had to be returned to their owners without Her Majesty's knowledge.

53 A Daimler trademark, laudaulettes were eight-seater limousines with a fixed roof for front occupants and a folding rear roof section.

54 This particular shade of green for the royal cars, continued today, originated in 1905. As the Princess of Wales, the future Queen Mary was walking around the grounds of York Cottage at Sandringham one day when she noticed the contrast in green on the fir trees. She had a sample of the foliage sent to the coachbuilders H.J. Mulliner and ordered that her first Daimler be painted in the shade.

55 Although she does not use a surname in everyday life, this was one occasion on which Her Majesty needed one, and she drove as Second Subaltern Elizabeth Alexandra Mary Windsor, No. 230873.

56 Her Majesty and Prince Philip laughed at the incident later, and days later the dumbfounded bobby received a commendation.

57 In February 1971, Rolls-Royce went into receivership, following the expense incurred in the development of the RB211 aero engine. The motor-car branch remained solvent and production of Rolls-Royces continued under a new public company called Rolls-Royce Motors Ltd. It was bought by Vickers in 1980, which sold it to Volkswagen in 1998. Today Volkswagen controls the Bentley brand and facilities at Crewe while the Rolls-Royce marque was acquired by the BMW Group. In a way, the royal cars have come full circle — back to a Germanic influence.

58 After that, phones were installed in all royal cars and the chauffeurs were sent on defensive-driving courses. In March 1979, the Princess's chauffeur attended the Rolls-Royce School of Instruction at Hythe Road and brought along a Royal Phantom VI to familiarize himself with the instruction techniques.

59 His valets know that, when he is driving, His Royal Highness likes to listen to classical music and they load the appropriate CDs in the car.

60 The Silver Birch DB5 has become firmly identified with James Bond, who used it to escape enemy agents in the movies *Thunderball* and *Goldeneye.* Like Prince Charles, OO7 would remain with Aston Martin through the years, driving a DBS in *On Her Majesty's Secret Service* (1969), a V8 Volante in *The Living Daylights* (1987), and a V12 Vanquish in *Die Another Day* (2002).

61 The Sykes family created each mascot themselves until 1948, when Rolls-Royce took over the casting procedure. Originally "The Spirit of Ecstasy" was silver-plated, and often stolen. Today, it is a nickel-plated alloy. A word of warning: the name "Spirit of Ecstasy" is never used by owners, who have nicknamed her "Emily." Rolls-Royce is a favourite among the Arab royal families; they thought that the standing mascot was too sensual, and, for their cars, the lady was redesigned in a kneeling position.

62   Sowerby and Frost, eds. *A History of The King's Flight & The Queen's Flight: A Celebration of Royal Flying, 1936-1995* (Bognor Regis: Woodfield Publishing, 2003), 1.

63   He was later to become Air Chief Marshal Sir Richard Peirse, and his son would be Deputy Captain of The Queen's Flight in 1969.

64   Edward Windsor, *A King's Story: The Memoirs of the Duke of Windsor* (London, Cassell and Company, 1951), 240.

65   He remained all his life very proud of serving in the Guards. Many years later, an American reporter asked the Duke of Windsor what was the tie he was wearing. "Guards," was the reply. The reporter, hearing "Gawd's," printed the story as such.

66   Edward Windsor, *A King's Story: The Memoirs of the Duke of Windsor* (London: Cassell and Company, 1951), 240–41.

67   Miss Jean Batten was the British aviatrix who three years later would fly solo in a Percival Gull from Britain to New Zealand in eleven days, one hour, and twenty-five minutes.

68   There might have been one more flight by RAF aircraft in the Duke of Windsor's future. Early in the war, when he and the Duchess were in Portugal and there was the very real possibility that the German secret service was going to kidnap them, the RAF secretly sent two Sunderland flying boats to pick them up off the Portuguese coast. Their vacillation and the media attention that the pair drew to themselves forced the aircraft to leave empty, and the Duke and Duchess took a ship to the Bahamas instead — their Elba, as the Duchess called it.

69   In 1916, Wallis had married U.S. Navy Lieutenant Winfield Spencer, a tall, bulky Texan and one of the U.S. Navy's first aviators, but to his wife a drunk and a sadist. Psychologists have speculated that she always associated flying with him.

70   www.royal.gov.uk.output/page 2612.

71   As always before leaving Britain, the King signed a warrant under the Great Seal appointing five Counsellors of State to act for him in his absence. They were Queen Elizabeth, Princess Elizabeth, the Duke of Gloucester, the Princess Royal (the King's sister, Mary), and the Duchess of Fife, widow of Prince Arthur of Connaught. This occasion marked the first time that Princess Elizabeth, who had turned eighteen in April, could act as counsellor.

72 During the war and after it, the royal family strictly observed food rationing while it was in place. Eleanor Roosevelt would write of dining at Buckingham Palace on meagre rations eaten off plates of gold. But this was an especial problem for stewards on The Royal Flight's Vikings as the bread, meat, and egg ration had to be kept fresh and cooked on board — all in an unpressurized aircraft.

73 It was on September 3, 1941, that the nineteen-year-old Magee wrote the words, "Oh! I have slipped the surly bonds of Earth" in the poem "High Flight." Two months later, on December 11, the pilot-poet was killed in a mid-air collision over Lincolnshire.

74 http://www.airforce.forces.gc.ca/

75 In gratitude to his poor instructor for all the anxieties he endured, Prince Philip presented Gordon with a silver locket, engraved "A reward for diligence," with the date of the first solo flight.

76 Brian Trubshaw would go on to be Chief Test Pilot at Vickers and later British Aerospace and would test-fly many aircraft, including the Concorde.

77 So impressed had the Princess been with the service on board that she remembered the name of the senior stewardess on that flight. Seven years later, on June 24, 1962, former stewardess Billie Houseman, now flight-training supervisor, received an invitation to dine with Princess Margaret at the Park Plaza Hotel in Toronto.

78 Perhaps because of the success of the Canadian flight in February 1963, Her Majesty and HRH Prince Philip took a Qantas Boeing 707 to Australia. Unimpressed, the Australians thought it lacked the grandeur of the *Gothic* entering Sydney Harbour.

79 Blount would be killed that December 7 when The Queen's Flight Whirlwind helicopter crashed on a flight from RAF Benson to the Westland factory at Yeovil.

80 His Royal Highness, Prince Andrew, the Duke of York, visited The Helicopter Museum in Weston-super-Mare on June 24, 2002, to officially open the new Exhibition Hangar. While there, Prince Andrew renewed acquaintance with the Westland Whirlwind, XR486, in which he flew as a child, and the Wessex, XV733, in which he flew to the museum in November 1989 to perform the original opening ceremony.

81 Her Majesty graciously invited the Duchess to stay overnight at Buckingham Palace. While in her room, her hairdresser remembers the Duchess saying in a little voice, "I wish David could see me now."

82 The first prime minister to use 001 was Paul Martin, who flew from Ottawa to Halifax on October 10, 2004, to attend the funeral of Lieutenant Chris Saunders, who died in the fire on the submarine HMCS *Chicoutimi.*

83 Department of National Defence officials say that they are unable to put a price on royal flights, but that the Challenger cost (in December 2004) $2,129 per flying hour and the Polaris $6,603 per flying hour, which includes the cost of fuel and maintenance. They cautioned that crew wages, hotel and meal costs, catering for passengers, and landing fees are not included in these hourly rates. The Canadian Taxpayers Federation estimated that the Challenger costs were closer to $7,000 per hour and noted that Bombardier charges its high-flying customers $15,500 per hour to lease one of its Challengers.

84 The red-carpet treatment had been adapted to the times. On getting off the Polaris, His Royal Highness had to step into a disinfectant mat to prevent the spread of foot-and-mouth disease. Because of the outbreak in Britain, Prince Charles could not visit any farms in Canada.

85 Her father was the same. In 1938, embarking by royal yacht on a state visit to France, on the way to Portsmouth, it was discovered that His Majesty had forgotten his hot-water bottle. A frenzied phone call preceded the Daimler through the streets to the dock and a child was sent by bicycle to Boots (the chemist) to buy one. No one expected him to make it back in time through the crowds and security, but he did, no doubt contributing to the success of the French visit.

86 If any member of the royal family is flying abroad, his or her valet or maid always packs a suit of mourning clothes, in case there is a death in the family and he or she has to return to the funeral.